MUSIC IN AMERICAN LIFE

*Volumes in the series Music in American Life
are listed at the end of this book.*

Club Date Musicians

Club Date Musicians

Playing the New York Party Circuit

Bruce A. MacLeod

University of Illinois Press
Urbana and Chicago

Library of Congress Cataloging-in-Publication Data

MacLeod, Bruce A.
    Club date musicians : playing the New York party circuit / Bruce
A. MacLeod.
        p.   cm. — (Music in American Life)
    Includes bibliographical references and index.
    ISBN 0-252-01954-7
    1. Musicians—Employment—New York Metropolitan Area.   2. Music
trade—New York Metropolitan Area.   3. New York Metropolitan Area—
Social life and customs.   I. Title.   II. Series.
ML3795.M14   1993
780'.23'7471—dc20   92-10010
                                                                          CIP
                                                                          MN

Contents

Acknowledgments

I would like to express my most sincere gratitude, first and foremost, to the many musicians in the New York metropolitan area who gave of their time, knowledge, thoughts, and suggestions during the course of my research. Without their aid this study would not have been possible. My hope is that, as an outsider to their world, I have been able to portray that world in a way they would consider fair and accurate.

A special word of thanks goes to the professors who worked closely with me in the early stages of my research and writing: Mark Slobin, David McAllester, William Barron, and Philip Ennis. Sociologists Howard Becker, Charles Nanry, and Robert Stebbins also offered useful comments and suggestions as I began my work. As the manuscript neared completion, I received perceptive and valuable criticism from two scholars in particular: my brother, Glen MacLeod, and sociologist Robert Faulkner.

Gratitude is also due to those people who were especially helpful in the technical aspects of the work: Bill Dillon, for his aid in procuring copies of unpublished works, Susanne Javorski, for invaluable assistance in editing and proofreading, and Bruce Bethell, for his fine job of copyediting.

Introduction

"There are a lot of guys who are really good, down-to-earth musicians—club date musicians . . . people who are a special kind of entertainer themselves—people who can do club dates. It is an art! And it's certainly not appreciated. You know, there's never going to be a TV show on the greatest club date band in the world. It's a joke. . . . You know Good-bye Columbus, *where they've got the bar mitzvah with the corny accordion player goofing off in a wedding band?"*

—a club date guitarist

New York musicians call them *club dates.* In Los Angeles the term is *casuals;* in the Boston area they are *G.B.* (general business) jobs; elsewhere they might fall into the general category of *jobbing.* Whatever the terminology, the performance context referred to is familiar to musicians and nonmusicians alike—formal social gatherings for celebrating ritual events: weddings, bar mitzvahs, debutante balls, anniversary parties, retirement parties, holiday dinner-dances, or charity balls. This book is about New York musicians who make a living by providing music for such occasions. How the musicians themselves define and evaluate their work is the primary focus.

It may come as a surprise to many readers, for one, that it is even possible to play music for private parties as one's sole occupation. Beyond that, few would expect that the field is at all specialized or that there is an art to doing the work well. The bar mitzvah scene in the movie *Good-bye Columbus,* noted by the guitarist quoted in the epigraph, is humorous because it is so familiar to most viewers: a band of middle-aged party musicians, one of them about to fall asleep, playing watered-down versions of well-worn popular songs to an audience that is hardly even aware of the music. Consider your own experience: can you remember anything about the band or the music at the last wedding reception you attended? Do you even recall whether there was a band? If there was a band, the music may not have been very exciting or memorable, but then, you didn't expect otherwise.

After all, the musicians were probably just weekend players out to make a few extra dollars, no? For better or worse, this is the image much of the public has of musicians who play music for private parties—a curious situation, considering the importance of the events involved and the amount of money spent to make the occasions "just right."

Now imagine for a moment a different scenario: a nephew of yours is getting married. He lives in Manhattan, and his fiancée is from New Jersey. You have been invited to the reception, which will take place at a posh country club in northern New Jersey. Social and familial obligations, as well as plain curiosity, compel you to go. Upon arriving, you realize that this is a *big* event—more than two hundred guests. The band is a twelve-piece group, and the music, you note, is not bad at all. In fact, some of it actually sounds pretty good. There is the usual mixture of styles you'll hear from any wedding band, though perhaps a bit more current Top 40 material than you would expect, considering that many of the musicians are "graying around the edges."

It isn't until halfway through the party that you notice a couple of other interesting points about the band: first, they never seem to stop playing, and second, they aren't using any written music. No music stands on the platform where they are standing, yet you hear harmony on every song, and some arrangements sound fairly complex. What's going on here?

Out in the hallway, on your way to the rest room, you see one of the musicians on a break. You approach him and begin by complimenting him on the band's sound. Then, what you really want to ask: "How do you guys play all those arrangements? You must rehearse an awful lot."

His response is not at all what you expected: "Well, don't let the leader know I told you this, but this isn't really a 'set' group. Sure, we've all played for this guy before, but this is probably the first time we've all been together in one group like this. I don't usually play for this leader, although there are probably six or seven others in the band who do play for him on a regular basis. The rest of the band is in my position—just 'add-ons' for this job. We play what the leader calls—that's it."

"But how do you know what to play on each song—what key, what arrangement?" you ask, a bit dumbfounded.

"Oh, it's not that big of a deal, really. The contractor wouldn't have called us in the first place if we didn't know the tunes. We all know the tunes, plus the kind of arrangements the leader usually wants to hear.

We follow his signals and just fill in the harmonies as we go. *Faking,* we call it."

This is not to say that every club date band in the New York area is an astonishing musical phenomenon; certainly a good percentage of them are mediocre or worse. But the New York club date scene *is* unique in many respects, and your chances of witnessing a wedding band that is very professional and musically satisfying are probably much better in the New York area than elsewhere in the country. Providing music for private parties is a large and sophisticated part of the music industry in New York, and in terms of the number of musicians it employs, it is by far the busiest area of professional music performance in the city.

At the same time, the club date business has much in common with any business, regardless of its location, that specializes in providing music for private parties. First of all, the work is neither high profile nor high status. A musician in a club date band is pretty much an anonymous employee. You may need very specialized musical skills just to get the work, but you aren't going to impress any new acquaintances at cocktail parties by announcing that you are a club date musician. Club date musicians, particularly those who do the work on a full-time basis, are well aware that the public knows them by the company they keep—and that company seems to include the accordion player goofing off at the bar mitzvah in *Good-bye Columbus.*

The occasions for which such musicians provide music are also not considerably different from place to place. A wedding reception in Oshkosh includes many of the same elements found in a wedding reception in Manhattan or on Long Island—a cocktail hour, dinner, dancing, and ritual events such as throwing the bridal bouquet, the bride's dance with her father, and cutting the cake. A society ball in Philadelphia is not very different from a society ball in Manhattan— indeed, the same band may be performing at each one. The particular songs that a band plays at a private affair will naturally differ from party to party and locale to locale, but there is a certain amount of general repertoire that is undoubtedly familiar to any musician who has played more than a few private parties, wherever those parties take place. Also, whatever the occasion and wherever it is celebrated, the bandleader's objective remains the same: to select music suited to the particular audience and occasion. To an experienced and dedicated bandleader, wherever he or she may be, this objective is both an art and a science.

There are also basic similarities in the organization of businesses that specialize in providing music for private parties. Wherever the business, the majority of its engagements will naturally fall on weekends, and the busiest months of the year will be May, June, November, and December. The person who books the engagements is almost always both a bandleader and a booking agent, and the money he or she receives is accordingly somewhat more than that received by other band members. Because of the weekend-intensive and seasonal nature of the business, it is always only a small minority of musicians who can rely on private party work as their primary source of income.

The New York club date business differs from others in size, for one. The exact size of the business is impossible to determine with any accuracy, but it is almost certainly the largest business of its kind in the United States. The jurisdictional area of American Federation of Musicians Local 802—the largest musicians union local in the country—includes not only New York City proper but also all of Long Island, and club date musicians based in this area will routinely work in central and northern New Jersey, Westchester County, New York, and southwestern Connecticut as well. This area has by far the largest population concentration of any metropolitan area in the country.

What this means in terms of club date jobs per year is difficult even to approximate, both because nonunion work is very common in the field—representing perhaps as much as 50 percent of the work, according to estimates from musicians and union officials—and because the area is covered by more than a single union local. The example of the largest club date booking agency in the New York area, Steven Scott Orchestras, does, however, give a general indication of the volume of work involved. In an average business year Steven Scott provides music for over 5,000 events.[1] Officials of the musicians union estimated that the Scott organization accounts for "about one-quarter" of union club date work in Local 802's jurisdictional area. There are perhaps a dozen or more smaller such agencies in New York and on Long Island, each one representing a business partnership between two or more bandleaders and known by musicians as a *club date office*.

In addition, there are scores of independent bandleaders who book their own services and those of other bandleaders. These independents include a handful of leaders in an area of the business unique to New York—the "society" field. These leaders have established reputations among a largely wealthy, upper-class clientele, and they work not only in the New York metropolitan area but also on a national and even international level. Lester Lanin, Peter Duchin, and Meyer Davis are the names most frequently mentioned by musicians working in the society field (Meyer Davis Orchestras is presently led by Emery

Davis, son of the founder). The Peter Duchin organization claims to be the busiest in the society field, booking over 1,000 engagements each year.[2]

The six or seven leaders generally known to musicians as "society" leaders stand at the top of an informal hierarchy in the business. Musicians will commonly refer to two other levels in the hierarchy—upper-middle class and middle class, grouping leaders together according to the socioeconomic status of their usual clientele. The total number of leaders working at these two levels may number 100 or more, including part-timers and nonunion members. A core group of perhaps two dozen at each of these levels handles most of the middle- and upper-middle-class work.

One aspect of the club date business that, although not exclusive to New York, is probably more prevalent and complex there than elsewhere is the free-lance hiring structure. Nearly all club date musicians work on a free-lance basis, and it is not unusual for a busy player to have more than fifty withholding slips at the end of a tax year—each slip representing a different leader or agency for which the musician has worked. The personnel working for one bandleader can be very different from night to night, depending on which musicians are available. "Set" groups, whose personnel remain relatively constant, have traditionally been the exception in the club date business.

The absence of written music during performance, which you noticed at your nephew's wedding reception, *is* completely standard practice throughout the club date business, regardless of the size of a band. Of course, there are musicians playing private parties or nightclubs outside of New York who have large memorized repertoires, but in New York memorized repertoire has become a prerequisite for getting any work in the club date field. Brass, woodwind, and violin players must also be able to play harmony parts for most of the songs if they hope to work in any bands that use more than a single melody instrument. Again, this practice is not limited to the New York club date scene; many jazz musicians, for instance, can play harmony parts for songs in their repertoire, and there are surely many musicians playing private parties in cities throughout the country who are able to improvise harmony. In none of these areas, though, is the ability to play harmony without written music a standard requirement. New York musicians refer to the practice as faking harmony. The term *faking band* normally refers only to an ensemble with two or more horns or strings, not to smaller groups that simply use no written music.

Club date musicians, and their counterparts elsewhere throughout the United States, play an essential role in American social life.

Contemporary mainstream American society, as "modern," secular, and sophisticated as it may seem to be, continues to recognize the importance of gathering together to celebrate significant life events in formal, ritualized fashion. Music in this context acts as a kind of social cement—a shared body of cultural experience that enhances the celebration, whether it is used for dancing, listening, or simply as a background. We are willing to pay for the services of club date musicians because we consider live music to be an integral part of a successful celebration.

The vast majority of performing musicians in the United States play some variety of popular music, and very few of these musicians have *not* played at private parties at some time during their careers. Indeed, outside of major urban areas, private parties may often be the only available performance venue other than nightclubs. As for nonmusicians, who hasn't attended a wedding reception, an anniversary party, or a holiday dinner party given by an employer where a band provided popular music for dancing? In any case, club dates, casuals, G.B. jobs—whatever they are called—are familiar to most people, probably more familiar than any other form of live music.

The very familiarity of the subject may explain in part the general lack of interest it has had for writers of any kind, popular or scholarly. You may find an occasional newspaper or magazine article on what to look for when hiring a band for your wedding, but that's about it. As for serious scholarship, only a handful of articles address the subject at all. From 1941 to 1968 various scholarly articles considered the role of "dance musicians" in our society.[3] These articles occasionally mention casual or club date work, but the emphasis throughout is on the relation of commercial dance music to the music that the musicians would really like to be playing—jazz. This focus leaves the reader with the impression that no one really likes casual work; indeed, the musicians all seem to be pretty miserable. Beyond that, we learn little of the work in itself or whether any condition other than misery is possible on the bandstand at a private party or a nightclub.

In one respect this lack of scholarly literature is not really surprising, for popular music itself has only during the last ten or fifteen years come to be accepted as a legitimate field for scholarly inquiry. Naturally enough, nearly all the studies that have appeared during this time are concerned with popular music at the *macro* level—the producers and products of the international recording industry. These studies are both necessary and enlightening, but we must bear in mind that they do not tell the whole story of popular music and its significance in our society. One song I heard repeatedly during my research provides a particularly good illustration of this point: the rather provocatively titled "Like a Virgin," recorded by Madonna. Listening to the song is certainly a very different musical experience if we imagine some different contexts for hearing the piece: in performance by Madonna herself, with thousands of devoted fans filling an auditorium; as part of a music video, seen and heard with one or two friends in the family living room; on a radio, while driving alone; in an instrumental version as part of the programmed background music at the workplace; or—as I once heard it—as a dance song at a wedding reception, with the bride's grandparents dancing along with everyone else. Musical meaning and even the sound itself can change as the piece is employed in each new context. We miss the full significance of popular music if we fail to look at what the sociologist Iain Chambers has called "the heterogeneous musical practices that coexist within the social and cultural structures of advanced industrialized society."[4]

Club date music exists in what H. Stith Bennett has called the realm of "secondary popular culture."[5] The music here has already reached the consumer through another medium. Recorded popular music becomes raw material from which appropriate "product" is selected, reworked, packaged, sold, and presented. Musicians and audience may represent all age groups, not simply the youth market. Nor is current music the only consideration: popular music from any period is fair game for inclusion in a club date musician's repertoire. The musicians who work in the field leave no artifacts such as recordings, and what few written records they keep are scanty or inaccessible. Consequently, oral accounts provide virtually the only sources for studying this secondary arena of popular music performance. Research at this level of popular performance has been minimal. The only book that considers the area specifically is Bennett's *On Becoming a Rock Musician,* a sociological study of rock bands working at the local level. One other book that deals with occupational issues commercial musicians meet at any level is Robert Faulkner's *Hollywood Studio Musicians* (though that book's focus is not entirely local). There are also a few articles that begin to address this local performance scene as it is experienced by both popular and "folk" musicians.[6] The particular performance contexts these writers treat differ considerably from the club date context, but many of the problems faced by the musicians and their strategies for solving them are similar to those of the club date scene.

Both the nature of the music and its meanings may change in these secondary manifestations. Similarly, the terminology commonly used in describing and analyzing music performance may come into question when it is applied to local performance scenes generally and to the club date context in particular. The term *performance,* for instance, usually evokes a presentation that is the main focus of an audience's attention, where the audience members have paid an entrance fee specifically to witness the event. In contrast, a club date band's presentation is only one part of a larger event, the audience does not pay to see the band, and for much of the "performance" time, the audience may be quite unaware of the music. The presentation *is* a performance, but only in the broader sense of the term as it is used by anthropologists, folklorists, or ethnomusicologists, who accept as performance a wide range of formalized presentational behavior.[7]

We also speak of music as an "art" and of musicians as "performing artists," yet we might feel less than comfortable applying those terms to club date music and musicians. Those concepts, as we normally use them in Western culture, have a very narrow range of reference that excludes a wide variety of music and musicians. We listen to "art" music with full attention and evaluate it—or at least think we do—as a purely aural experience. Club date music, on the other hand, is valued by both musicians and their audiences not only as pure sound but also in terms of its functional significance—its "fit" in a particular social context. We tend to view such an attitude toward music making—a "functional aesthetic"[8]—as characteristic of "folk" or non-Western societies, not of our own. We should, however, look at ourselves a bit more closely, for in our own culture *most* of the music that people hear—at the office, on the car radio, on recordings, at parties or nightclubs—is *not* listened to and judged as sound alone. The kind of critical listening we engage in at concerts or while attending closely to a recording is the exception rather than the rule.

My own understanding of club dates is based on interviews and conversations with more than 100 club date musicians and observation of more than forty of their performances. There are thousands of musicians in the New York area who play club dates at one time or another; perhaps 2,000 work in the business on a fairly regular basis. A core group of between 300 to 500 musicians relies on club dates as their sole or primary source of income. This core group is the focus of this book.

The central chapters of this book concern the specialized knowledge that allows these musicians to operate successfully in the club date world, as band members and bandleaders on stage and as employees and employers in conducting business. The performance and business contexts are not neatly separated in actual practice, but they do represent two distinct spheres of activity for club date musicians.

The two contexts require different kinds of cultural knowledge, and they are normally separated in space and time as well. A musician applies knowledge of club date performance at a catering hall, hotel, private club, or private home in the evening or on a weekend day. For the most part, the same musician will apply business knowledge during the week while at home, at an office, or at the musicians union hall.

Chapters 2 through 4 focus on the performance context. Chapter 2 describes the characteristic features of a club date performance—what actually goes on at a "typical" club date, who is involved and why, and what an observer sees and hears. Chapters 3 and 4 consider the roles of bandleader and band member in performance. The primary responsibilities of bandleader and band member in the performance context are very different, although the two roles require a certain amount of knowledge in common. The band member is first and foremost an instrumentalist or vocalist whose main responsibility is to perform whatever music the bandleader chooses. The knowledge required is almost exclusively musical: he or she must know what is considered "good" (or at least "adequate") music in the club date context and what the conventions of club date performance practice are. The bandleader is usually a performing musician also, but his or her main concern is to adapt the performance to its social context. The bandleader is the liaison between the band and the party guests, selecting music suited to a particular audience at a particular time, encouraging guests to dance, answering requests, and handling complaints.

In the business context—the focus of chapters 5 and 6—the two main roles discussed are those of employer and employee. Employees are either band members or bandleaders who are involved in neither booking nor hiring. Their main concern is to know and use the freelance hiring structure to control both the number and type of jobs they perform. The employer is the person responsible for booking engagements and hiring musicians. This is often, but not always, the bandleader in the performance context as well.

The musicians' views on particular aspects of the club date business are evident from quotations throughout the book. Chapter 7 considers their perspectives on their work as it relates to the various other social groups to which club date musicians belong: musicians, workers, businesspeople, families, and communities. The club date musician in society at large is a paradoxical figure, one who possesses specialized skills, is fairly well paid, and shares some of the glamour accorded to any of the performing arts yet is often treated as little more than a servant, ignored entirely, or even ridiculed. There are incredibly brilliant musicians among them, but they happen to be part of a field that includes a large number of musicians (perhaps the majority) who are minimally proficient, playing for a public that gets precisely what it pays for and probably expects no better.

Both the performance context and the business context experienced significant changes since I first studied club dates in 1978. My research from that year later became a doctoral thesis, which I set aside for nearly a decade. In 1989 I revisited the club date world, observing performances and conducting interviews once again, and I discuss the important changes over this period in chapter 8.

To introduce the reader to the club date business, I describe in chapter 1 how I myself first learned about club dates. I encountered my share of difficulties along the way, but these were easily outweighed by the many small joys I felt in discovering more and more about a fascinating world known to very few people other than its inhabitants. This world interested me from the start because I was myself a free-lance performer; it was only much later that I realized why it was that others found the club date scene equally intriguing.

The sociologist Robert Faulkner, having read an early draft of the book, pointed out to me that the club date world is really not so different from the various social "worlds" we all inhabit. We are all trying to succeed on some sort of social circuit—learning what is expected of us; internalizing unwritten rules, rituals, and formalities; adjusting to changing fads and fashions; presenting ourselves to others as best we can, with accompanying rewards and penalties; hoping we will be called back; and judging others and being judged all along the way. Ultimately, it's all a series of one-shot transactions that we hope will connect into some sort of continuity and make sense in the long run. Of course, it doesn't always work as well as we might like. Free-lance performers—or private entrepreneurs of any sort—conduct work on this basis daily; for them, the process *has* to work more often than not, because their livelihood depends on it. The stories of those who have managed to survive and even prosper as free-lance performers hold a certain fascination for us, for the nature of their work is familiar to us all from daily experience. Whether or not we are immediately aware of it, the business of the free-lance musician is a metaphor for the business of life.

Notes

1. Alan Breznick, "Bookings for Orchestras Swing into the Big Time"; Bernice Kanner, "Strike up the Bands"; interviews with Steven Scott partners.

2. Marilyn Bethany, "The Duchin Touch"; Alan Bunce, "When His Orchestra Plays, Society Sways"; interviews with managers at the Duchin office.

3. The group of articles, in chronological order, includes Carlo L. Lastrucci, "The Professional Dance Musician" (1941); Howard Becker, "The Professional Dance Musician and His Audience" (1952; the data from this and related articles also appeared later in Becker's *Outsiders* [1963]); Alan P. Merriam and Raymond W. Mack, "The Jazz Community" (1960); Phillip S. Hughes, "Jazz, Jazzmen and Jazz Audiences" (1962); and Robert A. Stebbins, "The Conflict between Musical and Commercial Values in the Minneapolis Jazz Community" (1962), and "Class Status and Power among Jazz and Commercial Musicians" (1966).

4. Iain Chambers, "Some Critical Tracks" 32.

5. H. Stith Bennett, *On Becoming a Rock Musician* 113.

6. Clinton R. Sanders, "Psyching Out the Crowd"; George H. Lewis, "Take out My Guitar and Play"; William P. Nye, "The Social Organization of Time in a Resort Band"; Stephen B. Groce and John A. Dowell, "A Comparison of Group Structures and Processes in Two Local Level Rock 'n' Roll Bands"; and Kenneth Mullen, "Audience Orientation and the Occupational Rhetoric of Public House Performers" and "The Impure Performance Frame of the Public House Performer."

7. For an overview of the various conceptions of performance from these fields, see the introduction to Gerard Behague's *Performance Practice*.

8. The term *functional aesthetic* in this sense comes from the field of ethnomusicology and was first used by David McAllester in his 1960 article "The Role of Music in Western Apache Culture," cited by Merriam, *The Anthropology of Music,* 271.

1

Discovering the Club Date Business

"You a union rep?" the musician asked in a not-too-friendly tone of voice. He had good reason to be suspicious of my presence—he had seen me earlier speaking with the bandleader, plus I was scribbling notes into a pocket-sized notebook that I kept in the outside pocket of my tuxedo.

"No, not at all," I replied, laughing a bit self-consciously. "I'm just a student trying to learn about private party bands here in New York."

His look changed quickly from suspicious to incredulous. "Why would anyone want to study *this?*" he asked, gesturing to indicate the whole scene—catering hall, party guests, musicians, and food service personnel.

I fumbled my way through as brief and cogent an explanation as I could muster. Along the way, I did drop one phrase, "music and society," that apparently made some sense to him. His expression still said to me, "What will they think of next?" but as he put out his cigarette and prepared to return to the bandstand, he remarked, "Music and society, huh? Well, you've come to the right place."

This brief exchange took place at a catering hall on Long Island in early 1978. It points out some of the problems I encountered in trying to learn about club dates and club date musicians. Access to performances was one of these. Although I did have permission to attend every affair I observed, usually from the bandleader or from the office for which the bandleader worked, that was not always sufficient. The incident just described ended on a neat, even humorous note, but reactions to my presence as an observer at these private affairs ranged from mild curiosity to open hostility. The head of security at Manhattan's Waldorf-Astoria was not nearly so understanding: he simply told me to leave in no uncertain terms. (Fortunately, the same man was not on duty during an earlier performance at the Waldorf.) At a

posh country club in Westchester County I was again asked to leave—
in that case, by the bandleader, albeit in a gracious and understanding
manner. His office had not informed him that I would be attending,
and because he was not familiar with the caterer, he felt it would be
better for me to see his band at a later date.

Most bandleaders were very helpful in finding appropriate occasions for me to observe. "Appropriate" meant those occasions where
the leader was familiar and comfortable with the catering personnel
and where, from the leader's knowledge of the sponsors and the nature of the party, my status as an observer would be least intrusive.
A few leaders, although they readily agreed to be interviewed, would
not even consider my attending a performance. "These are all private
affairs," I was told again and again. Other leaders allowed me to observe their performances on the condition that I not arrive until
the affair was well under way—usually one or two hours after it had
begun.

The bandleader has a commercial rather than personal relationship with the party sponsor and guests. And quite naturally, because
the sponsor and guests represent the leader's best source of future
business, the leader is careful about exceeding the bounds of this relationship. To some, introducing an outside observer would have ex-
ceeded those bounds. In retrospect, I find it surprising that the
people paying for the party were never, as far as I knew, informed of
my attendance *before* the event. In some instances bandleaders introduced me to the sponsors, and in all these cases I was welcomed, but
most often I was anonymous to the party sponsors and guests. I did
wear a tuxedo to most performances, and that allowed me to blend in
with the scene fairly well. People would often mistake me for either a
waiter or a band member, because my tux was basic black—standard
apparel for club date musicians, and for the waiters as well at many
locations. Party guests might ask me for directions, and if I was familiar enough with the location, I would direct them accordingly. If a
guest asked me about food or drink, I either relayed the question to
a waiter or waitress or, if the catering personnel already knew me,
went to the kitchen myself to retrieve the item.

Those musicians and guests who did ask direct questions about my
"outsider" status were almost always very interested and helpful once
I explained my project, with a few glaring exceptions. My explanations were probably overly brief and somewhat less than lucid, because for one thing, I at first did not know the term *club date—private
party bands* was the best I could come up with. When musicians or

party guests went on to ask what academic field I was working in, my answer—ethnomusicology—provoked some hilarious responses. One person, upon hearing that ethnomusicology is concerned with world music, exclaimed in disbelief, "But this isn't the world! This is Long Island!" Another, who had heard something about the field elsewhere, asked, with a look of genuine concern on her face, "But shouldn't you be in Africa or somewhere like that?" I found myself explaining again and again that the *ethno* part of the work could refer to *any* cultural group, not necessarily an exotic one.

"It sounds like sociology" was another common response. And true enough, my general area of interest, American popular music, is most often the domain of sociologists, just as non-Western music is the usual domain of ethnomusicologists. The weight of these associations makes it difficult to convince anyone that things could be otherwise. The two fields do differ, both in emphasis and methodology—sociology of music stressing human relationships in a musical context while rarely discussing the sound itself, and ethnomusicology describing and analyzing sound product, social context, and the interrelation of the two—but I often felt that my attempts to explain the difference served to confuse rather than elucidate the matter.

My initial interest in the club date business was not scholarly at all; rather, I first observed a New York club date band in performance for practical and economic reasons. In 1977 I was the leader of a small band in Connecticut and, as such, was responsible for securing work for the group. One of the band members suggested that we try booking engagements through his father, a caterer in Westchester County, New York. That was two hours away, but the considerably higher pay scale in the New York area supposedly would have made up for the extra driving time. His father arranged for us to observe a band at an outdoor wedding at a private home. We donned waiter's jackets and poured water for the guests, and as long as the water glasses were full at our respective stations, we were free to watch the band.

What we saw and heard made it obvious that we were far from ready to break into the party circuit in metropolitan New York. The bandleader in particular was very impressive. He was an excellent singer and entertainer in addition to being proficient on trumpet and flugelhorn, and from the beginning it was clear that he was "running" the party. He acted as master of ceremonies, introducing the wedding party, announcing the dinner courses as they were served, and guiding the cake-cutting ceremony, the throwing of the bridal bouquet, and the couple's first dance. He would coax guests to the dance floor, talk and joke with them while they danced, build enthusiasm and momentum with his selection of songs, and have the dancers laughing and applauding again and again as they returned to their seats.

The band itself—a six-piece group—used no written music, and though we had all seen and played in small jazz groups where this was the case, the range of the band's repertoire was very impressive. They performed authentic-sounding versions of Top 40 hits—much more current than anything we did—as well as rapid-fire medleys of swing, Latin, Jewish, and Broadway show music. The leader was apparently choosing songs to play as he was singing or playing, because the music seemed to go on continuously, with no break lasting more than a few seconds.

Performing at a party in New York was clearly a far more sophisticated venture than any of us had envisioned. On our trip home, I recall feeling like the proverbial country bumpkin having visited a relative in the big city and then returning somewhat sheepishly to the simple and familiar life. Still, the experience did at least leave me with a strong desire to learn more about these bands, if only for my own education as a performer of popular music.

Later that year, when I decided to conduct a research project dealing with these bands, I had doubts about the project's feasibility. I had no idea what to call these bands or whether there was a term that specified them as a separate genre. *Society bands* was the only term that came to mind. Also, my only access to the music and musicians was through my friend's father, the caterer. In fact, he became my first source, giving me the names and phone numbers of three bandleaders and one "music organization," all of whom provided music for private parties such as the one I had seen the previous summer. My proposed topic title betrayed my ignorance of the subject: "An Ethnomusicological Study of Society Bands in Westchester County, New York."

The first two bandleaders I contacted by phone seemed interested in my subject, but neither of them could meet with me for at least another month or two. With only two numbers left, I was beginning to wonder whether the project would ever get off the ground. Fortunately, the next two men I spoke with were extremely helpful. I simply told them of my interest and asked to arrange an interview. Both of them agreed readily.

The first interview turned out to be not with the originally scheduled bandleader, who had another engagement at our appointed time, but with another musician who was in charge of payroll for the same office. The questions I asked were necessarily very general and uninformed, but this man was kind enough to spend nearly two hours with me explaining the workings of their "music organization," as he called it. I soon realized that my proposed title was not at all workable. For one thing, the office where the interview took place, Steven Scott Orchestras, was located on Long Island, and most of their work took place within the jurisdiction of Local 802, which did not include Westchester County. Also, when I mentioned the phrase *society band,* although the man did recognize the term, it was obvious that it was the wrong label for the general field of party performance.

As I was preparing to conclude this first interview, I asked if I would be able to see any bands in performance. The musician I was speaking with was not in a position to grant me permission, but he had his doubts about the proposition. "These are all private affairs, you realize," I was told for the first time. I was starting to feel a little bit foolish, even helpless, when the president of Steven Scott, Marvin Kurz, unexpectedly stepped in. When I mentioned my desire to see bands in performance, he immediately gave me permission to observe any of the bands working through his office—thirty-five of them at the time. Mr. Kurz did make one stipulation, that I could not tape-record any of the bands; the musicians union would not allow it, plus he felt that neither musicians nor party guests would appreciate it. During the next two months, armed with notebook and pencil only, I observed performances by ten different bands and met most of the members of each band.

I also conducted interviews with five or six bandleaders during this time, and between the interviews and the performances I began to get a better idea of the nature of the work these musicians did. For one thing, I learned that the phenomenon I was dealing with was not limited to New York City and Long Island but rather involved the entire New York metropolitan area, including Westchester County, much of New Jersey, and even Connecticut. Also, I learned that the term *club date bands* referred specifically to bands performing at private parties. After the first interview, I had begun using the general term *dance bands* in talking with bandleaders and band members, adding that party performance was my main interest. Not until I observed the third or fourth performance did I learn that *club date* was the generally accepted term among musicians. One musician asked me, after I had introduced myself and described my project, whether I meant "dance bands in general or just club date bands." After he explained the usage to me, I began using the term among other musicians. They all recognized the term, and it apparently had a common meaning for them.

My interest during these first months was focused on the band-leaders, because they were responsible for dealing with both the audience and the musicians. In addition, the bandleader had to comply with the wishes of the caterer in charge of a party's food service. In short, it seemed that the leader was responsible for the success or failure of any party. If any one of the three other groups involved—musicians, audience, or caterer—was dissatisfied, the party could flop and the bandleader would be held responsible. I began to appreciate the complexity of what it was these leaders were doing and found their ability to "read" an audience and adapt the performance accordingly quite remarkable.

At the same time, this initial focus had its limitations. For one thing, it disregarded the other musicians in the band, and what they were doing was equally remarkable in its own way. I had learned fairly early on that club date bands, almost without exception, did not use written music. That in itself was amazing, but two other features of the work made it even more so: the art of faking harmony and the free-lance hiring structure. When I first observed a fairly large club date band in performance, I could hardly believe my eyes and ears. Here was an ensemble with full brass and saxophone sections, presenting the music in the same nonstop format, playing everything from current Top 40 to Dixieland jazz, *and* playing in harmony! And as if that were not enough, while the rest of the band took a break, four of the horn players took out violins and strolled the floor playing waltzes—again, in harmony throughout.

Trying to figure out how these musicians were able to do this, I assumed that much rehearsal was surely part of the answer. What I discovered instead was that *no* bands rehearsed, because nearly all the musicians worked on a free-lance basis. The actual personnel in a bandleader's ensemble for one night could be quite different from the same bandleader's group on the following night. This aspect of the club date business was something I simply could not ignore.

I also had no real perspective from which to view the statements of the leaders I had interviewed, because I did not know the size, constituency, or interests of the world about which they were speaking. I had until that time been in the position of trying to understand the workings of an industry by consulting management alone, entirely disregarding the employees and their contribution to the workings of the business. My focus changed from a treatment of one specific aspect of a larger whole—the role of the bandleader in club dates—to a more general consideration of the whole itself—the club date business. My goal was to gain an understanding of the overall structure of this "world": who belonged to it, what its components were, and how the members defined and evaluated their participation in it.

I soon learned that, although the musicians occasionally used the words *bandleader* and *band member,* the words were very general in their designation. There were four main roles that musicians played in the business: leader, subleader, sideperson,[1] and contractor, and it appeared that there was considerable fluidity among the roles. *Leaders* are the employers; they are in charge of booking work and hiring musicians to fill the other roles. In the performance context, all leaders fill the role of bandleader. If a leader is sole proprietor of a business, he or she is known as an *independent leader.* Leaders who form business partnerships with other leaders are known as *office leaders.*

Sidepersons are employees: band members with no supervisory responsibilities. If a leader books work for more than a single band, *subleaders* are hired to direct those bands other than the leader's own. The subleader stands somewhere between the leader and sideperson in terms of both pay and responsibilities. The subleader's role in the performance context is that of a supervisor; in the business context it is more closely allied to that of the sideperson, both sidepersons and subleaders being employees. The general term *bandleader,* then, refers to the person actually leading a band on stage: this person can be a leader or a subleader.

Club date musicians most often work in just one of these roles, sometimes doing one exclusively, but they may play all three roles at one time or another. This is especially true of the subleader: it is common for musicians to switch from subleader to sideperson frequently, depending on the type of available work. Many sidepersons will also book some of their own work, and in that case, they are temporarily in the leader's role. The leader's role is the most constant; it is exceptional for an established leader to work as either a subleader or sideperson for other leaders.

The *contractor* is the person paid by a leader to hire musicians once engagements have been booked. The role of contractor is an ambivalent one. On the one hand, the hiring decisions made by contractors are clearly managerial in nature, which places them on the side of employers in labor-management relations. Many contractors, however, are sidepersons or subleaders in the performance context, which makes them employees as well. Contractors may or may not be union members, but they are excluded from voting as sidepersons in pay-scale negotiations with leader/employers.

Musicians may fill additional roles beyond the basic four, although these are business-related activities that do not require the person doing the work to be a musician. These roles include such work as payroll preparation, sales, bookkeeping, or equipment management, and I will refer to them under the general designation of office personnel.

Club date employees and employers work together in a relatively small world in which both news and gossip travel quickly by way of the grapevine. The free-lance sideperson's livelihood depends in large part on maintaining good relations—on the surface at least—with leaders and contractors. This explains in part why many of the musicians agreed to be interviewed only on the condition that they remain anonymous. I decided in the end to leave all the musicians anonymous, giving all the speakers equal weight and ensuring at the same time that no one could be positively identified. Quotations are identified instead by the speaker's role in the business, general age (for example, 30–34 = early 30s, 35–39 = late 30s), and primary instrument.

In 1978 I conducted interviews with forty-two club date musicians. The interviews ranged in length from one hour to two and one-half hours. The general format I used for the interviews—a combination of open-ended and directed questions—is described in appendix A. Informal questioning and conversations with musicians before and after performances and during breaks also provided much useful information. I spoke with at least forty musicians in this context. These brief talks often proved to be as fruitful as some of the shorter interviews (if not more so), probably because of their more casual nature. I was certainly more at ease, since I was not expecting anything particular from the conversation nor was I trying to direct *its* course. No tape recorder was present, and I refrained from taking notes until the band resumed performing.

My main criterion for choosing musicians to interview formally was the extent to which they were involved in the club date business, simply because musicians who had spent more time in the field were certain to know more of its inner workings. All the musicians interviewed relied on club dates for at least 50 percent of their income; about half of them worked in the club date business exclusively. Beyond using this single criterion, I chose musicians to interview according to age, instrument played, and role performed within the business so as to achieve a variety of viewpoints. Appendix A includes a statistical breakdown of these categories.

In 1989 I conducted another nineteen interviews and spoke with at least twenty more musicians at performances. Some of these followed the same format described in appendix A; others, however, used more directed than open-ended questions, because I was seeking to fill what seemed to be gaps in my knowledge of the business left from the initial study. When I quote from the 1989 interviews I include the year in the identification.

When I began observing performances, I was not particular about the *kind* of occasion involved, because I knew so little about the business. As I learned more about the nature of the business, I tried to be more selective in attending performances, hoping to achieve a final sample that would be representative of the club date business as a whole. What the business as a whole included, though, was not clear at first, for there seemed to be some discrepancy as to what the term *club date* signified. There was no question that the performances I was observing were club dates; the question was whether these were the only kind of performances signified by the term.

None of the musicians were sure about the origin of the term in reference to private party engagements, nor were they in complete agreement as to its meaning today. They did all agree that club dates have nothing to do with nightclubs, even though the term *is* frequently used to refer to nightclub engagements. The *club* part of the club date business must have originally signified some sort of private organization, country clubs or upper-class private clubs such as Manhattan's Union Club being the most likely initial references. Upperclass "society" affairs were and still are held at such clubs, as well as in hotels or at private estates. And because catering halls did not always exist to the extent that they do today, even parties among the less affluent often took place in halls owned by local civic or fraternal organizations—all "clubs" of various sorts. If much party work did take place in such locations, it is understandable that such dates or engagements came to be known as club dates. The performance settings have changed, but the term itself remains.

There appear to be two usages of the term *club date* among New York musicians, one more or less official and the other colloquial. The New York musicians union local publishes a handbook entitled "Single Engagement Club Dates: Wage Scales and Minimums," which uses the terms *club date, single engagement,* and *single engagement club date* interchangeably. This includes one-night shows, concerts, and even recording dates, as well as private parties. The performances take place on one date and do not repeat thereafter.

Some musicians subscribe to this "official" meaning, but they seem to be in the minority. One club date sideperson, a member of a committee formed by union members to deal with problems in the club date field, described for me an article that the committee printed in the union newspaper, *Allegro,* dealing with this matter of definition:

> We decided we'd start a column in *Allegro* . . . called "What Is a Club Date?" The idea of it was to illustrate the range. For instance, the Philharmonic doing a single job in the park is in a sense a club date, a one night thing. We tried to show that a show with a big entertainer . . . was also a single engagement. [Note the change in terminology.] Of course, we ran into a lot of resistance all over. They like to keep things simple, the way they are.
> —*sideperson, early 50s, piano*

Union members reading the article had their own meaning for the term, and it apparently did not include the Philharmonic playing in Central Park. The members of the Philharmonic are being paid a regular salary, and they are using written music—a context unfamiliar to the club date field as most musicians know it.

Another sideperson, a pianist in his early 40s, gave his opinion of the terminology that, in the end, appeared to be the generally accepted definition: "A single engagement is not necessarily a club date. I think of a club date as a private party in the nature of a wedding, bar mitzvah, dance, banquet—a celebration of some occasion." This colloquial definition, used by the majority of the musicians with whom I spoke, excludes any work done on a steady basis, as well as single performances for shows by nationally known performers. I asked one musician what kinds of musical work he had done, and he subdivided it this way:

> Club dates are about 50 percent of my income. The rest is from Broadway shows, playing for stars—Tom Jones, Engelbert Humperdinck, Liza Minelli. And I've done some recording.
> —*sideperson, early 30s, drums*

The colloquial usage specifies one area with a generally consistent set of characteristics, and this is the definition I have used throughout: private parties that are usually a celebration of some occasion.

Within this colloquial definition of a club date performance, musicians categorize the various types of parties in at least two different ways, depending on what aspects of a party they are considering. There is, first of all, a categorization according to socioreligious criteria, which divides the club date business into five different fields or areas: Jewish, Gentile, society, ethnic, and corporate/industrial. This group of categories seems to be the one most frequently used in describing the business as a whole. Musicians will also speak of types of parties according to the apparent economic status of the party guests: middle-class, upper-middle-class, and upper-class—the latter identical with the society area.

It should be obvious from the names of the two classifications that there is much overlap between the areas and that not all parties fit neatly into a single area. A corporate party—one sponsored by a business as part of a convention, for example—might well include a majority of upper-class, "society" guests, and a party given by middle-class clients may take place in a facility that musicians would more often associate with upper-middle- or upper-class clientele. And of course, the boundaries from one class to the next are a matter of perspective. These categories are thus less than foolproof, but musicians use them because they notice significant differences from one category to the next, and those differences affect the nature of their work.

Jewish parties constitute the largest single category of club date work in metropolitan New York. The general consensus among the musicians I spoke with was that, in terms of numbers of parties per year, approximately 40–50 percent of club dates could be considered Jewish work. This large percentage is explained in part by the importance of the bar mitzvah and bas (or bat) mitzvah celebrations, which often can be as elaborate as wedding celebrations among either Jews or Gentiles. Certain leaders have reputations for doing mainly Jewish work, but none performs exclusively for Jewish clientele. There are two distinct types of Jewish parties, American Jewish and Hasidic. The label *American Jewish* covers a wide range of clientele, from middle-class to very upper-class (the Jewish high society) and from very orthodox to reformed. Hasidic work is considered part of the ethnic area, for it requires a repertoire completely different from that used for American Jewish parties.

Gentile parties account for a somewhat smaller percentage of parties—perhaps 30 to 40 percent of the business. When club date musicians refer to Gentile parties, they usually mean non-Jewish parties that are not upper-class. The boundary between Gentile and society parties may be unclear at times, because the basic distinction between them is one of money and social status. Also, the large amount of intermarriage between Christians and Jews blurs the Gentile and Jewish categories. Most Gentile parties are either weddings or dinner-dances, the latter often sponsored by civic, church, or labor organizations. Strong ethnic affiliations are evident at many of these parties, and the musicians will speak of Italian, Polish, or Irish affairs under the general rubric of Gentile work, but the area still remains distinct from actual ethnic work, because most of the music for a Gentile affair will be of the American popular variety.

The society field accounts for between 5 and 15 percent of club date work, the number varying depending on the definition of the term *society*. Society clientele need not be members of the old "400," nor must they be listed in the *Social Register*, although many of them are. Most work in the society field is for a Christian audience, if only because so-called high society itself has traditionally been exclusively Christian. Two types of parties are characteristic of the society area: debutante balls and charity balls, the latter signifying the beginning or completion of fund-raising drives for charities such as the Heart Fund, the Cancer Fund, schools, or museums. The prevalence of engagements outside the New York area, on a national or international scale, is also characteristic of the society area.

Ethnic parties require a specialized repertoire suited to the particular ethnic group sponsoring a party. Little or no American popular music would be played at an ethnic Italian job, for instance, distinguishing it from a Gentile affair with a predominantly Italian-American audience. Although there are many bands that specialize in the music of one ethnic group—usually composed of musicians from that ethnic group—much ethnic work is contracted by leaders who work also in the Jewish and Gentile areas. One or two specialists in the desired ethnic music will be hired for a performance, and the other band members will be drawn from musicians who generally work in other areas of the business but have enough familiarity with the repertoire to provide support for the specialists. Ethnic parties, though very important for the musicians who can do them, form probably the smallest segment of the club date business—5 to 10 percent at most.

The corporate area covers a wide range of performance contexts, many of them falling outside the musicians' colloquial definition of club dates and often including entertainment other than dance music. The events are sponsored by businesses, often as part of a convention. The events may include dinner-dances or parties given by executives in an organization, but much of the corporate work involves "shows" of various sorts: fashion shows, promotional shows for new products, or shows featuring nationally known performers backed by New York musicians. Such shows will often require rehearsals and the use of written arrangements, placing them outside the club date field. Offices and individual leaders who do a large amount of corporate work will distinguish their club dates from the corporate engagements as two separate categories, although there is certainly some overlap between the two. The amount of corporate work similar to work in other club date areas accounts for a small percentage of the club date business as a whole.

The second classification system, according to economic class, parallels the hierarchy of leaders. A few points about this classification need to be mentioned here. For one, class distinctions are, of course, not always easily drawn, and there are bound to be parties that do not fit exactly in either category. In addition, the classification makes no provision for parties that take place at any level below that of the middle class. This reflects in part the limitations of my research method and in part the nature of the club date business. I focused my efforts on musicians for whom club dates were their main or sole source of income; these musicians tend to work at those economic levels of the business offering the most and best-paying work—the middle class and above. Even at that level, only a small percentage of musicians are able to support themselves from club date work alone. Finally, the club date business is a luxury business. The business survives only if a large enough portion of the local population has the requisite disposable income to pay for the services of a club date band. People at lower economic levels certainly celebrate ritual events and include live music, but they do so on very limited budgets. The musicians they hire are probably playing for much under union scale and certainly do not survive on their income from party performance alone. The portion of the business that I discuss throughout this book serves a middle- to upper-class clientele because the business as an ongoing operation employing hundreds of individual musicians on a full-time basis could not survive at a lower economic level.

I asked a number of leaders, for instance, whether they ever played for parties where the guests were predominantly black or whether there was a separate club date "circuit" of sorts that served the large black population in the New York area. The response I received was invariably put in economic terms. As one leader put it, "We *do* play black parties from time to time, but not frequently. It's not really a question of race—it's a question of whether they have the money and are they spending it." I also spoke with a number of black sidepersons and one black bandleader, and their responses were not very different from that of white leaders. Although they had all played all-black private parties, there seemed to be general agreement that there was not enough of the work to make specializing in black parties a viable business.

I attended a total of twenty-eight parties in 1978. I observed thirteen of these for their full four-hour duration; for the other fifteen, I observed portions of the performances between one-half hour and two hours in length. Fifteen of these parties were Jewish affairs, eight were Gentile, and three society. Two were not easily classified, one where the audience was primarily Egyptian, yet the band neither knew nor played any Egyptian music, the other a Jewish-Christian wedding. Of the thirteen full-length affairs I attended, seven were Jewish, three were Gentile, and two society—the last being the Jewish-Christian wedding. Of the eleven nonsociety affairs, at least half took place in locations that most musicians would consider middle-class and the remainder in upper-middle-class facilities. In 1989 I attended thirteen affairs altogether. Five of these I was able to observe for their full length, four Jewish functions and one mixed Jewish/Gentile dinner-dance. These were all upper-middle-class affairs. Of the remaining eight, four were Jewish, three Gentile, and one a society dinner-dance. Most of these nonsociety events were held in what would be considered middle-class locations.

My observations, then, were concentrated on the bulk of the business, the Jewish, Gentile, and society areas. Most of the musicians I interviewed or spoke with at performances did have experience playing for ethnic and corporate parties; indeed, it was rare that a club date musician had not performed in all five areas at one time or another. Individual musicians, though, tend to work primarily in one or two areas exclusively, since their contacts with clients, leaders, and other musicians have been established in those areas.

Note

1. The term *sideperson,* as opposed to the traditional *sideman,* is used today by both men and women in the club date business, although it is not by any means common parlance. I have chosen to use the former throughout the text because it is more precise, considering the number of women in the business today.

2

The Performance Context

Every social event—including every club date—is unique. The time, place, participants, and reasons for any event will never again coincide in exactly the same way. At the same time, it is possible to group together under a single label those events that seem to have common elements, compare and contrast the many individual events, and generalize about human behavior in that social context. This allows the club date musician, while pointing out the relative merit of particular types of parties, audiences, locations, or musical groups, to speak of club dates in general as a single performance context with characteristic features. The purpose of this chapter is to identify those characteristic features. In becoming acquainted with the context in which club date musicians present their musical product to the public, we can better appreciate the musicians' overall understanding and evaluation of their occupation.

A wedding reception is the best example of a "typical" club date. Every club date musician has performed for wedding receptions at one time or another, regardless of which area of the business he or she works in most frequently. Weddings, along with bar and bas mitzvah celebrations, are the bread and butter of the club date business; the two types of celebrations probably account for more than half of all club dates in the New York area. So closely are weddings and club date musicians related in the public mind that the term *wedding band* is commonly used, both in the New York area and elsewhere, to refer to any group of musicians that performs mainly at private parties, even though weddings are most likely only one type of event for which the band plays.

At the same time, some basic characteristics of wedding receptions are totally absent from other types of club date performance contexts. The guests at a wedding reception, for instance, are usually a very heterogeneous group, representing relatives, friends, and business associates and spanning all age groups from the very young to the very old. The guests at a charity ball, in contrast, will generally be either business associates or friends as well as age-peers, the very young almost certainly excluded. Also, formality and ritual are more clearly displayed at a wedding reception than at charity balls or company dinner-dances.

With these qualifications in mind, let us consider the context of a wedding reception as one example of the social environment in which club date musicians ply their trade. What is the setting, who are the participants and what are their various perspectives, and how is the event arranged and executed—these are the questions to be answered here. The reader will note that, although some aspects here may be unique to the New York area, many more elements of the performance context are common to private party engagements wherever they may take place.

First of all, consider the planning of the affair. A formal affair with catered food service and live music for dancing *can* be held for any number of reasons, or even no apparent reason at all. One musician, for instance, recalled playing a party given by a man who had been convicted of tax evasion—evidently quite a lot of it—to celebrate his final days of freedom before his jail term began. Others described elaborate parties put on by very wealthy clientele where there seemed to be no central event or celebration involved—a party seemingly for its own sake. These are the exceptions, however. For individual party sponsors, as opposed to organizations, only once-in-a-lifetime occasions such as weddings, confirmations, or anniversaries are important enough to justify the large investment of both time and money required to put on such a formal affair.

Sponsoring a large formal party with a sit-down dinner and live music is not easily done on the spur of the moment, even if you have the money available to do so: the hall where the event is to take place, the catering service, and the musicians often must be hired many months in advance of the event—sometimes a year or more for popular locations, caterers, or musicians—and none of these comes cheaply. Take as an example an upper-middle-class wedding reception for 150 people, the total price to include a formal dinner, photographer and florist fees, and a seven-piece band. To accomplish this for less than $10,000 would be nearly impossible. $15,000 is a more reasonable figure. Nationally syndicated financial advice columnist Sylvia Porter quotes the "price tag for a traditional wedding now [March 1991] at an average of $16,000."[1] And the sky is the limit. One leader showed me initial arrangements for a wedding reception that had already reached $250,000 in catering, music, and other entertainment fees. The rule of thumb might be that if you are going to pay for a fairly large private party in the New York area, expect to invest nearly as much as you would on a midrange automobile.

Whether it's for a wedding reception or an automobile, whoever is paying is going to consider carefully just how that sizable bit of money is spent. There are, however, a couple of major differences between the two investments. There is very little reliable, unbiased information on the basic ingredients for a wedding reception—no *Consumer Reports* on catering halls, photographers, or musicians. Plus, many of the people making the arrangements are doing so for the first and perhaps the only time in their lives. A poor choice of automobile can be avoided the next time around. A wedding, on the other hand, is— at least in theory—a once in a lifetime event. If the reception doesn't go right the first time, you don't normally get a second chance.

Consequently, a certain amount of decision making will have to rely on the good faith of the caterer, photographer, or bandleader. The sponsoring family, concerned as they may be that everything be picture perfect, can never be completely sure of the exact nature of the services they have hired until the reception actually takes place. If they are lucky, they may already be acquainted with a number of different halls and different bands and can make informed choices for each. Failing that, they will talk to friends to get suggestions and then do a bit of research on their own. In any case, it *will not* be a matter of just looking in the *Yellow Pages* and making a few phone calls. Every effort is made to ensure that what is taking place is not an everyday occurrence but *special.*

Of course, the invited guests may have a very different view of the affair, and this is all part of the social dynamics of any formal party. As special or "once-in-a-lifetime" as the event may be for the person footing the bill, guests attend such an affair for a variety of reasons, which may only nominally include the wish to celebrate an event important to the sponsor. For business associates or friends, social obligations may be involved; for relatives, familial obligations; for children of the adult guests, parental obligation. Beyond these various obligations, which in themselves may be enough to bring guests to the occasion, there is always the attraction of a good meal cooked and served by someone else and live music for dancing—all of it "free," although a gift is often expected almost as an obligatory entrance fee.

All the party guests know the bride or the groom, or at least their families, but they seldom know everyone else at the reception. As a guest at the reception, you may find yourself among many relatives, close friends, and acquaintances. If you like large parties—and the relatives and friends—it can be a very pleasant, even joyful event. If large parties are not your cup of tea, and you find yourself in a room full of strangers or people you would rather not see, you will be glad to leave at the first opportunity. Guests will also be expected to arrive in formal attire—an enjoyable aspect for some, a trial for others. The invited guests who do arrive do so with a mixture of motivations and expectations. For some, the event is a thoroughly happy occasion they have anticipated for months; for others, the reception is simply the highlight of an otherwise uneventful week; and to still others, it is a formality they would rather do without.

The kinds of facilities where these functions are held tend to reflect the "special" nature of the occasions. The celebrations can, of course, take place in virtually any kind of hall large enough for guests, music, food, and dancing, but there are certain types of facilities where the majority of parties are held. In the Jewish and Gentile areas of the business, catering halls are a common location. These range from large, relatively inexpensive halls capable of holding multiple parties simultaneously (known to many musicians as "budget halls" or "function factories") to fairly exclusive and expensive halls. The less exclusive halls serve a lower-middle- to middle-class clientele; the expensive halls cater to the upper-middle class. Country clubs or hotels are common locations among wealthier Jewish or Gentile clientele. Jewish affairs may also take place in the halls—some of them very elaborate—connected with some synagogues or Jewish centers. Society affairs are most often held in either exclusive Manhattan hotels (the Plaza or Waldorf-Astoria, for example), private homes, or private clubs.

Many of these buildings are very imposing structures—catering halls hundreds of feet long and three stories high with wide expanses of glass, or clubs and hotels with dark wooden doorways twice the height of mere mortals and flanked by stone pillars. All the locations have an air of exclusivity: anything less than formal dress and a written invitation would seem very inappropriate. Valet parking is the norm, and the main entrance is usually staffed by uniformed door attendants (and even security guards, as I discovered at the Waldorf). These attendants perform a valuable service beyond keeping out the uninvited: arriving guests need directions once inside the building, because there are often two or more parties taking place in the same location. A friend of mine recalled arriving at one Long Island catering hall, misinterpreting the directions given to her, and spending nearly half an hour at a stranger's party before realizing her mistake.

The decor of the lobbies and hallways generally conveys a sense of wealth and elegance in very traditional terms. No modern, bright furnishings or wallcoverings, no twentieth-century paintings on the walls. Instead, there will be staid and formal furniture, large chandeliers, wide staircases, and perhaps an indoor fountain complete with an imitation classical statue. Burgundy seems to be a favored color for carpets and drapery. This conservative and traditional emphasis is hardly surprising; the events being celebrated are themselves very conservative and traditional reaffirmations of the social order.

Of course, both the very special event and the very elegant surroundings are commonplace to club date musicians. Providing music for special events is their occupation, and the location is their usual working environment. The musicians, along with the catering personnel and the photographers, are simply anonymous employees providing specialized services. Their relation to the celebration and the participants is professional rather than personal. The social dynamic between the providers and the users of the services is common to most other service occupations: what is a relatively unique event to the user is an everyday occurrence for the provider.

Performing musicians in other contexts share a similar relation to their audience, but the nature of the relationship is fundamentally very different in the club date context. Concert performers in whatever musical idiom may view their performances as "just another gig," while their audiences understandably regard the performance as very special. In the concert situation, however, the music and the musicians themselves are the focus of the event—what makes it special. Club date musicians and their music are, in contrast, appendages to an already special event. Their performance may make the occasion *more* memorable or significant, but the event itself remains important regardless of the music.

Both the dress and decorum of the musicians are in keeping with the formal nature of the events. Most arrive at the performance location in formal attire. For male musicians this is simply a black tuxedo. The requirements for female musicians are somewhat more flexible, depending on both their role in the ensemble and the socioeconomic class represented by both the location and the audience. Female instrumentalists will usually dress in black as do the male musicians, but there seems to be a bit more leeway in dress requirements for female singers. Rather than sporting a tuxedo, which a female piano player might wear, a singer is more likely to wear a dress. The style of dress can range from dark and conservative to brightly colored and knee-length or shorter. There do seem to be limits to the spectacle created, however; explicitly revealing, "sexy" clothes— as one might expect to see on a female nightclub performer—are uncommon.

Most musicians arrive wearing their formal clothes despite the fact that moving amplifiers, instruments, and microphones into the hall can be both physically taxing and dirty work. If they are lucky, the room where the band will play is on the same level as the entrance, or there may be a freight elevator if the room is above entrance level. Otherwise, the equipment must be carried up a flight or more of stairs. There are no "roadies" to do this for them, nor are dressing rooms available. If band members *do* need to change clothes, a bathroom or a storage room is the only choice.

Formal wear is the club date musician's work uniform, one that often may be worn continuously from early Friday evening through late Sunday night—driving to jobs, eating meals in between, moving equipment, and performing. The musician is expected to appear neat and clean once on stage, but that is not always a simple task:

> I wear my glasses, not contacts; I don't wear makeup; I wear a polyester tuxedo—something you can get axle grease on and still not notice. You *are* going to get dirty—the stuff weighs a ton, you have to take it upstairs, you go through the kitchen. You can't look pretty. . . . You're at the cocktail hour, pumping out "The Girl From Ipanema," people are knocking over your stuff trying to get to the food, the plants are in your face, the sterno burners are heating things up.
> —*sideperson, late 30s, vocals and piano*

In most locations, musicians are expected to use service entrances—often through the kitchen—rather than the main entrance used by the party guests. Catering hall and hotel managers can be very strict in forbidding musicians the use of the same entrances used by party guests. (It also seems that the more exclusive the party location and, along with that, the wealthier the clientele, the stricter the managers are about musicians mixing with guests.) There may, of course, be some utilitarian reasons for this—more direct access to the rooms via the service entrance or freight elevator, for instance, but the musicians' status as employees is certainly a major reason for this restriction. Many club date musicians, understandably enough, resent this treatment, especially at those locations where it would simply be far easier to enter through the main door.

The room where the musicians first set up their equipment is separate from and smaller than the room where dinner will be served. The space is used only for serving cocktails and hors d'oeuvres, and once the cocktail hour is over, the band will move the equipment once more to the main dining room. Musicians usually arrive at least half an hour before the party is to begin in order to begin precisely at the contracted time. The sponsor of the party has reserved the hall for a specified time period—normally four hours—the caterer times the food preparation within this time frame, and the music, with rare exceptions, begins and ends precisely as specified by contract. There is little or no allowance for tardiness in arriving at the job.

During the half-hour or so between arriving at the party location and beginning to play the musicians have some opportunity to socialize with one another. The talk among them tends to center on experiences from previous gigs. In addition, some of them may not have worked together for a while and may be reacquainting themselves and catching up on one another's lives. Because most of the musicians work on a free-lance basis, they travel to work alone, and this is one of the few times when they have an opportunity to meet and talk with other musicians. Once the job begins, their social interaction is limited to onstage communication plus a few five-minute breaks during the four hours.

As the musicians are unloading and setting up their equipment, the other service employees—waiters and waitresses, bartenders, and photographers—are going about their last-minute preparations. There is not much time for social interaction among the musicians and these employees, but when they do interact, a certain camaraderie is often evident. Many, after all, know one another from previous parties, and there seems to be a recognition of and respect for one another as employees in the same enterprise, as different as their roles may be. Their common status as employees entails some basic rules of decorum. Number one is that socializing with party guests is not allowed. When not performing whatever service they are being paid for, all employees either leave the dining room or stand at its edges. Eating food prepared for the party guests is also forbidden, although some caterers may allow employees to eat as long as they are not in the room where the party is taking place. (At one party I attended, a waitress delivered a complete meal for the entire eight-piece band to the storage room where they were taking a break. At the same time, she cautioned them not to tell anyone she was doing so, since she was apparently stretching the rules somewhat.) The situation is similar in regard to drinks, although it is generally permissible for musicians to order a drink from the bartender and then leave the room. Soft drinks only are the rule; alcoholic beverages for employees are strictly forbidden.

Again, these rules of decorum for the various employees are more strictly enforced at the more exclusive locations serving a very wealthy clientele. At the opposite extreme, as musicians recalled from their early performing experience and I, too, remembered from some of my own work at parties, the lower on the socioeconomic scale that the party location and guests seemed to stand, the less likely that such restrictions existed or had much significance. At a lower-middle-class affair held at the local Elks Club hall, with a buffet of cold cuts as the main meal, the party sponsors may go so far as to offer the musicians a table of their own in the dining room itself, a free meal and drinks, and sufficient time to enjoy both. In such a situation, the musicians are not seen as lower in social status; indeed, they may come from the same community and know personally both the sponsors and many of the guests. Further up the socioeconomic ladder, the musicians become anonymous and separated by class from the party guests, and that separation is clearly delineated.

The physical arrangement of the musicians and their equipment is governed by practical considerations—the available space and the need for the band members to hear one another. In the cocktail room, the band frequently stands at floor level rather than on a raised platform or stage. Drums are in the rear, with guitar, bass, and keyboard nearby. Whatever horns there may be will generally stand to the side and forward of the rhythm section. Singers and the bandleader "front" the band, standing forward of the other members; consequently, they are the musicians most immediately visible (and approachable) to the party guests. The bandleader is, with very few exceptions, an instrumentalist as well, most often a horn player or guitarist. There *are* keyboard player–bandleaders, but they seem to be in the minority. Drummer-bandleaders are a rare breed. The bandleader, after all, needs to communicate with the other musicians, the party guests, and the caterer, and playing an instrument that requires the leader to remain seated and behind the other band members inhibits the ability to do so.

A seven-piece band at a wedding would most likely include drums, guitar, bass guitar, electric keyboard, singer, trumpet and a woodwind player who doubles on sax, clarinet, and flute. The singer is probably the only female in the group. Assuming that the group represents a cross-section of club date musicians as a whole, the age range of the musicians will be fairly wide; this is neither a group of high school players nor a group of swing-era veterans. The youngest members of the group will most likely be the guitar and bass players and the singer—all in their twenties to mid-thirties. The horn players are more likely to be older, perhaps well into their fifties. There does not seem to be any typical age for drummers, although most I saw were forty or younger. Nor is any age group usual for keyboard players. The bandleader will almost always be at least thirty years old, for the role requires a certain amount of experience in the field.

The musicians will usually represent a broad range of backgrounds and motivations. Of the seven musicians in this hypothetical typical band, only one or two will be involved in the club date business on a more or less full-time basis. The bandleader is probably one of these: he plays every weekend, probably makes a few jobs during the week as well, and does a certain amount of office work—booking or contracting, for instance—during the week. Perhaps the sax player is also in club dates as a sole source of income, although he—I never saw a female sax player on a club date—is a performer only. To keep his schedule as full as possible, he most likely works for a number of different band leaders. The remainder of the musicians do club dates primarily on weekends. The keyboard player and the singer are the two who are most likely to rely on music performance as their sole source of income, working either in recording studios or in nightclubs during the week. These two musicians, singer and keyboard player, are also the ones who would most likely be female, if any women were included in the band. The others work day jobs outside of music performance—most often teaching music in public schools.

Almost certainly, none of the band members are self-taught. The younger ones in particular are likely to have college or conservatory degrees in music. Of course, what they learned in school may have very little to do with what they need to know on a club date. All the musicians, whether or not they studied music in college, have learned the requirements of club date playing mainly through performance experience in the field itself. Each of the musicians has his or her own reasons for working in the club date business: some do it for extra money as a sideline to their day jobs; others find it necessary if they hope to piece together a living from performance only; and still others find it preferable to other areas of performance and rely mainly on club date work for their income. Some like the music and the working environment; others dislike it intensely and feel trapped in the business. The motivations and expectations of the musicians as actors in the performance context are no more simple or singular than those of the party guests.

The band begins playing at the appointed time for the beginning of the party—for instance, precisely at 8 P.M. for an eight to twelve o'clock evening event—even though few or even no guests may be in the cocktail room yet. The room is set up to encourage guests to mix, being relatively small and generally having fewer tables and chairs than the total number of guests. Most guests remain standing after entering the room, greeting friends and relatives and generally warming to the occasion. The music and the physical presence of the band may be noticeable to the guests, but it is hardly the center of attention. Both music and musicians are, at this point, very much background and are expected to be so. More than one musician referred to their presence and performance at this point as "wallpaper," more a decorative element than an integral part of the proceedings. Indeed, the noise level of guests arriving and conversing at this point in the party can almost completely obscure the sounds coming from the band.

Normally, the first guests at a wedding reception to "check out" the band both visually and aurally will be the teenagers. They will stand close to the band, ask questions of the bandleader or other band members, eye the instruments closely, and may even request particular songs very early on. Music is, after all, an important ingredient in their world; they listen frequently, develop very definite likes and dislikes, and often identify very closely with particular songs or performers. They can also be the harshest critics of a club date band's presentation. They all seem to have the same question running through their minds: "Can these musicians, all of them so much older than myself—and wearing tuxedos!—play *good* music?"

This teenage segment may be somewhat disappointed during the first hour or so of the party. Latin tunes and medium-fast show tunes are common choices during the cocktail hour. The songs are generally played at a low volume, and rarely do they include vocals. "Light and lively" seems to be the theme here; pleasant and pretty, but not really engaging. Dancing is certainly not openly discouraged, but neither is it common during this first hour. Little is said over the microphones, and consequently, exactly who is leading the band may not be obvious yet. The bandleader's main object—to get the people dancing—is not yet the focus:

> You don't really expect to get them dancing in the first hour. They want to hear you so they know they're getting their money's worth, but they don't want to dance. So, you wait until they get into the

dinner room and have some booze in them—you know, a little edge
on. That's when you hit 'em.

—*bandleader, late 30s, guitar and vocals*

A party guest who does happen to listen to the band at all closely
during this first hour might take note of the particular way in which
these light and lively songs are presented. "The Girl From Ipanema"
is very likely to appear, but it almost invariably will be part of a medley
of Latin songs, perhaps sandwiched between "Desafinado" and "Fly
Me to the Moon" (originally a waltz, but typically done in Latin
rhythm by club date bands). Burt Bacharach's "Look of Love" is likely
to be followed by one or two other Bacharach tunes, "Raindrops Keep
Falling on My Head" or "Close to You," for instance. This might not
seem an especially notable point, since many bands elsewhere around
the country use a medley format for at least part of their repertoire,
but there are a couple of big differences here. First, the medleys are
rarely prearranged. Without referring to written music, the band
members switch from one song to another following signals from the
bandleader, and the signal for the next number may come only during the final measures of a song. The musicians learn which songs are
part of the medley only as the medley is being played. Second, the
medley format is used for nearly all the repertoire, not just a small
portion of it. Generally speaking, if the band begins a song suited to
one particular dance style, it will segue to at least one or two similar
songs before moving on to another rhythm.

If rock music is used at all during the cocktail hour, it will often be
the final number before the band moves to the main dining room. Although there are exceptions to this sequence, it is common enough
that, upon hearing a rock number begin after forty-five minutes or so
of "cocktail" music, I was nearly always correct in assuming that the
bandleader would announce the move to the dining room at the end
of the song. Exactly when this move is to take place is communicated
to the bandleader by the caterer, either verbally or by hand signal.
The musicians, much as they may dislike moving all their equipment
once again, accomplish the move quickly and efficiently. In fifteen
minutes or less, drums, amplifiers, microphones, and instruments are
ready on stage in the main party room.

When the band resumes playing in its new location, it is clear that
the nature of the party is about to change. The music is now in the
foreground both aurally and visually. Whereas there is often no bandstand in the cocktail room, here the band is on a raised platform

directly in front of the dance floor and also directly across from the head table, where the important participants of the affair will be seated—in this case, the wedding party. The music is perceptibly louder and more conducive to dancing. Current rock songs or up-tempo foxtrots are common at this point, the choice depending on the type of occasion and makeup of the audience. The band will usually play a short group of engaging dance songs—ten minutes or so—while the guests enter the dining room.

Just who is leading the band is obvious now. As the guests filter into the room, the bandleader welcomes them and encourages them to dance. The bandleader is also the only one on stage who will frequently turn away from the dance floor to communicate with the other musicians, again through verbal or hand signals. He or she is also the representative for the band in communicating with the caterer or with party guests who have particular songs or styles to request.

The dance floor will be at least partially filled with dancers by the time all the guests have entered the dining room. Then, responding to a signal from the caterer, the bandleader will request that the guests take their seats. The music stops briefly, and the bandleader announces the names of the members of the wedding party, who are greeted by a short fanfare and applause from the audience. Finally, the bride and groom enter to the "Wedding March." Once they are seated, the minister, priest, or rabbi recites a prayer before the meal begins.

These short periods while ceremonies take place—entrances, prayers, and speeches—are the only time during the remainder of the party when there is no music. The music begins again once the prayer is over and the guests begin to eat their first course. This time, however, it is even more obviously background than it was during the cocktail hour. Only one or two of the musicians may be playing, while the others leave the room for the five or so minutes it takes for the first course to be eaten. These interlude periods are generally the only time during a party when very slow tempos are used, the message being: take your time, relax, enjoy your food, the dance music will come later.

The caterer signals the bandleader to resume the dance music. The music returns to the foreground, and the bandleader once again encourages the guests to dance. The shift to dance music once a dinner course has been served and eaten does not, of course, mean that everyone immediately gets up to dance and that the band is suddenly the center of attention. There are few party locations where the dance floor is large enough that *all* the party guests could dance even if they wanted to. The dance floor may be completely filled at some points during the party, but this still means that a large portion of the guests are *not* dancing: they are visiting friends at other tables, talking, eating, drinking, or taking pictures or videos of the event, and they may be quite oblivious to the music. In the private party context, the music is rarely if ever the sole focus of everyone's attention.

In the course of a four-hour party, a band will play sixty or more individual songs, covering a wide range of dance styles and musical genres. Within this broad range, there is one characteristic common to all the songs: familiarity. The bandleader selects songs with an eye first and foremost to those that are known by the largest number of guests and consequently have associations and meaning for them. It *is* all popular music of one sort or another, but it is more specifically popular music that party guests are going to recognize. Obscure songs or styles of music—even if they would still be classified as popular—are avoided as much as possible; if they do appear, it is most likely a result of a specific request from a guest.

Although a group of younger party guests at a club date might like the music of Talking Heads or Led Zeppelin, they aren't likely to hear either. They *will* hear rock music—and it will often be performed in a manner almost indistinguishable from the original recordings—but it will be *commercial* rock music, that is, music familiar to a broad audience through extensive radio exposure. Nor will a jazz fan be likely to hear the music of Miles Davis, Charlie Parker, or John Coltrane, even though the musicians in the band are probably quite capable of playing the songs *and* improvising excellent solos as well. Instead, the jazz fan will have to be content with show tunes or other "standards" that are both familiar and danceable. The same tunes may be common in jazz repertoire, but the improvised solos played in the club date version will be concise and conservative. The keyboard player in the band may be an accomplished composer of popular or jazz tunes, but the band won't play any of that music on a club date. The club date stage is simply not the place for musicians to display originality, much as it may be valued in other contexts.

It really is not until the final hour or hour and a half of the party that the band and its music come to the full attention of the party guests. All the dinner courses have been served, and all or most of the rituals and ceremonies are over (at a wedding reception, the throwing of the bridal bouquet and the groom's removal of the bride's garter are usually saved for the last hour.) Other than conversation, listening or dancing to the music are the only diversions left. By this time, the bandleader has a pretty good idea of what kinds of music will draw the most dancers to the floor and chooses songs accordingly. The band will play more rock music at this point than at any earlier time during the party, and if songs that require group participation are appropriate—"The Alley Cat," "Never On Sunday," or a medley of horas—they, too, will be included in this final hour or so. The bandleader's goal is to get and keep the party guests' attention, to have as many of them as possible dancing or listening to the music.

It is also at this point that the bandleader may be besieged by requests for specific songs or styles from individual guests. The bandleader honors the requests as closely as possible while keeping in mind how each request suits the general course of the party as it has gone so far. A request for a slow ballad while the band is playing a rousing rock number for a packed dance floor may have to wait a while. Likewise, a cha-cha request may have to be postponed if the bandleader has already seen that few dancers are willing to display their unfamiliarity with the step.

Many party guests prepare to leave well before the actual end of the event, and it is not unusual for nearly half of the guests to have left by the time the band stops playing. This isn't at all a sign that the band has failed in some way; musicians expect a certain percentage of any group of party guests to leave early. The dancers remaining on the floor are the focus, and there are usually quite a few of those right up to the very last song.

The band plays according to contract—four full hours, no more and no less. They begin at the contracted time for the party's beginning, even though few guests have arrived, and they end precisely at the appointed time for the end of the party, however many guests remain. Requests to have the band play beyond the contracted four hours *do* happen, but not frequently. Such requests are a rarity at afternoon club dates, most likely because everyone at the party—musicians, catering personnel, and party guests—may have other engagements later on in the evening. An evening affair lacks the same restriction, but extending the party still requires either a very generous sponsor or an informal collection taken up among the guests. The musicians have ambivalent feelings about overtime: it means more money, of course, but it may also rob them of an hour or more of much-needed sleep in preparation for an afternoon job the following day.

The bandleader will preface the final number of the party with a brief announcement thanking the guests for their presence and wishing them a safe drive home. The title and lyrics of the last song often continue this closing message: "The Party's Over" or "Last Dance," for example. Almost immediately after finishing the last song, the musicians quickly and efficiently set about packing up their equipment. They don't have the luxury of leaving their equipment set up for the next night; each job requires complete set-up and tear down. And again, many of them may be on their way to another job elsewhere in metropolitan New York, either in a few hours or early the next afternoon. Consequently, few of the musicians choose to socialize following the conclusion of the party, and few of them indulge in alcoholic beverages.

The bandleader will usually be seen at this time talking with the host/hostess for the affair, receiving both whatever compliments he or she may have and also a check to cover the balance of payment for the band's services. Other party guests may also approach the bandleader or other band members, either to compliment them or to ask about their availability for future parties. Band members may also use this time to talk over practical matters with the bandleader—future jobs and musical or financial questions. The two brief periods before and after the party are often the only times when it is possible to deal with such questions in person rather than by phone.

What conversation there is among the musicians after the party always seems to be a bit less animated than it was four hours and sixty or more songs earlier, especially if the party is in the latter part of the weekend. A busy club date player will often do four or five jobs from Friday evening through Sunday evening, and it is not uncommon for them to feel a bit punchy after the last job. First there is equipment to pack and put in the car, and then there is the drive home, perhaps thinking over the upcoming week's schedule and finances; once home, there is time only to put away the equipment, perhaps grab a bite to eat, and get some needed sleep. If you talk to busy club date players on a Monday morning you will probably hear very little right away about what led them into their occupation in the first place and what the public pays them for—the music.

Note

1. Sylvia Porter, "Wedding Costs" 11.

3

The Music

It's a really tough business. I don't mean to get the work, but to learn the craft. I have seen some really good players go right down the tubes on a club date. It reduced them to children. And I'm talking about some really good jazz players—guys who really knew what they were doing. I know a really good jazz piano player who's a quasi-name, and I did five or six club dates with him. He was just awful. It devastated him. He just didn't know the tunes.

It would be easier to replace myself on a Broadway show than a club date. And on a show I may have to play three or four different instruments. But it's easier to find one guy who can read and play those instruments than one guy who can play one saxophone and know the tunes."

—sideperson, late 30s, saxophone

Repertoire

You either know the tunes or you do not work in the club date field. This has been the case since at least the early 1950s. Surprisingly, as radical a change as it must have been at first—especially for those musicians working with large ensembles—no one who was active in club dates during the forties and fifties was able to give me a clear picture of exactly when and why the change took place. My own understanding of the process comes from a kind of composite oral history, culled from interviews and conversations with leaders and sidepersons who were part of the process.

It seems that, following World War II, a particular set of social, musical, and economic circumstances made it possible—even inevitable, some would say—for club date bands to do away with written music entirely. Older club date musicians generally agree that there were always some smaller bands that could perform for an entire evening without reading music, but they were in the minority before the war. Most club date bands, large and small, played from written music, using either fake books or stock arrangements:

Every band took a book on the job before the war. [Only one leader] didn't bring music on the job. I remember doing small jobs with him . . . when you did jobs with five or six men, you never used music. It was only the larger bands.
—*sideperson, early 60s, saxophone*

When I first started [in the mid-1940s], you would say, "If you have the music I'll play it." That seemed to be the proper thing to say. Not today.
—*sideperson, early 50s, piano*

The move away from written music evidently became a trend some time during or directly following the war. Musicians who were working in the club date field directly after the war had conflicting views on exactly *when* the change took place, but it is clear that all the major bandleaders had stopped using written arrangements by the mid-1950s. An individual musician's perception of the situation would depend on which leaders he worked for at the time. A trumpet player in his late 50s in 1978 remembered the change as having taken place while he was in the service: "Right after the war I came back and was astonished that everything had changed. Nobody was using music anymore. You had to play everything from memory." A violin player who began doing club dates in 1952 recalled some instances of using written arrangements, but these were exceptional:"Some leaders still used the stocks and then faked around it . . . but the [Lester] Lanin and [Meyer] Davis bands had already moved away from that. I worked for those bands when I first started in club dates. Sometimes you would have music, but only for new shows. Even so, you would learn the tune and arrangement after three or four times of playing it." Musicians who entered the club date field after the war recalled very few or no instances of using written music at performances.

The move away from written arrangements took place first in the bands that played for high-society clientele. Relying on written arrangements was not always practical or possible because of the nature of society parties. The parties would often last eight or more hours, and the bandleaders prided themselves on being able to satisfy nearly any request from the party guests. Of course, not every requested song would be in the book of arrangements, but usually some band members would be at least familiar with the song. So, to satisfy the request, part of the band—perhaps just the lead trumpet and the rhythm section—would "fake" its way through as well as it could. Also, the performance format known as continuous music, introduced first in the society field, compelled bandleaders to rely less and less on charts (musicians' slang for written music). The term *continuous music* means exactly what it says: the music is continuous; it never stops. The client is getting more music altogether but is also paying substantially more for the service. The extra cost explains why the format was limited at first to society affairs, even though it is standard throughout the business today. In any case, keeping the music going continuously was not always a practical possibility if twenty or more band members had to search through their books of arrangements for the next song. Consequently, more and more "faked" tunes needed to be fit in between the written medleys:

> Dates might run from nine o'clock to four, six, seven o'clock in the morning, and they couldn't carry that large a library . . . it was just more convenient for the leaders. . . . Somebody comes up and they want to hear a particular song while the band's playing. Now, if ten or twelve men are going to have to go digging through a library for number 585 or some silly number, it doesn't work.
>
> It probably started with the smaller bands and then gradually evolved to where the bigger bands didn't bother with it either. It's also easier for the leader not having to haul a big case of arrangements on the job.
> —*sideperson, early 60s, saxophone*

Even if the entire repertoire could have been included in a leader's library, the arrangements would still have been inadequate, because the size and constituency of bands changed from night to night. An arrangement written for a ten-piece band will not work for a sixteen-piece band, and vice versa. The number of musicians in a band depended both on the desires of a party's sponsor and on the minimum number of musicians required at the party location by Local 802. One union official felt that these "minimums" were the main reason why playing from memory and "faking" harmony became standard practice in the club date field: "Where faking harmony really took hold was probably due to the minimum number of musicians required in the hotel ballrooms. If you've got to hire ten or twelve people (and you don't have appropriate arrangements), somebody's got to know how to fake. Once a few leaders figured out that they didn't have to buy the music, others followed."

Another major factor in the change to a no-music policy was the availability of stock arrangements. The bulk of the society band repertoire came from Broadway shows, and the charts that society bands used were the same stock arrangements used by big bands throughout the United States. There was one big difference, however: the publishers would commonly provide these arrangements free of charge to the society leaders. It was good advertising for the Broadway shows, and also good for sheet music and record sales. But with the breakup of the big bands following World War II and the demise of the genre's market, the publishers drastically cut back their output. They stopped giving away arrangements to society leaders, and by the late 50s, they stopped publishing stocks altogether:

> After the war, these companies stopped making stocks on all of their tunes. Before the war, every show that came out, every publishing company made stocks for. Occasionally, they'd have to pay for them, but the publishers were tickled to death to get their songs played, so they sent orchestrations to the bigger leaders.
>
> Naturally, through the rest of the country they sold them, but in the big cities they just gave to the leaders. The leaders would go down there once a week or month and pick up a whole stack of orchestrations. A lot of them were current songs, or some were just older songs that they had too many copies of.
>
> —*sideperson, early 60s, saxophone*

Obviously, maintaining a library of arrangements once such complimentary stocks were no longer available could add considerably to a leader's business expenses. If leaders wanted charts for current hits of any sort, they would have to pay someone to write them. The leader who could do without arrangements at all not only had a new selling point for his bands but also stood to save a lot of money.

Probably the most important factor in bringing about the change is that the number of steady location jobs at hotels and ballrooms diminished rapidly as the popularity of big bands waned during the 1940s. While steady engagement work was still readily available, the number of musicians in the club date field who could play without music remained relatively small.

> In a ten- or twelve-piece band, there would be two or three older guys who could fake the old tunes, and they would sandwich them in between the new stuff . . . at that point [before the war], they didn't have that many men who could fake harmony parts. It was a thing that evolved over years.
>
> —*sideperson, early 60s, saxophone*

The club date field attracted many musicians who no longer had steady work yet wanted to continue performing music in New York:

> During the Swing Era, most of the musicians who could play were playing in the swing bands. It was after the demise of the swing bands that we all gravitated to the floor [the union exchange floor, traditionally used as a hiring hall]. It [the club date business] was, in effect, the last refuge for musicians, the only source of steady work.
> —*sideperson, late 60s, violin (1989)*

The musicians who had played in hotel or ballroom bands were well acquainted with the standard dance repertoire, and many of them knew not only melodies but also harmonies from memory:

> They played the same stocks day after day, year after year. And the same man would be playing second part all the time, and after a while he might not even be able to play the melody, but he could play the second part to almost any standard song he'd ever played. You had a whole slew of people who, as the hotels were closing out, could play in sections.
> —*sideperson, early 50s, piano*

When I asked one saxophone player how he had first learned to fake harmony parts, he explained it exactly that way. He had played in swing bands and in the house band at WNBC radio, always on the third alto part:

> So, being third alto for those couple of jobs, I learned the harmonies just by osmosis. I didn't make a point of it, but I began to know the harmonies for all the tunes of the day. When I began working with other people, I could play third alto or lead. . . . The other guys probably [learned] the same way—they learned it by osmosis.
> —*sideperson, late 60s, saxophone (1989)*

The more that musicians with this ability entered the club date field, the less that leaders had to rely on arrangements. Just which leader first made the step of presenting an entire evening of music with a large orchestra and no written arrangements was unknown to the leaders and sidepersons I interviewed. It seems most likely that a number of different leaders, all of them drawing from the same pool of musicians, were experimenting with the idea simultaneously. In any case, once the major leaders made this practice a standard policy, all the others soon followed suit. The sidepersons, in turn, realized that memorizing the repertoire was going to be necessary to continue working in the club date business, and some apparently chose to leave the field at that time:

> So it just evolved: if you want to work, you have these tunes under your thumb. Gradually the ones who could do it got the jobs, and the others either dropped by the wayside or went into other work like shows or things where you'd be reading.
> —*sideperson and union official, early 60s, saxophone*

By the late 1940s written arrangements had become the exception rather than the rule in the club date business. Each song came to be played in its "standard key," which was normally the original key of the sheet music or stock arrangement of the song. Without a standard key for each song, leaders could never be sure that all band members would know a particular song in the same key signature. Knowing a song in the wrong key signature became equivalent to not knowing the song at all. A. Ray DeVita's *Standard Dance Music Guide*, first copyrighted in 1939, became a standard reference tool for club date musicians. There is no written music in the book, but there are lists of thousands of songs with their standard keys and starting notes, making it quite valuable both for remembering previously learned songs and adding new ones.

Each song in the repertoire also came to be phrased in a style that was more or less standard throughout the club date business, a style reminiscent of the phrasing used by the large swing bands. Lead trumpet, saxophone, and violin players became responsible for keeping the phrasing as standard as possible so that other musicians in their sections could anticipate the correct phrasing from previous experience.

The musician who first described the "standard phrasing" concept to me used the song "C'est Magnifique" as an example. Figure 1 shows the melody first as it appears in a sheet music version of the song[1] and then as it was sung to me by this man, a trumpet player. After singing these four bars of the melody to me, he added,

> If the first trumpet player didn't do it that way, I'd consider him an inferior first trumpet player. I would consider his playing unpredictable, and I would not consider him a good experienced first trumpet player capable of organizing and laying down a pattern that the rest of the orchestra can follow.

Figure 1: "C'est Magnifique" (from *Can-Can*)

Line 1 = sheet music
Line 2 = club date phrasing   Cole Porter 1953

> Sometimes there is a certain amount of ambivalence, but most of the time there is pretty much of a standard way. If I'm playing second trumpet, and I anticipate the lead player, most of the time I'm right.
> —*sideperson, late 40s, trumpet*

For some standard songs, melody notes may be added or subtracted in club date usage; others lend themselves to "tag" endings, where measures 29 and 30 of the thirty-two-bar song are repeated twice before proceeding to the final resolution note in measure 31 (assuming, of course, that the song is the last in a medley). All these rhythmic and melodic devices are typical in dance band arrangements of songs that were originally vocal numbers, especially ones from Broadway shows. (Before rock music entered the club date repertoire, vocals never accounted for a large portion of the music.) Nonetheless, a musician can learn which particular changes in phrasing are common practice on individual songs only by performance experience in the club date field.

Some leaders will specify a song's phrasing according to their own tastes, and musicians are obliged to change their phrasing accordingly. As long as the personnel in the band does not change too radically from night to night, the leader can expect the band to play in the desired manner. One particular leader was noted by a number of sidepersons for his tendency to phrase nearly all songs except waltzes in a sharp staccato style, which was, they assumed, his way of "jazzing up" a melody. A sideperson who worked for this leader for over twenty years recalled the treatment of "On the Street Where You Live" as a flagrant example of this approach. Whereas most club date

Figure 2: "On the Street Where You Live" (from *My Fair Lady*)

Line 1 = sheet music & normal club date phrasing   F. Lowe 1956
Line 2 = society leader X's phrasing   Chappell & Co., Inc.

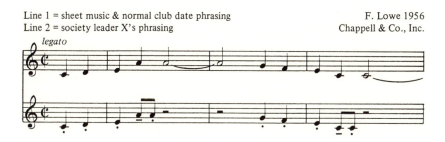

bands would follow the legato phrasing indicated on the sheet music,[2] musicians in this leader's band were expected to play the song with short, staccato phrasing and also at a somewhat faster tempo than one might expect (see figure 2).

Conflicts in phrasing were bound to occur if musicians were unfamiliar with a leader's style, but musicians who worked for a number of different leaders soon learned which phrasings were peculiar to certain leaders and which were common to most. Even the most experienced club date musicians do not always agree completely on the phrasing for every song in the repertoire, but as one trumpet player emphasized,

> Don't forget—we're not making recordings, and we do not need perfection. All we need is about 90 percent. That's enough because people are not listening to the music critically. They're not listening to every note, and if sometimes I might play a phrase differently from another man, it's not that critical. As long as we're together most of the time, and that's the way it is.
> *—sideperson, late 40s, trumpet*

If party guests were listening to the music critically, they might well find the less-than-perfect "head" arrangements less than acceptable. Club date bands can get by without charts, even though some mistakes are nearly inevitable, because the party context allows it. Music is not the sole focus, and consequently, the performance does not have to be perfect. The music's function—it's "fit" in the social context—can be as important as the actual sound in determining the audience's appreciation of it. If party guests enjoy the celebration as a whole, the bandleader is likely to be praised for his or her part in the scene. On the other hand, regardless of how good the actual sound of the band may be, if the party flops for any reason, the band is also less than successful.

The change to a no-music format took place before rock music appeared on the popular music scene, when the term "American popular music" still referred to an easily defined and stylistically consistent repertoire. The majority of songs used the thirty-two-bar, AABA song form and were easily adapted to a foxtrot dance rhythm. The homogeneity of this body of music, which musicians today refer to as "standards," facilitated the memorization process for club date musicians. A trumpet player known among veteran club date musicians for his vast knowledge of tunes recalled how relatively easy it was to learn this standard repertoire:

> I have the reputation of knowing more tunes than anybody in the business. I didn't work at it. I just have that kind of mind which retains melody once I hear it. . . . We grew up in an era when the average song was a thirty-two-bar song—eight bars repeated, then an eight-bar bridge, then eight bars again. So it was a hell of a lot easier. . . . [But] some of the rock tunes I've actually had to pick up the music for, because it doesn't have the kind of continuity that we're accustomed to . . . you have to look at them.
>
> —*sideperson, late 40s, trumpet*

For many standard songs, then, the musician needed to learn only sixteen measures of music, because the first eight measures would appear three times. Examples of this include such familiar songs as "I'm in the Mood for Love" (1935), "I Can't Get Started" (1936), "The Lady Is a Tramp" (1937), "Over the Rainbow" (1939), "Blue Moon" (1934), "Misty" (1954), "Satin Doll" (1958), and "More" (1962).

The large portion of this standard repertoire that came from shows on Broadway became almost synonymous with "society music" to club date musicians. Bill Harrington, a popular society leader, explained this association quite succinctly in this quote from a 1966 *New York Times* article: "These people are theatergoers, and what they've heard on stage is their notion of popular music. If they liked what they heard in the theater, they want to dance to it."[3] Or, as one sideperson and subleader explained it, a bit more crudely:

> Society people don't work; they go to the theater. So, naturally they're going to want to hear show tunes. They'll ask for show tunes you never knew existed.
>
> —*sideperson and subleader, late 30s, guitar and vocals.*

It was common practice at society affairs to play nearly all these show tunes at a bright foxtrot tempo—"bright" often meaning 100 or more beats per minute *in cut time*. Club date musicians refer to this almost undanceable tempo as "society tempo" or "the businessman's bounce."

> We had to play everything at that tempo. That's what the social secretaries wanted, and that's what the clients wanted. They did not want any variations—they just wanted wallpaper. . . . Everything should be like it was at the other party . . . no experimentation, even if the kids wanted something else.
>
> So we had to take every kind of tune and just beat this thing out—tune after tune at this tempo. And, I'm telling you, it was hard work, because many of the tunes didn't fit.
>
> People used to walk around to that because it was too fast to dance to. Some danced, but most just walked.
>
> —*society leader, early 70s, saxophone and vocals*

When I first heard a society band playing in this style I could hardly believe my ears. "Some Enchanted Evening" and "Bewitched" are two I remember particularly: try singing either one at a very fast tempo and you'll have a good idea of what the leader just quoted meant when he said it was hard work making everything fit that one tempo.

Latin American music was the first major stylistic addition to the standard repertoire. The music gained popularity throughout the United States in the 1930s, and Latin repertoire began to enter the club date scene in the 1940s, once both the music and its associated dances had become a national craze. Particularly in the Jewish area of the business, knowledge of Latin repertoire became a necessity:

> Latin music was almost half the repertoire, especially in the Jewish work. It has spilled over into society now. You never had Latin in society except the samba.
>
> There was a tradition for years of having a beautiful woman singer up front shaking maracas. The reason for the maracas is that we have minimums. They couldn't just have a singer on since she would be an additional person and the minimums go by instrument. So they'd join the union as maraca players, and there are still listings of maraca players.[4]
>
> Even before that, you had to have a man up front with a ruffled shirt and dark complexion playing maracas or timbales. That was because if you didn't do that there would be an all-Latin orchestra.

So the regular leaders would say, "Sure, I'll give you a Latin band."
Then he'd hire his regular men and put one Latin guy up front.
—*sideperson, early 50s, piano*

One leader who had spent many summers during the 1950s working in bands at various resorts in the Catskills recalled that there, too,
Latin music was strongly associated with the Jewish clientele:

> Every hotel had a dance teacher. . . . One night a week every hotel
> would put on a dance fiesta, where all the teachers in the area
> would come down to dance at this specific hotel. Now, these people
> became so interested in watching the dance instructors that they
> then were sucked into taking dance lessons. So, that's one of the
> big factors for the Latin music being so popular with the Jewish
> people. . . .
> These bands like Tito Puente and Noro Morales and Tito Rod-
> riguez were strictly playing in Jewish hotels and Jewish clubs.
> Every hotel had a major Latin band and a minor dance band.
> Whereas the Christian hotels did not have the Latin bands. They
> did not stress that kind of music, and they did not have the dance
> instructors.
> —*leader, late 50s, trumpet and vocals*

John Storm Roberts, in speaking of Latin music in New York in the
1930s, notes that there were many Jewish leaders and band members
in Latin bands throughout the city and that "Latin music's hardcore
non-Latin audience was almost entirely 'ethnic'—largely Jewish and
Italian—and black."[5] Exactly why this Latin-Jewish connection developed is not at all clear, but it seems to have a long history. Eventually,
Latin music filtered into the other areas of the club date business as
well, becoming part of the general repertoire. You will still generally
hear more Latin music at Jewish occasions than elsewhere, but Latin
tunes are common today at Gentile and society parties as well.

In the Jewish and Gentile areas, some knowledge of ethnic music
was also expected. An accordion player who came to New York from
Chicago in 1948 noticed this prevalence of ethnic music as a distinguishing feature of the New York scene: "Repertoire was only a
problem where it became international, since New York is such a
cosmopolitan place. You had to play music from all the countries of
Western and Eastern Europe. . . . I worked one summer for a bandleader who did a lot of work for weddings and bar mitzvahs for Jewish
clientele. We were at a hotel [in the Catskills], and the clientele were

largely Eastern European Jewish. I learned a great amount of repertoire that I never knew before." The musician who learned enough of a single ethnic repertoire could begin to accept strictly ethnic work, which was apparently readily available in the 1940s and 1950s:

> New York, because of its size and many ethnic groups, is different. At one time, you could make a full-time living doing just parties for Jewish clients or Greeks. The city offered a living for specialists in a variety of musics and also for those who could "cover all bases."
> —*sideperson, early 50s, piano*

One trumpet player, saying that he had "made a fetish" of learning the repertoire of different ethnic groups, cited some areas of ethnic work that are still available to the musician who is willing to learn the necessary repertoire:

> We get real Italian jobs, off-the-boat Italian jobs, where they aren't interested in American music. They want Italian songs, and they'll get musicians who are into heavy Italian music, not guys who can only play a few songs. . . . There are also the heavy Greek jobs. . . . There's also a growing market for Hasidic music, and they want only Jewish music. They don't want any American music. You play "Hello Dolly" at a Hasidic wedding and to say they'd frown upon it is an understatement—they're liable to throw knives and forks at you.
> —*sideperson, late 40s, trumpet*

Not all club date musicians who work in the society, Jewish, or Gentile areas have either the time or the patience to learn enough of a single ethnic repertoire to accept strictly ethnic work. Learning an ethnic repertoire can be much more difficult than learning the popular music used for other club date work. Discovering which songs are best to learn is a complicated task, since there are fewer available recordings, less reliable sheet music, and less opportunity to get on-the-job experience. Also, much of the ethnic music demands new and relatively difficult instrumental techniques for the outsider.

How many songs club date musicians in the 1940s and 1950s would know from each of the categories I have mentioned—standards, Latin and ethnic—would depend on the area of the business in which they worked most frequently. All of the older musicians whom I interviewed worked in all four areas—society, Jewish, Gentile, and ethnic—at one time or another, and most continue to do so today. A musician's general repertoire, then, would include songs from all three categories, with the most emphasis on standards, since they were useful for all three of the non-ethnic areas of the business.

Rock music, although it first appeared on the popular music scene in 1954, did not find its way into the general club date repertoire until much later. After all, sponsors of private parties are adults, and there were few adults in the 1950s who were rock music enthusiasts. Club date leaders succeed through selecting music that is familiar and pleasing to party guests, and rock music was at first both unfamiliar and unpleasant to most of their clientele. A few leaders did begin using rock guitar players in their bands in the late 1950s, in response to increasing demand from young party guests. One leader who first began using rock guitar players in 1958 and 1959 recalled receiving comments such as "How could you bring something like that into a country club?" A society leader described similar reactions from both audiences and musicians:

> The men said, "Hey, he's nuts." I said, "Well, I'm going to stay nuts." We started doing debutante parties with them [rock guitar players], and they all said it was premature [1958]. And we went to Newport. The people said to me, "We love you, but we think you're insane with this cannibal noise." Now, if I go to Newport and, depending on the type of occasion, if I don't bring any rock, I'd be out of luck.
>
> —*leader, early 60s*

The musicians were uncertain at first how to approach this new music. Not only was it completely different from the standard club date repertoire, but also few of the musicians felt it was anything more than a passing fad:

> I did a thing in the Garden [Madison Square Garden] in 1955, and a group played after us. I couldn't figure out what they were doing—it sounded like it belonged in the mountains. They told me it was rhythm and blues. It was a complete mystery to most of us old-line musicians. In fact, it's still a mystery to most of us, since we can't quite fathom its appeal. The beginnings of rock were completely out of the mental reach of the club date musician. And we acted as though maybe if we didn't bother with it it would go away. It hardly did that—quite the opposite. It engulfed us, really.
>
> —*sideperson, early 60s, saxophone*

We didn't think it would be around in 1960. We'd joke that some day it's going to be one of us old guys and a rock band instead of the one "rocker." I do jobs like that today, where I'm there to do requests for older things that the younger players can't do. So it's switched around in a lot of cases.

—*sideperson, early 60s, saxophone*

At first, rock music was not perceived as a major change by older club date musicians, who initially were not even expected to play on the few rock numbers the bandleader called for. The leaders who introduced rock into the club date bands did so simply by hiring a rock guitar player—a "rocker," as the musicians came to call him—and he was solely responsible for satisfying requests for rock numbers. The role of the rocker was precisely the same as that of the Latin musician in club date bands of the 1940 and 1950s: the specialist in a genre of music that the regular band could not perform authentically. This single rock specialist was a common feature in the Jewish, society, and Gentile areas of the business well into the 1970s. One of these guitarists, Bruce Bergman, even published a small book for aspiring rockers: *How to Make Money Playing Rock Guitar: The Complete Professional Club Date Rock Guide.* Of course, by the time the book was published in 1976, much of the author's advice was already somewhat dated, for by then the rock guitarist had become less of a specialist and more of an integrated band member, even a bandleader, as were many of the guitarists I spoke with both in 1978 and in 1989. Only in those areas of the business where large bands were the norm, the society field in particular, did the rock specialist remain a common figure. Bergman's description of rock's appearance on the club date scene points out very clearly the problems facing the leaders at the time:

At first the club date orchestras were simply unable to play any rock. Then, to meet the demand, they developed a few rock tunes. However, musicians schooled in show tunes and standards, no matter how good they may be, cannot play music which approaches authentic rock, particularly without a guitar sound. If you've ever heard piano, drums and trumpet try to copy the Rolling Stones you'll know what I mean. Most non-rock players have not grown up with rock music and therefore neither understand it, know anything about it or like it. Not only don't they play it, but they have no knowledge of the requests.

All this being the case, club date offices sought out a musician to meet the trend—the rock guitar specialist.[6]

The guitarist eventually came to be responsible for nearly all contemporary material outside of Broadway show tunes, even though much of the music would not have been considered rock by any youthful audience. Bergman refers to this nonrock contemporary material as "pop," "a special category of standards which are treated by club date leaders as modern standards which fall somewhere in between standards and rock. For example, when Burt Bacharach's 'Raindrops Keep Fallin' on My Head' came out in 1969, every club date band in the business started playing it. It came to pass that this modern type song was often sung on the job by the rock guitar player."[7] Other such "in-between" songs that Bergman includes in this category are "The Look of Love" (1967), "We've Only Just Begun" (1970), "Yesterday" (1965)," "Tie a Yellow Ribbon 'round the Old Oak Tree" (1972), "Sweet Gypsy Rose" (1973), "You Are the Sunshine of My Life" (1972), and "The Way We Were" (1973).

In the club date context these songs would not normally be played with a strongly emphasized rock rhythm and consequently would not be conducive to dancing in the nontouch styles associated with rock. The songs "The Way We Were" and "Yesterday," for instance, are usually accompanied by "slow" dancing—a general term for dancing that involves little more than moving in time to the music while in close embrace with one's partner. The songs "Raindrops Keep Fallin' on My Head," "Tie a Yellow Ribbon 'round the Old Oak Tree," and "Sweet Gypsy Rose" are often accompanied by foxtrot dancing. The rhythms for most of these songs do not really correspond to any one specific dance step; rhythmically, they are neither strictly rock, nor strictly Latin, nor strictly foxtrot but somewhere in-between. The dancers respond in a variety of ways. During one band's performance of "You Are the Sunshine of My Life," for example, I noticed three different dance steps being done: nontouch rock dancing, foxtrot, and what appeared to be a bossa nova step. In speaking of this category of music, club date musicians will use the terms *contemporary, pop, moderns,* or *contemporary pop,* but it is not always clear what the limits of the terms are. I have chosen to use the term *contemporary pop* to distinguish this music from rock because it is not usually accompanied by nontouch rock styles of dancing. Often, such music is used not for dancing at all but rather as interlude material while guests are seated for dinner courses.

Because the rock guitarist was at first solely responsible for both rock and contemporary pop songs, this material did not present any immediate problems for older musicians from the standpoint of learning new repertoire. The addition of a rock specialist did represent a threat, however, for he often replaced one of the other band members:

Let's assume that you have a six-piece band. Without a rock-and-roller, it would be drums, keyboard, possibly bass, and then three horns—sax, trumpet, trombone. Now they turn around and take that six-piece band, add a rock-and-roller to it. If they're keeping it six pieces, the first one to go is the trombone. In other words, you're replacing musicians. And it would go all the way down the line. You've got a five-piece band with sax and trumpet, you replace the trumpet player. And with a four-piece band, you'd replace the sax player.
  —*subleader, late 30s, guitar and vocals*

Common instrumentation for a four-piece club date band in 1978 included guitar/bass guitar, drums, electric piano, and sax/clarinet/flute, although this instrumentation did not become standard until the late 1960s and early 1970s:

It was a gradual change. . . . The instrumentation originally, when I started in the music business [in the 1940s]—say in a four-piece band—would be drums, piano—but usually accordion because the pianos were in terrible shape—and trumpet and somebody who played saxophone and clarinet. That's your standard four-piece band. If you had five, you had a bass fiddle.

As the years went by, you dropped the bass fiddle for guitar; then you dropped one of the horns for guitar. Some of the bands which are really far out on the rock have dropped both horns, so that now you have both guitar and bass guitar. And the keyboard instrument has become an organ/electric piano-type thing.
  —*leader, early 50s, piano*

Accordion players were those most directly affected by the increasing popularity of rock music. Some have continued to play accordion only, but their work opportunities have decreased sharply:

A lot of people did not want to buy a band that had something that looked like an accordion in it. It wasn't the sound but the sight of the thing that they cared about. Leaders would say to me, "You play very well, but the guy who played with me most of the time plays electric piano. And I can't very well sell my band with an accordion player in it no matter what it sounds like.

It looks wrong for today's concept, and my feelings on that for the longest time were to resist it. I like the way an accordion sounds, and I like what you can do with an expressive instrument as opposed to a cheap portable organ.

—sideperson, late 20s, piano and accordion

By the 1970s it had become very difficult to sell any band that could not consistently produce authentic-sounding rock music. At many affairs with predominantly young audiences, rock came to constitute nearly half the repertoire. And it was not only the younger guests who wanted rock:

Nine years ago, ten years ago, you could get away on a job without it. Now, you book a conservative-type client—even though they might want *one* rock-and-roll number out of four hours, if it doesn't have the right flavor, you've really delivered a job that was a turkey.

If you come in and do a wedding or bar mitzvah now—when I say wedding, I mean any kind of ethnic group: Italian, Irish, WASP, Jewish, anything—and do it without rock and roll, you've got a disaster. Because you didn't include half of what everybody wants to hear. And I'm including the sixty-year-old grandmothers too, because the whole thing has become a standard part of the scene. Now *that* has come about in the last six or seven years.

—leader, early 50s, piano

In addition, by 1978 most bandleaders expected that all members of a club date band, regardless of instrument, would be able to contribute something to a band's arrangement of rock material. This situation came about only gradually as it became clear to older musicians—both leaders and sidepersons—that knowing rock repertoire was an economic necessity:

For a long time all the offices hired a guitarist who showed up and sang his ditties, and many of the old-line players would leave the stand or be sent off by the leaders, which was a bad thing. Because as the rock and rollers became more polished, pretty soon people were saying, "Hey, more people are dancing to this than to that other band." And many rock players were approached for jobs while doing club dates and went to do their own thing. They could do it with only three guys, so why not?

Then some of the leaders decided that when the rocker plays you'd better stay on that bandstand so it looks like we're all doing something. And pretty soon they [the band members] realized that they could play many of the rock riffs on their instruments.

Now this took an awful long time. It took ten or twelve years for this to happen, because most of us would sit there like a bunch of carbuncles. It was embarrassing. The better club date musicians have finally accepted the fact that rock is here and it is possible to make it musical and even be a part of it.

—*sideperson, early 60s, saxophone*

Throughout the 1960s, the rockers themselves were becoming more versatile musically and could contribute more than just an occasional rock number accompanied by drums alone. Many were able to sing suitable background parts for the other players or even write them out beforehand for the players to memorize and this helped the "old-line" players adapt to the new music. Also, most of the rockers who stayed in the business began to learn the songs in the standard repertoire, often doubling on electric bass for the nonrock material. Eventually, the entire repertoire became everyone's responsibility, regardless of instrument.

Just how many songs an individual club date musician knows is a fascinating question but impossible to determine. The musicians themselves could only guess at the size of their repertoire. Many said that a basic knowledge of "about 300" songs would be a minimum for a beginner in the business. Veteran players felt certain that most of them knew 2,000 or more songs well enough to perform.

To give a general indication of the size and scope of the repertoire, I compiled song lists from nine performances in 1978—four bar mitzvahs, one Jewish wedding, two Gentile dinner dances, one society dinner dance, and one Jewish-Christian wedding. I have divided the total number of songs, 520, into six categories to give some indication of the repertoire. I have already discussed five of the categories: Standards, Latin, Ethnic, Rock, and Contemporary Pop. The sixth category, Group Participation, includes songs that involve either group dancing specific to the song ("The Alley Cat," "The Hokey Pokey," "The Mexican Hat Dance") or group singing ("Happy Birthday," "The Bride Cuts the Cake"). These categories reflect distinctions that are useful both to a bandleader in selecting songs appropriate for a particular audience and, in turn, to sidepersons in determining which types of music are most necessary for their repertoire. The categories are distinguished from one another by two factors: (1) the age group that is probably most familiar with a particular song and consequently most likely to appreciate it, and (2) the dance styles that normally accompany a song (see table 1).

Although the musicians use these names for the categories in speaking of repertoire, the terms do not necessarily mean the same thing to everyone. As noted above, *contemporary pop* is only one of a variety of terms that musicians use for nonrock contemporary music, and not even those terms have generally agreed upon meanings. All musicians used the term *standards,* yet what that category includes can vary from individual to individual. The club date musicians, after all, have no real reason to create theoretical labels or definitions for the music they play. Theirs is a practical understanding of the music. Bandleaders know which songs are useful for different audiences and at different times during a party, and sidepersons learn the songs that bandleaders are likely to select, whatever kind of songs they might be. As one subleader said when I asked him how he went about pacing a performance,

> Well, I've never really thought about it—I just do it. So if I stumble and bumble, you'll have to forgive me. It's a very interesting thing you're doing. I've never really consciously thought about it, but I'll try and do it right now. Look, that's why God created sociology.

Table 1. Song Categories and Associated Age Groups and Dance Styles

Category	Age Group	Dance Styles
Standards	older adults	primarily foxtrots, also two-step, Charleston, waltz
Rock	teenagers and young adults	nontouch or disco
Contemporary Pop	all age groups	no single step: nontouch, Latin, foxtrot, "slow," or all four
Latin	adults	cha-cha, merengue, tango, rumba, etc.
Group Participation	all age groups	steps corresponding to the song or none (sing-along)

At any rate, the first thing you realize is that within four hours you're going to have to give a fairly good mixture. And it's two mixtures—one is a mixture of kinds of music: 1930s, 1950s, 1960s; and the second one is kinds of dances: cha-cha, foxtrot, you know—what have you.

—*subleader, early 40s, trombone and vocals*

By "kinds of music" this man was referring to music directed to particular age groups—the first distinction I have used. "Kinds of dances" is my second distinction.

A few examples from my list point out just how fuzzy the boundaries between the categories can be. There are cases where a song is obviously derived from the tradition represented by one category yet, as performed, belongs elsewhere. "Fly Me to the Moon" is often used as a Latin number, and I included in that category; nonetheless, the sheet music for the song is in 3/4 time, and it is often played as a foxtrot in 4/4 time. Also, a few songs that are generally known to musicians as standards were performed as disco numbers: "Baby Face," "My Way," "Over the Rainbow," and "Our Day Will Come" are all examples of this. Songs played while guests were seated for dinner courses—known collectively as "interlude" songs—are all in either the contemporary pop or standards categories, where they would most likely be if used as dance numbers.

Because most songs were included in sets, with each set using the same rhythm and tempo, I could accurately categorize a song even though I did not recognize it immediately by title. The bandleader might also announce songs by saying "It's mambo time," or "Let's do the hora," or "Let's take a nostalgia trip back to the era of the big bands," which made the category clear whether the song was familiar or not. This was especially helpful, because I was often keeping track of songs while engaged in conversation with curious party guests or musicians on break.

Keeping these qualifications in mind, the 520 songs played at these nine performances distribute as shown in table 2.

The actual number of song titles was much less than 520, since many songs appeared at more than one performance. Of the 414 songs that I knew by title, there were only 237 different titles. Assuming that an approximately equal percentage of titles appeared more than once in the unknown group, this would account for 47 additional titles. (Because the percentage of repeated songs varied from category to category, I calculated this separately for each category.)

Table 2. Distribution by Category of Songs Played

Category	Number	Percentage of Total
Standards	210	40.4
Rock	107	20.6
Contemporary Pop	76	14.5
Latin	52	10.0
Ethnic	57	11.0
Group Participation	18	3.5
Total	520	100

To have performed at all the affairs in the sample—not an entirely unlikely occurrence—a musician would have needed to know approximately 292 songs. The breakdown according to category is shown in table 3.

A full-time club date musician certainly has a repertoire far greater than this sample represents. The area of the business in which the musician most often works determines the emphasis placed on the different categories. A musician who works primarily in the society field will naturally have a predominance of standard repertoire; one who plays many bar mitzvahs and weddings on Long Island will know a large amount of current rock and probably Latin material. There is, of course, a limit to the number of songs a club date musician knows, even though bandleaders surely hope to satisfy every request from their clients, however obscure the titles of those requests may be. But no leader can afford to rely on obscure or esoteric material, particularly if he or she does not have the same musicians in the band from night to night. Within each area of the business, then, there is a general repertoire with which all experienced players are familiar:

Table 3. Required Repertoire Size, by Song Category

Category	Number of Titles	Percentage of Total
Standards	130	44.5
Rock	61	20.8
Contemporary Pop	44	15.1
Latin	24	8.2
Ethnic	25	8.6
Group Participation	8	2.8
Total	292	100

If you've learned the style and repertoire for one of these society offices, you've pretty much learned the same for all of the society offices. It's pretty much the same with the Hasidic work. If you learn the repertoire for one office, you can be pretty sure that the same tunes and arrangements will be used by the other offices. Because what they [leaders] choose to play is determined by what the people in the band happen to know.

There's not much new on the horizon. It's much like military hardware: one nation has something; the other nations follow through rapidly. So you learn different repertoires which will accommodate any office in that particular field.

—*sideperson, late 50s, saxophone*

As Bergman describes the situation, "The thing to remember is that the club date business is an inbred subculture with everybody in it doing just about the same thing, the only difference being that some do it better than others."[8]

Many musicians noted that, because most of them perform in more than a single area of the business, there is a tendency for songs to "spill over" from one area to another:

One thing about repertoire: when a musician in the club date business learns a variety of different areas—say society and Jewish and Italian—there's always going to be a spillover. Tunes become part of a general repertoire, and there's going to be situations where you'll play show tunes although they may mean nothing to the people at the party. So these people get acquainted with other styles, even though they may not have wanted to hear them in the first place.

That may be one of the ways in which Latin music made it into the society area . . . there was a tendency on the part of the players to use the repertoire that they had, not to limit themselves as narrowly as one would be required to [for an individual area].

—*sideperson, early 50s, piano*

Regardless of their instrument or age, musicians who hope to sustain themselves through club date performance must have a repertoire large and varied enough to allow them to play for various leaders in different areas of the business. Guitarists, though they remain the specialists for rock material, must be able to play standard nonrock songs. Trumpet, saxophone, and trombone players, as well as drummers, must be able to contribute to rock arrangements;

otherwise, they limit the amount of jobs available to them. The musicians most in demand in the business are those who have, in a sense, specialized in diversity.

The Learning Process

Discovering which songs make up this general repertoire is no simple task for musicians entering the field. The task was certainly easier, though, before rock music came on the scene, for the bulk of the repertoire consisted of standards and Latin American music, which were both current genres familiar to working musicians into the 1950s. Even so, a certain amount of on-the-job training was unavoidable:

> The only way you learn what the requirements are is by going on a job and not knowing. Then you go and get the music or find somebody who can show it to you. So your repertoire is constantly expanding as you work.
> —*sideperson, late 50s, accordion*

> When I began in the club date business, I had a fake book on my music stand in my basement for about two years. And any time a leader called a song that I didn't know—and there were plenty that I didn't know—I would make it a point to assume that that tune would be called again in the near future and I'd better learn it. Because I had in effect been told that that tune is called and that tune is played. And I did learn it.
> —*sideperson, late 40s, trumpet*

Club date bandleaders do not expect newcomers to the business to know every tune called, as much as they might like that to be the case. Still, for the novice club dater, pleading ignorance too often can be both very uncomfortable on the bandstand and harmful to one's reputation:

> I could go on a club date and not know a tune, and those in the orchestra will just smile—it means nothing since I am established. I can get by with it, since he [the bandleader] knows that I have most of the repertoire down, and he feels secure with me in the band.
> If I was a new person on the scene, that one tune might seem to be catastrophic, since the leader would be afraid to call tunes I

wouldn't know. It would make him nervous, uptight. And maybe
that would mean an X in his book.

—*sideperson, late 50s, saxophone*

A certain amount of the music *must* be memorized before the first
job, but where to start? Fake books and recordings contain nearly all
the songs ever used on club dates, but how is a musician to know
which of the thousands of popular songs from the turn of the century
to the present are useful club date material? And some of the music
played at a club date is hardly ever played elsewhere. A female singer
who got into club dates in the mid-1980s after working nightclubs for
a number of years recalled feeling very much out of her element at
first. "Many of the songs," she said, "seem to be indigenous to club
dates. You find that every bandleader calls for them, so you learn
them, but you never hear them anywhere else." On the society circuit,
bandleaders will routinely call for songs from Broadway shows of the
1930s and 1940s, some of which certainly *seem* obscure. Yet party
guests will dance by the stage singing along as the songs are played.

In the 1940s or 1950s club date repertoire was fairly consistent stylistically and probably did not differ considerably from the music
played at nightclubs or heard on the radio. By the 1960s, though,
rock music had become the nightclub staple, and musicians working
the nightclub circuit were less and less likely to be familiar with
Broadway show tunes and other standards. But the show tunes and
standards remained very much in the club date repertoire, as they
still do today. Outside of the club date business, perhaps the only contemporary context where musicians can gain at least a minimum familiarity with standards is playing jazz.

In reality, the only way to learn the basic repertoire requirements is
to talk with club date musicians themselves. Not surprisingly, most of
the musicians I spoke with who had entered the business after the
mid-1960s had relatives, teachers, or friends who were already active
in club dates. Indeed, well over half of the sixty-one musicians I interviewed had relatives in the business who provided the novices not
only with repertoire information but also with initial business contacts. It isn't quite a hereditary occupation, but because repertoire requirements as well as the general workings of the business are known
and transmitted mainly by word of mouth, players with family contacts certainly have a natural advantage at the start. The situation was
a bit different for those guitarists who were first hired as rock specialists, because they were expected to play only a small part of the repertoire. They could keep track of which songs were called without

being required to play on all of them. The rock repertoire learned from work in areas outside the club date field was sufficient to secure some work in club dates; the rest could be learned on the job simply by listening.

> I worked from about 1967 going around from club date office to club date office, and gradually word got out that myself and a few others were good at what we did. People *needed* us for the rock stuff, so they hired us, paid us union scale. Then, by *being* there, and if you had a mind to, I would watch and learn by being a side-man . . . when there wasn't a rock tune, I sat down and waited until he said "play." So I'd spend the time, instead of just daydreaming, I'd watch. I'd watch the leader and watch the tunes he called . . . and learned from there.
>
> —*sideperson and subleader, late 30s, guitar and vocals*

For younger musicians trying to get into the business with no personal contacts at all, there is no simple method. There are, for instance, club date workshops given occasionally by active club date musicians, but the few younger musicians I spoke with who had attended them felt that the workshops were not very helpful as far as repertoire was concerned. One sax player recalled attending such a workshop and becoming increasingly frustrated that the workshop's leader was unwilling to give the participants lists of songs, as if he were protecting secret information. Eventually, he did manage to collar the teacher one night when no other students were in class and got him to check off songs in various fake books. Beyond these workshops, the only way to learn about repertoire requirements is to establish contacts with active club date players. Bergman, for instance, has this advice for the novice guitarist: "Go to the largest catering hall in town. Wander around the building. Listen to as many bands as you can to get the feel of what's going on. Then, when a group is on a break, talk to the guitar player . . . and tell him you'd like to get into club dates. Musicians really are good people and almost any one of them will be glad to advise you."[9]

Musicians have two ways to determine whether they have acquired enough of the general repertoire to work regularly in the field. One is to audition for an office or independent leader. Some offices schedule formal auditions on a regular basis at catering halls or hotel function rooms; others may simply quiz the newcomer briefly at the office itself. The second method is to find an office or leader—again, through advice from other club date musicians—that is willing to hire a novice without an audition. Such offices will not be the best-paying or the most prestigious in the business, but this is just as well, because less is at risk if the first job does not go well. Still, the formal audition is the least risky, for the leaders or contractors in charge are accustomed to musicians failing once and returning later after learning more material. In either case, through audition or on the job, whether the musician's repertoire is sufficient will be clear from the reaction of the leader in charge.

The goal of learning the necessary repertoire is never completely attained, because new songs are constantly being added. In my repertoire sample from 1978, for instance, seventeen of the song titles had first appeared on the *Billboard* charts less than six months before I heard them, some only a few weeks before. Forty of the songs were less than five years old. Currency of repertoire is important, and both bandleaders and sidepersons are obliged to keep abreast of changes in the popular music scene on a monthly or even a weekly basis to satisfy the rapidly changing tastes of their audiences.

Most active club date musicians listen to popular radio stations on a fairly regular basis to be at least familiar with current hits. Guitarists especially need to know current repertoire, because they play the instrument most characteristic of the music, and they do vocals for most of the songs as well. They will not only listen to Top 40 radio but also record songs from it, buy sheet music, or buy the recordings themselves. One guitarist described his regular procedure for learning new material as follows:

> On Sunday mornings I listen to the Top 40 on one of the local FM stations. If I'm working in the afternoon, I'm usually listening to that on the way in the car. . . . I'll also look in the newspaper to see which songs are moving up in the charts in popularity. Then I'll either tape from the radio or go out and buy the single. We keep pretty fresh that way—constantly trying to work new songs in . . . I feel it's my responsibility to break in new tunes. For the bar mitzvahs especially. Those kids can drive you crazy requesting new songs.
> —*sideperson, late 20s, guitar and vocals*

Another guitarist said he would buy recordings immediately when they appeared on the market if he felt they would later be used on club dates:

> Not that I love the music, but I know it's good product. I'm a product, and I'm offering a product. Leaders like it when you're up on

the tunes; it gives them security. They represent the band, and if
you're up on the current tunes, so are they.

—*sideperson, late 20s, guitar and vocals*

Yet another guitarist had a rather methodical approach:

I more or less have myself on a schedule as far as rehearsing the
current tunes. I try to do about three or four hours a week and
learn three, four, or five tunes, although I'm more of a jazz player.
With the help of my wife, who likes the disco things and rock or
whatever you want to call it. She tells me what's current. Once in a
while I'll switch over to a commercial or rock-type station, but most
of the time it's my wife who tells me. I rehearse them by myself.

—*sideperson, early 30s, guitar and vocals*

Because it would be virtually impossible and not at all practical to
learn every song on the Top 40 each week, club date musicians—and
guitarists especially—need to be very selective in deciding which current tunes to learn. They use a number of criteria to determine which
songs they will spend the time and money to learn:

1. Has the song been requested? This is usually the most reliable
means for determining whether a song is "good product," even
though it does mean that the musician is always one step behind the
current tastes of the audience.

2. Does the musician already know a representative selection of
songs by the same performer? If a musician already knows two or
three songs by Bruce Springsteen, learning songs by other performers will probably take precedence over learning yet another of his
songs. If a new song of his *is* requested, the request can be at least
partially satisfied by playing another Springsteen song. Of course, if
the song is requested often enough, it will be clear that it must be
learned after all.

3. Has a particular leader suggested that a song ought to be in the
repertoire? Some offices and independent leaders will keep current
libraries of sheet music for the use of musicians who work for them.
If it is obvious that the leader had decided to do a particular song, a
musician who works regularly for that leader is obliged to learn it.

4. Have other musicians mentioned the song in conversation? The
grapevine is a fairly reliable source for information on current trends
in the club date business, and a musician can be certain that a song
title mentioned among other club date musicians is current in the
minds of a few leaders as well. If more than a few musicians have

played the song already, it is almost certain to become part of the general repertoire, at least for the near future.

5. Is the song danceable? The Top 40 charts include a wide variety of musical styles, and not all songs that reach the top of the popularity charts are useful for anything other than interlude, nondance material in the club date context. The important music on a club date is the dance music, because leaders, clients, and party guests tend to judge the success of an affair by the number of people dancing. It doesn't make sense to spend too much time learning nondance material when the time would be much better spent learning current dance tunes.

An inherent problem with keeping the repertoire current is that songs remain current for a limited time. As selective as a musician may be in deciding which new songs to learn, many of those songs will drop out of the repertoire as other hit songs replace them. This is an unfortunate fact of the business, and it affects both guitarists and nonguitarists, since everyone must be familiar with current material. The rapidly changing nature of rock repertoire can be very disturbing, especially for the older musicians in the business who began before the arrival of rock music:

> I feel that it's an imposition on me to have to learn every transient piece of trash that comes along on the charts. And some leaders are absolutely hysterical about learning all this. A lot of times it's just a question of a lot of silly words and two chords.
>
> —*sideperson, late 40s, trumpet*

> I find some of these things it's really distasteful to spend the time on. Then sometimes you don't get much mileage out of it. Three, four months, and you spend three, four hours to learn it from a record.
>
> —*leader, early 50s, piano*

> The rock repertoire, unlike the repertoire of the thirties, forties, and fifties, is a constantly proliferating one. A constant turnout, a constant newness. . . . I think it's ludicrous for a conventional older musician to try to keep up with all of this.
>
> —*sideperson, early 50s, piano*

> Rehearsal doesn't really make sense anymore, since by the time a piece has been polished up and worked into the repertoire, there's a new hit song and the one we learned is old.
>
> —*subleader, early 40s, trombone and vocals*

Probably the most complicated problem for nonguitarists, especially horn players, with learning the current rock repertoire is that their instruments were not often included on the original recording of rock songs. If the original recording of a song did happen to include horns, the club date horn players will learn the appropriate parts. If no horns were used on the record, the horn players will either provide background lines or simply not play for that song, partly depending on the preference of the leader on a particular job. The majority of current repertoire for the horn player consists of introductions, background parts, and endings. Many of these players, since they do not need to know the melody or lyrics for the songs, may not even know the title for many of the songs, though they can play the correct horn parts:

> Personally, I don't take the time to learn most of them. I play behind many I don't know the name of. But you get the intros and endings after playing them a few times with the guitarist.
> —*sideperson, early 50s, trumpet*

> I know many rock and roll tunes, but there are some that I can't give you the title for. For example, I know the whole score to *Saturday Night Fever* [a club date staple in early 1978], but I can't tell you the titles of the tunes. "Stayin' Alive" is one of them, but I don't know any of the other titles.
> —*sideperson, early 50s, saxophone*

Authenticity in rhythm and phrasing is another significant problem for the older club date musicians in dealing with contemporary repertoire. Some of the busiest players in the business, all of whom have extensive repertoires including much rock material, willingly admit their limitations when it comes to playing rock music. A trumpet player and contractor in his late forties noted: "I do rock music, but not what the youngsters want. So I hire a rock specialist." A saxophone player with thirty years of experience in the business recognized the musical difference in rock music, yet he did not feel that he had been able to adapt to it: "I'm not a rock player. I'll play a jazz chorus on a rock tune, but I'm just stuck with my style."

The different rhythmic sensibility needed for rock playing has compelled drummers especially to keep abreast of the current repertoire, even though they need not know chords or melody for the songs. The drum rhythms on a recording of a rock song become part and parcel of the song itself, in the same way that bass lines can come to characterize particular rock songs:

> The kids want it as close to the truth as possible. So it is important for the drummers to listen. In fact, it's more important for the drummer and the guitar player to know what's happening than anyone else. If the rhythm is not what they want to hear, the drummer is on the spot.
>
> What I try to do as a drummer is to assimilate what's going on in the rhythm section on a record. And you might have five or so guys playing rhythm on new records. What I try to do is pick out three or four rhythms and put them together on my drum set to try to get the sound. You have to keep up.
>
> I fell back recently. Like I was draggin' it and not learning the things. And I found out that even the dumbest leaders were starting to turn around and say, "Hey, man . . ." So I figured if these cats are hearing it, I'd better get down and do it.
>
> If you don't play the right rhythm for [a current song] or are at least getting close, forget it. They'll come close to booing you— you can see it on their faces. They'll just sit down . . . it's a different ball game.
>
> —*sideperson, early 40s, drums*

In performing current popular songs, club date musicians meet with the same audience expectations as do Top 40 or "copy groups," such as those studied by H. Stith Bennett in *On Becoming a Rock Musician.* Young listeners may have heard a single recorded version of a particular song scores or even hundreds of times, and *the actual sound* of that recording is what they want to hear. Simply playing the right melody and harmony for the song is not sufficient. The "truth" that the younger crowd wants to hear is the record: "the reproduction now functions as the original, the live performance is judged against the recording."[10]

Adding current songs to the repertoire becomes a very different process—"a different ball game"—from learning standard tunes. The sound of a current recording is often the result of sophisticated electronic manipulation of the sounds originally produced by a group of musicians, making it nearly impossible in many cases for even the original group to reproduce the sound of the recording in live performance. The task for a club date band is to give "the *impression* of precise reproduction,"[11] to approximate the recorded sound well enough to be accepted as "authentic" by young audience members. Musical memory is still at work, but the memorization process must include awareness of specific sound textures that can be duplicated exactly only in a recording studio.

The ability to memorize music is a combination of both natural talent and acquired skill. Only one musician I spoke with felt that his command of repertoire was largely a result of a natural gift, whereby he could repeat a melody exactly after a single hearing, even if many years passed from the time he first heard the song until he was asked to perform it. This same man was cited repeatedly by his colleagues for this uncanny ability of his. Memorization comes less naturally to the others, but they still have repertoires that are astounding in size and scope. Most seemed to feel that the process of building a repertoire, although difficult and even forbidding at first, becomes at least somewhat easier as the skills are exercised more often:

> In the beginning, if you don't know anything, it's hard to learn even one. You know, after you know over a hundred tunes, and you're into the thousands now, it's easier. The more you know, the easier it is to learn new ones. It's some function of memory which I don't understand, but it seems to work that way.
> —*sideperson, late 50s, trumpet*

Arrangement

Simply knowing the tunes is the first and certainly the largest obstacle to overcome for the novice club date musician. There are also certain conventions for arranging the music that the player needs to know; ultimately, these must be learned on the job. Some of these conventions reflect standard arranging techniques from the big band era, as do the conventions of phrasing; others are peculiar to the club date context. The purpose of all the conventions is to produce arrangements that closely resemble written arrangements—at least closely enough that club date audiences find the music acceptable. The conventions are, in the sense suggested by Howard Becker, "negotiated" between performers and audience, and only those conventions are used that can render a final product "familiar enough that audiences have no difficulty in responding appropriately."[12]

Even in a small club date band with only one melodic instrument— normally sax or trumpet—arrangement of songs, however minimal, is necessary to avoid boring both audience and musicians with one continuous sound texture. The arrangement on a thirty-two-bar song may be nothing more than a stipulation from the leader that the sax will play the first sixteen measures and the last eight, with the piano taking the melody during the eight-measure bridge. If the leader decides to repeat the thirty-two bars, one instrument may solo for sixteen bars, with the melody resuming at the bridge. A vocal chorus is another way of varying the arrangement. A common club date arrangement for two choruses of a thirty-two-bar song with the usual AABA structure is to play the first verse in the manner just described, with a horn taking the A sections and the piano the bridge, and to have vocals for the entire second verse, with horn background throughout.

Contemporary songs tend to be arranged in a manner that closely resembles original recordings. If a song as recorded includes a solo chorus, the club date arrangement will also include a solo. If the song has four verses of lyrics, these will usually be sung in their entirety. Particularly in the minds of teenage party guests, the recorded version of a song *is* the song, and they will make it quite clear to the musicians if their club date version of a recent hit is not satisfactory, either in so many words or by leaving the dance floor. As a general rule, the less contemporary a song is, the less true to the original recorded version the band needs to be. Not only are people less familiar with the original recordings after ten or fifteen years, but often the same songs have been performed and rerecorded by various musicians since the original version appeared.

The arrangement of any song must be flexible enough to change according to the number of musicians in the band and the audience reaction to the song. Each leader and subleader does, however, arrive at fairly predictable methods of arranging songs in the repertoire, and these are known by musicians as the leader's "routine." After working for one leader or subleader a few times, the sideperson will come to know what songs to expect, as well as their arrangement and phrasing. Even the order of songs can become predictable in some cases. If leader A, for instance, begins a set with a Glenn Miller tune, musicians familiar with the leader's routine will expect to play one or two more Miller tunes immediately after the first to form a medley. If leader B begins a set with "Mame," more often than not this will be followed by "Hello Dolly" and/or "Cabaret"—all show tunes similar in style.

The leader's routine for arranging the music obviously works best with musicians who are familiar with the leader's work, but both leaders and subleaders often find themselves directing bands with one or more unfamiliar musicians. In that case, the bandleader needs to direct arrangements constantly, either by hand signals or verbal explanations. Fortunately, certain methods of arrangement are relatively standard and known by any experienced club date musician. Only when a leader's routine is radically different from this standard approach will any significant musical conflict be apparent to the audience, even though the musicians may never have played together before. In particular, subleaders who work with different groups of musicians at every job must rely on this standardization of routine:

> If you don't have a set group, then you pretty much follow certain cliché formulas—four-bar intros, endings pretty much patented. Most bands end songs the same way. The melody is pretty much played straight. It's hard to ask a musician to change his phrasing to suit your needs. If he doesn't know your work, how is he going to know whether you want staccato or legato phrasing, long lines or short lines? And the tempos will change the phrasing, sometimes meaning that you have to add or subtract notes from the melody.
>
> The leader has to know how to ask for and get from the musicians what he wants with no rehearsal.
>
> —*subleader, late 40s, piano*

A bandleader will begin a set—a group of songs using the same rhythm and tempo—by telling the band members the title of the first song. A leader who either sings or plays a melody instrument can begin a second song in the same key with no indication given to the band members; on hearing the first measure of the new song the other musicians will switch to it. If the second song happens to be in a different key, the leader will indicate the new key with a hand signal: one finger pointing upward signifies one flat—the key of F major; two up, the key of B-flat major. Fingers pointing downward refer to the number of sharps in a new key. This system may at first seem illogical, since you might expect raised fingers to indicate sharps, which "raise" notes, and vice versa. The majority of popular songs in the standard repertoire, however, are written in keys using flats. Because raising the hand and fingers is a much more natural and more easily seen motion, flat keys are indicated in that way. Minor keys are not common in popular song, and the key indication is usually spoken if the next song will be in a minor key.

These signals are given during the last measures of the first song. When the keyboard, guitar, and bass players see these signals, they will either:

1. play a subdominant to dominant chord progression leading to the new key;
2. simply play the dominant chord of the next song on the last measure;
3. arrive in the new key "unprepared," merely playing the new tonic chord on measure one of the new song; or
4. play a four-measure introduction to the next song using a cadence to the new key (usually a two-measure I-vi / ii-V progression repeated).

The fourth method is used most often in large bands. It allows the full band to begin the new melody without any hesitation. It is not so difficult to communicate the key change quickly in a smaller band with only one or two melody instruments, and some hesitation at the beginning of a song is less obvious to listeners.

These rapid modulations are less common when bands are playing contemporary songs. This is primarily because current songs take more time to perform in their entirety than do standard thirty-two-bar pieces. One or two rock songs alone can constitute a "set" of eight to ten minutes, whereas four or more standards would be needed to fill the same amount of time. Also, medleys are not always appropriate with current music, since, in keeping as close to the recording as possible, drum rhythms, bass lines, and instrumentation may have to change along with the key signature when moving to a new song. Fifties rock-and-roll and Motown songs, being more standardized formally, are exceptions to this general rule and *are* often presented in a medley format.

The number of songs in each set will depend on both the bandleader's personal taste and his or her perception of the audience reaction to the set. Just two or three songs can constitute a set. At the opposite extreme, bands will play sixteen songs in as many minutes as a continuous medley. A club date band under the direction of an experienced leader will rarely take more than five or ten seconds between sets, because the longer the interval between sets, the more likely that dancers will leave the floor.

The size of the performing unit in the club date context can range from one—a solo guitarist or pianist, for example—to twenty or more. Most bands have between three and ten members, and four-piece bands are probably the most common unit throughout the business. Larger bands will build from the basic four-piece unit—guitar/bass, drums, piano/elecric keyboard, and horn—mainly by adding more wind instruments. Another guitarist is often added so that both electric bass and electric guitar can be used for all arrangements. A ten-piece band, then, might include guitar (vocalist), bass (vocalist), drums, piano/electric keyboard, two trumpets, trombone, and three saxes. The instrumentation can be varied depending on the wind players' "doubles." Most saxophone players, for example, double on flute and clarinet. Some brass and woodwind players also double on violin, although this was becoming a rarity even in 1978. Larger bands will add violins as well, all depending on the preferences of the leader and the sponsor of the party. I interviewed one leader, for example, who rarely used saxophones because he felt that a single accordion served as a suitable substitute for an entire sax section. One contractor preferred an all-brass horn section, feeling that he could achieve a more contemporary sound that way: "We don't use saxes . . . that's the style that is better for today's type of playing. Riffs with brass background behind contemporary rock is better. Saxes are an old-fashioned thing." (Apparently, no one had pointed out to him that the saxophone is easily the most common solo wind instrument in contemporary pop music.)

Especially for bands that include more than a single melodic instrument, leaders try to hire only those musicians who are familiar with their particular routine. This allows not only the necessary agreement in phrasing and order of solo versus ensemble passages but also harmony and/or counterpoint. Although the musicians refer to the ability to improvise harmony or contrapuntal lines as *faking*, the term is not meant in a literal sense, for the musicians *are* familiar with the standard harmonies for each of the songs they perform. The harmonies they use are arrived at through a combination of listening, memory of the chord sequence, and theoretical knowledge of harmony. It is not unlike the seventeenth-century use of continuo parts, the main difference being that the chordal structure is not written in the club date performance context.

Literal faking, where band members know a song only vaguely yet proceed to perform it, does occur on club dates, but leaders with established reputations avoid the practice. One subleader remarked that he would now and then try to fake his way through an unfamiliar song to satisfy a request from the audience but that he usually regretted having done so, since the result generally sounded very amateurish. One sideperson recalled certain club date leaders who would attempt to fake their way through any song requested by a party guest. Their willingness to do so, he added, explained why their bands often sounded "like a series of train wrecks."

In the late 1940 and early 1950s, when faking harmony first became standard throughout the club date business, many of the musicians had the advantage of knowing harmony parts from the stock arrangements used by hotel and ballroom bands. At the same time, faking in the club date context was not merely a matter of playing memorized stock harmonies. Not all the harmony parts from the hotel bands were directly applicable to club date faking, because the size and instrumentation of club date bands could vary considerably from night to night. Also, not all musicians who worked in the club date field when faking became common practice had equivalent experience in steady hotel bands. These men had to learn the art of faking harmony on a trial-and-error basis, relying on their ears and their knowledge of chord structures to guide them. For most, it took time to learn the art of faking, and the process of learning made for quite a few embarrassing musical moments:

> It was pretty bad for a long time, but everything is experience, and it's a habit actually. It's no reflection on a musician's ability or ear or anything. There are lots of musicians who come in now who can't fake parts, but not because they can't do it—they just don't know where to start. They don't have the background of goofing up a lot of jobs, whereas the older guys do. That's the way you learn. It takes a little time. It's not that simple.
> —*sideperson, early 60s, saxophone*

The lead trumpet, saxophone, and violin players are the key players in a good faking band, since they must lead the phrasing of all the harmonized parts. The actual arrangements are arrived at through a combination of the leader's and the lead players' ideas of phrasing and balancing the use of the band's sections (saxes, brass, strings, rhythm) for each song. After two or three performances of a new song, the arrangement becomes more or less finalized for a particular leader. As long as the lead players know this standard arrangement for each song and enough other members of the band are familiar with the leader's routine, the leader can expect at least a close approximation of the standard arrangement from job to job.

Figure 3 provides an example of the harmony lines that a four-person saxophone section might play for the standard song "Just In Time." The example was written out for me by a sax player who had been playing club dates since the late 1930s. He originally notated the parts in the key signatures used by each of the saxophones, because I had simply asked him to write out the parts as he would normally play them as a member of a saxophone section. I have transposed the parts into concert key to make their harmonic relationships more immediately apparent. The separate parts from top to bottom on the staffs correspond to (1) alto, (2) alto, (3) tenor, and (4) baritone sax.

Figure 3: "Just in Time"

Jule Styne 1956

The writer of this harmonization did not specify the chords that the saxophone players would expect the piano, guitar, or bass to use throughout the piece. The chord symbols I have written above each measure represent only the basic harmonies that the saxes seem to be outlining from measure to measure. A second symbol in parentheses stands above those measures in which the sax harmonies are either ambiguous or perhaps oversimplified.

It must be remembered that the example has been written out by just one musician, who would play but a single one of the harmony parts in performance. The actual harmonies played by a club date faking band are only as good as the musicians in the band. In the words of one trumpet player in his late forties, "Harmonies depend on who is in the section at that date. Sometimes it can be excellent; frequently, due to thousands of things, poor." Even with experienced musicians, though, there is not always general agreement as to what is "good" improvised harmony. As one saxophone player with over forty years of experience in the business described the basic approach to faking,

> What a club date band tries to do is stay together and play mainly what the lead men are laying down. This is a very brutal process, as many lead players couldn't care less whether the other horns are able to follow them. Sometimes you need a butterfly net, better than that, a shotgun.
>
> When I play lead and have the luck to have a fairly able section—those who will pay attention to what I am doing, I try to make things as simple as possible. The melody phrase should be as consistent as you can make it.
> —*sideperson, early 60s, saxophone*

Another factor in the harmonization created by a section is the chords used by the rhythm section. The saxophone player just quoted also wrote out a harmonization of "Just In Time" for me, though only for the first eight measures of the piece. Below these measures he wrote "approximately—due to what I hear throughout the other horns, bass, and keyboard . . . I use my ear for harmony parts: it says when I am right or wrong." The writer of the complete harmonization in figure 3 also noted that "the harmonies might change depending on the piano player's chords. Sometimes they [the piano players] alter them, and we try to listen and change with them." This written harmonization, then, is only one possible approach that a club date sax section might choose. Even so, there are general features of the harmonization that are common to faked arrangements throughout the business.

One thing that is clear from this example, for instance, is that the harmony parts generally move in parallel motion to the melody throughout the piece. The baritone part does move in contrary motion at times, but according to other horn players whom I interviewed, this is exceptional. Normally the fourth saxophone part, whether it is played by tenor or baritone sax, doubles the melody at the octave below. There are apparently very few club date players who can play a fourth part without simply doubling the lead line. One player made a particular point of his ability to do so:

> In my case, I can play any harmony chair—even four parts. I'm probably the only guy in New York who can play fourth tenor part, and that's because I write.
> —*sideperson, late 50s, saxophone/composer-arranger*

Another experienced sax player felt that, even though there are sax players who will try to play a nonmelody fourth part, it would usually be better if they stuck to the melody:

> The second tenor [fourth part] or baritone is a source of much annoyance to me. . . . There are very few players who can do it without falling all over the other harmony parts or who have the musical taste to retreat to the melody. Usually that chair becomes the musical sandbox while these happy characters entertain themselves, much to my discomfort.
> —*sideperson, early 60s, saxophone*

Another feature of the harmonization in figure 3—and one that is understandably typical of club date faking—is that none of the parts strays very far from chord tones. The only notes in the middle two parts that are not chord tones are the lower neighboring tones following the repeated lower neighboring tones (C-sharp and F-sharp) in the melody line. The baritone part is, again, the exception to this rule, since it does use scalar motion to a limited extent in measures 4, 10, 12, and 24—all four times leading to the root of the following chord in typical bass line fashion. Sticking to chord tones may produce a very conservative harmonization, but it at least ensures that the harmony will be acceptable and that individual parts will not conflict. Only performers who have played together frequently will attempt more "daring" harmonic devices such as passing chords or substitute chords, since all the parts must be using the same devices for them to work well at all.

The writer of the harmonization in figure 3 pointed out that, although the members of a saxophone section must be able to play harmonies for all parts of a song, the entire section will not necessarily play the song from beginning to end. Different leaders, after all, have different routines:

> Most of the time, the brass and saxes play concerted for the first sixteen bars, then the saxes or piano or solo instrument plays the release, depending on what the leader calls for. Then either ensemble or saxes finish the chorus.
>
> If we play a second chorus to the tune, it is saxes or a solo again, depending on the leader. Release again, whatever is called for. Generally, ensemble finishes the second chorus again—it's up to the leader. He generally tells us a couple of bars ahead or points or makes signs.

As if playing harmony parts for the melody of a song and following the leader's signals were not difficult enough, this man wrote out, in addition to the harmonization of the melody, "a little unison background which we use sometimes behind the brass or a solo instrument." This particular unison line, which is written out in figure 4, is one of any number of possible background lines that might be used for the song. The lines are initiated by section leaders—sax, trumpet, or violin, and eventually those lines that work best come to be standard background material throughout the business. A violin player explained to me how this happens:

> I will set an obbligato line for the fiddles to play behind the trumpets or saxes . . . certain tunes lend themselves to that more easily than others, where there are moving lines in half or whole steps. I've initiated a couple of these lines on standard tunes over the years which gradually spread and get picked up by other guys. After a while, all the bands use them—lines they got from another office, since the personnel in the groups mixes over time . . . I'm talking about the real free-lance part of it, the guys who aren't tied up with one office. They'll work for Lanin, Davis, Steven Scott. This is a sort of a floating contingent of sidemen who will pick up whatever they can, and they will use it and pass it on to whatever band they are working with, especially if one of them is playing lead sax or trumpet. He'll set down a line or background that he's picked up from

Figure 4: "Just in Time"

Line 1 = melody   Jule Styne 1956
Line 2 = sax unison

*The chord symbols are derived from the previous sax harmonization.
(Brass or full ensemble on melody last 8 measures)

other bands. So, in that way, it's a continually spreading repertoire of phrasings, obligatos, and so on.
    —*sideperson, early 60s, violin*

These background lines may begin as unison lines and become harmonized lines later on as more players become familiar with them. Learning to play the lines, whether or not they are harmonized, must be done entirely by ear. They are created and transmitted aurally, unlike the melodies of the song, which can be learned from their written form.

The concept of faking harmony does have practical limitations. For one, not all popular songs lend themselves to improvised harmonization. Although the large majority of standards are relatively simple harmonically, others, such as "Stardust," "Laura," "I Concentrate on You," or "Body and Soul," are fairly sophisticated harmonically and less easily faked. A wise leader, when calling such songs, will ask for either solo or sectional unison statement of the melody or a solo supported by sustained chord tones.

Another practical limitation in faking harmony is that the pool of musicians who are able to fake well is diminishing rapidly. This was true in 1978 and was even more so in 1989. The practice began, after all, at the tail end of the swing era, when saxes, trumpets, trombones, and even strings were all part of the sound of contemporary popular music. Rock music, which has since taken over the popular music scene, rarely uses any of these instruments in large combinations. Club date bands have gotten smaller since the advent of rock music, partly because of economics, but mainly because the music itself does not need a big band to achieve its characteristic sound. Why should clients who primarily want to hear rock and other contemporary music hire a fifteen-piece band? There are still large faking bands around, but they will be found mainly where they first appeared—at high society affairs, where the audience is both willing and able to pay for a band large enough to reproduce the big band sound, even though more of the band's time may be spent on rock material. The only place for a younger player to learn the art of faking is in a club date band itself, and few contractors want to take a chance on a musician who has never tried to fake harmony. There is, thus, both less demand for the art of faking and less opportunity for players to learn it.

A good faking band in performance can be an amazing musical phenomenon: if you close your eyes you would swear that the musicians were playing from written arrangements. One particularly remarkable example of faking that I witnessed involved the caterer for the affair, who also happened to be an experienced trumpet player and bandleader and at one point took over the direction of the band for half an hour or so. He led the band through a fast-paced medley of songs from the swing era—the musicians, of course, having no idea which songs he would call. I learned later that the musicians rarely played a couple of the songs on club dates. Cues for songs were given by hand signals only as the caterer/leader/trumpet player finished the final bars of one song and was about to begin another. I could see the horn players leaning close to each other to hear the harmony lines, yet the resulting arrangement was full and the phrasing very clean. On a few of the songs, the saxes provided contrapuntal lines against the note-for-note brass harmonies. Again, the result sounded like well-rehearsed arrangements. A contemporary song requested by a party guest was familiar to only two or three players in the band, but the band produced a surprisingly polished version of the piece. Fortunately for the band, the two men who knew the song were the guitarist and the lead trumpet player. The lead trumpet player sang and lightly played the necessary lines for the other horns before beginning the piece, and he led the section through the number with no apparent faltering.

As if this display were not enough, while dinner was being served the four brass players took out violins and proceeded to stroll the dance floor playing waltzes. And, of course, they were playing in harmony the whole time.

I was not alone in being thoroughly amazed at the ability of these horn and string players to harmonize a seemingly endless number of popular songs. Club date guitarists, drummers, and keyboard players expressed again and again the greatest admiration for the art of faking harmony. "These guys are incredible" or "They are simply geniuses" were the kinds of comments I frequently heard. The faking musicians themselves also realized the uniqueness of what they do, yet they were generally very modest in speaking about this skill. Many of them pointed out to me that, given the same opportunities and conditions they themselves experienced, most musicians would also eventually acquire the skill.

The faking bands I observed were, to be sure, some of the best such bands in the club date business. When I asked for permission to observe large bands, the leaders naturally wanted to show their product at its best. Throughout the business, though, there is much variation in the quality of faking bands. The ability to fake harmony does not come easily, and lack of such ability can lead to "gross musical abuses," as one saxophone player put it. Yet such abuses evidently do not offend the ears of many party guests. If they did, faking bands would have disappeared from the club date business long ago. As long as the party is a success, and the band fulfills its function, the music is good—or at least good enough.

Notes

1. The sheet music version here is from *The Best of Cole Porter.*

2. From *The Chappell Collection of Great Theater Composers, Volume II.*

3. Virginia Warren, "They Call the Tune for Society's Dancing Feet."

4. The 1978 Local 802 directory listed over fifty maraca players, 90 percent of them female.

5. John Storm Roberts, *The Latin Tinge* 130.

6. Bergman, *Rock Guitar* 6.

7. Bergman, *Rock Guitar* 53.

8. Bergman, *Rock Guitar* 54.

9. Bergman, *Rock Guitar* 74.

10. Peter Wicke, "Rock Music: A Musical-Aesthetic Study" 236.

11. Bennett, *On Becoming a Rock Musician* 155.

12. Howard S. Becker, "Art As Collective Action" 771–72.

4

Entertainment:
The Bandleader's Art

Serve the public! Whoever you play for, try and make sure you were part and parcel of something happy, so if a woman whose party it is sees you on the street 15 years from now, she'll say "Lester, you made my party."

—Lester Lanin, society leader[1]

How the sound of a club date band is presented is at least as important as the strictly musical quality of that sound. The most musically proficient group of club date players can be a total flop at a party under the direction of an inexperienced bandleader. Many club date musicians—both leaders and sidepersons—go so far as to say that the presentation is far more important than the music itself in determining a band's success at a party. The bandleader is completely in charge of the nature of presentation. The choices that he or she makes—what music to play, at what tempo to play it, when during a performance to use certain types of music, how to respond to direct requests from the audience, to what extent verbal interaction with the audience is appropriate—can be *the* most significant determinant of the character and ultimate success of the social/musical event. The objective throughout is to have the performance cater as much as possible to the tastes of the audience at a particular affair—to adapt the performance to its social context.

The club date performance context is distinguished from other contexts for musical performance in our society by two factors: first, the affairs are private, "invitation only" events, and second, the affairs commonly involve some kind of celebration. These two characteristics provide the framework within which the bandleader organizes the presentation. The private aspect of an affair means that the guests have some common social bond exclusive of their interest in music,

dancing, drinking, and eating. The bond may be one of family relation, friendship, or simply membership in an organization. The celebration is the primary purpose behind the event. Food, drink, and
music may add to the enjoyment of the celebration, but the celebration can take place without any of those ingredients.

In fact, many people choose to have no music at all; eating, drinking, ritual ceremonies, speeches, and conversation with friends can be
sufficient entertainment for the guests. Adding live music to a private
celebration, however, changes the very nature of the event. Party
sponsors are well aware of this difference, whether or not they verbal-
ize it; otherwise, they would not invest what can be a large portion of
a party's expense in live music. Bandleaders will frequently hear comments after a party, either in person or in writing from the host or
hostess, such as "A band definitely makes or breaks a party" or "The
band really *makes* the wedding," followed by praise for a job well done.

Without a band at such an affair, the celebration itself is the central
focus of visual and aural attention. The important participants in the
celebration—the bar mitzvah boy and family, the wedding party, the
president of the organization, the featured speaker—are normally
seated facing the other guests, emphasizing the focus of the affair. A
group of musicians provides a second focus for audience attention.
The musicians are not direct participants in the celebration, and they
are quite anonymous to most if not all of the guests; in a sense, they
are intruders at the private affair. The physical placement of the musicians further emphasizes their separation from the guests. A dance
floor extends outward from the band to the tables where guests are
seated, and the band is usually further separated by a bandstand one
or more feet above the rest of the floor.

The bandleader is the visual focus of the band, normally standing
in front of the other musicians, and is also the only person on stage
who speaks to the party guests. In essence, the bandleader *is* the
band—the representative for the group, and the only one whose personality is presented to the audience. Indeed, the main distinguishing
feature from one bandleader to another is personality. This is the
main product the bandleader has to offer to the public—a personality
and the ability to project it successfully. Even bandleaders who emphasize the importance of playing high-quality music readily admit
that without a strong and pleasant personality to deal with an audience there is little hope of success on a club date:

> A *very* important thing is—even more so, and I hate to say this,
> even more so than talent, is to be personable . . . is to be likable.
> To go up to people and shower them with "hello" and "You look

beautiful today" and "You're lovely" and kiss her hand and shake the host's hand. Show them good attention. "Anything you want, I'll be most happy to do it for you." *That* would be the most important thing.

—*subleader, early 40s, trumpet and vocals*

In most cases, it is the bandleader and not the band itself that clients hire. A client has a good idea of what music will be suitable for a party, but this can usually be provided by a number of different leaders. The personality of the particular bandleader is the distinguishing feature. One musician, who works alternately as sideperson, subleader, and contractor, illustrated the importance of the bandleader's personality in the following way: "Suppose you saw and heard a band led by Lester Lanin or Peter Duchin tonight. I could take a picture of the band to assure you that every member was the same for your party *and* hire them for you for $2000 instead of $4000. The average client would not take the offer, since to them, the band *is* the leader. They're buying a name, just as everyone buys brand names in the supermarket instead of lesser names of equal quality for the same or less money."

Successful bandleaders can adapt their personality and style of presentation to a variety of circumstances, even though they may perform at certain kinds of events more than others. A bandleader may play a small dinner dance for a sedate, older group one night and the next day be leading a band at a loud and lively wedding with 200 guests. The extent to which bandleaders project their personalities and interact with audiences will differ considerably from case to case. The role of entertainer changes from party to party.

In speaking of their role at private parties, many bandleaders prefer not to think of themselves as entertainers at all. The word *entertainer* implies to them the kind of bandleader who will put on a visual and verbal display at a party:

I think that people hire a band to play music. If they wanted a floor show they would hire it rather than have it intrude on their affair. An entertainer is a Tom Jones, a Frank Sinatra. We *do* entertain, but we are in a different bracket.

—*subleader, early 30s, piano and vocals*

When I do singles on accordion, I do think of myself more as an entertainer. Otherwise, I'm just calling the tunes. I'm not an entertainer in the sense that I'm actually performing on the stage.

—*subleader, late 50s, accordion*

I'm not an entertainer; people don't expect it. I sell good music and momentum and tempo and keeping a party happy and getting the people exhausted and feeling they've had a good time . . . without having to stand on my head or wear a funny hat.

—*subleader, late 40s, piano*

The more ostentatious types of entertainment were at one time very common in the business. In the forties and early fifties, a club date band's performance often included a complete floor show during dinner. Older musicians recalled bands that did pantomime, impersonations, and comedy routines. More than a few also recalled the use of blackface well into the 1950s:

They'd do pantomime in blackface to recordings, imitating Al Jolson or whoever. They'd even have strobe lights to make the lips and gloves shine. It was a cakey kind of entertainment, but it was part and parcel of the whole thing.

—*sideperson and subleader, late 40s, piano*

Vestiges of this showy type of entertainment can still be seen on club dates. One instance is the bandleader's teaching dance steps to the audience. On a song such as "The Alley Cat" it is standard practice—though, again, depending on audience response—for the leader to sing the first few verses of the song using dance instructions as lyrics while demonstrating the steps. This was done for the cha-cha at one time, later for early rock steps—the Frug, the Mashed Potato, and the Swim—and for disco dance styles in the 1970s. Also in this category are the many game songs such as "The Bunny Hop," "The Hokey-Pokey," or "Simon Says." The types of game songs or dance instruction songs change over time, and some are revived by bandleaders now and then as novelties, given the appropriate circumstances. Even some of the actual "floor show" types of entertainment can be seen—one bandleader doing impersonations or playing two instruments at once, another getting the audience to "name that tune"— but it seems that fewer and fewer audiences want such routines, or *shtick,* as the musicians refer to it. Written or verbal specifications for parties will often note that the client wants *no* "Alley Cat" or other game-song material:

They will intimate this when you talk to them, but they're a bit embarrassed to come out and say it. So I'll say, "You don't want any corny stuff, right?" It puts them at ease, or so I think.

—*subleader, early 40s, trombone and vocals*

When I do things, I perform, but I try not to run what we call—
or Jewish people call—a "kishka" job, with all that garbage like
Alley Cats and Bunny Hops. Here's, for instance, a letter about a
job this weekend. They say: "Do not do: 'The Alley Cat,' 'The
Bunny Hop.' "

—subleader, early 40s, trumpet

If no mention is made of game songs or shtick directly, the type of
audience will often be enough to tell the bandleader whether such
material will be well received. As a general rule, the more money
spent on a party, the less likely that shtick will be desired by the client
or guests. All bandleaders noted, for example, that shtick was totally
out of the question at society affairs or country club dances. An audience that is upper class, or at least considers itself to be, tends to see
such material as lower class and corny. Probably the very idea of having a bandleader who is, after all, only a hired employee lead them
around in party games goes against their grain. If shtick is used, it will
usually be at parties where the audience is either predominantly
young or at least more middle than upper class.

The wane in popularity of this kind of entertainment throughout
the club date business was attributed to a number of factors. Musicians noted the rise of television as an entertainment medium as one
significant factor. People could see the same kind of show performances on television on a regular basis at no cost, making club date
floor shows both less necessary and often weak by comparison. Some
older leaders also mentioned that the addition of rock music to the
repertoire necessitated devoting more performance time to music
rather than routines, since wider representation of styles was needed
to please all segments of the audience. Another factor mentioned
frequently was the increasing affluence of club date clientele in the
decades following World War II. As people became more affluent
they wanted to dissociate themselves from what was considered lower-
class entertainment.

Bandleaders today are still playing the role of entertainer; that is,
their goal is still to arouse and sustain interest and enthusiasm in the
audience. Generally speaking, the role no longer requires a display of
histrionics, but verbal interaction with party guests is still very important, for it adds a personal touch to the performance, identifying the
individual bandleader with the band and with the success of the party
as a whole. In talking with the party sponsors and other individual
guests while off the bandstand, in answering specific requests, in
introducing songs or groups of songs, and in acting as master of

ceremonies, the bandleader's personality—his or her main "product"—is in full view. The bandleader's goal is to leave a consistently
favorable impression in each of these situations.

The quality of the music—the actual sound presented by the
band—is not exactly *un*important to bandleaders or party guests.
Bandleaders certainly have minimal technical/musical standards that
they expect their musicians to meet. What is equally important to
them, though, is the way this musical raw material is adapted to the
social context of the private party. *Which* songs the bandleader selects
and *when* he or she calls for them can make or break a party:

> I can show you a dozen different bands where the musicians are
> terrible. I mean, they can play, but not well. But, they know when
> to play a certain song—when to do a rock set, when to do a cha-
> cha, and get the people riled up so they have a good time. Musi-
> cianship plays only about a 50 percent role—the rest is knowing
> how to control the people.
>
> —*subleader, late 20s, guitar and vocals*

In a sense, the musical tastes of the guests at a party "control" the
selection of songs, but it is the bandleader's interpretation of these
tastes and how this interpretation is applied that determine the success of the affair. Bandleaders will speak in terms of "controlling the
people" and "running a party,"[2] and even party guests will use similar
terminology. "He really knows how to run a party" was a comment I
frequently heard from guests in talking about a particular bandleader. Satisfied clients will also occasionally include a short thank-you
note with the balance of payment, and these "testimonials," promi-
nently displayed in many club date offices, make it clear that party
guests appreciate the art of bandleading. Some such letters that I
came across included the following comments: "Your talent to play
the right tunes at the right time made for a swinging affair." "You
have great insight and picked up on every cue." "You presented a perfect selection of melodies suited to the celebration and the composi-
tion of the audience." "The band was outstanding and could play
any type of dance or show music . . . (you) sensed the mood and responded to it."

Direct requests for particular songs do not usually account for a
large percentage of the music played, but each one of these requests
is very important nevertheless. Every party guest represents a future
client and thus cannot be ignored:

To play one of these songs for someone who may be a potential customer will make him happy, and he'll remember us as the band that played his song. That guest may become a client of mine, so you've got to keep everybody happy.

　　—*leader, early 50s, trumpet and vocals (1989)*

That single song may be the only thing the party guest remembers about the occasion, but it may also be enough to compel the guest to call on the leader in the future. A drummer I spoke with during a break at a performance laughed at first as we talked about certain leaders who would do almost anything to satisfy a request. He was saying how ridiculous it could be, playing totally obscure tunes for the only person in the room who knew them. Later on in our conversation, though, he recalled an instance when, as the band was playing a requested number, an elderly woman danced by the bandstand singing along to the tune and smiling. "You knew by the look on her face that, if she ever gave a party, she was going to call that leader. He made her evening with that request."

There are situations where direct requests must be politely ignored or at least saved for use later during the party. If, for example, the band has just completed a twenty-minute rock set and the younger party guests want more of the same, an experienced bandleader may find it wisest to change the pace to please the older segment of the audience while taking note that more rock numbers will be useful later on. Or a request for "The Alley Cat" may have to be disregarded if the host or hostess has previously specified that the song *not* be played under any circumstances. One leader described a party where the hostess had said that she wanted to hear nothing but Cole Porter songs all evening, which he did not believe she meant literally. When he finally acceded to a guest's repeated request for a cha-cha, however, the hostess ran up to the bandstand and told him to stop the song immediately. An exceptional situation, to be sure, but it illustrates the impossibility, at a party or elsewhere, of satisfying all of the people all of the time.

The most reliable indication that the bandleader is successfully entertaining an audience is a dance floor filled with dancers throughout most of the party's duration. Keeping the people "on the floor" is the main objective in deciding which songs to play and when to play them. Satisfied party sponsors again and again mention the bandleader's ability to get a crowd dancing as a major reason for a party's success, as can be seen in these additional excerpts from testimonial letters: "A band's success can only be measured by its ability to get people away from the tables and onto the dance floor. By that definition, your group was a rousing success." "Even the 'older folks' found they couldn't sit by and watch—they too crowded the dance floor." "To me, a sign of a good party is if everyone is up and dancing. The dance floor was packed all afternoon . . . and there was music for every taste. Even our older relatives were dancing to contemporary music. What a feat!"

The goal of keeping dancers on the floor explains why there are virtually no breaks between songs or sets of songs.[3] With little or no silence between songs, dancers are less likely to return to their seats once a song has ended. Once they return to their seats, it is that much harder to get them up again.

There *are* parties where the number of dancers on the floor is not necessarily a clear indication of a bandleader's success or failure. Some audiences, for instance, simply prefer to dance less than others. The dance floor might never be crowded during an entire party, yet the clients and their guests are quite satisfied with the band's performance. Then there are people who love to dance and will dance regardless of what music is played. The styles, songs, or tempos may not be especially to their liking, yet they will continually fill the dance floor. I observed one party where the dance floor was packed from the first song the band played. The bandleader didn't quite know what to make of the situation, since anything he did seemed to have the same enthusiastic response—a packed dance floor. How does one gradually "build" enthusiasm at a party if it is there from the very beginning, without the help of the band?

The general guiding principle, though, is to keep people interested and dancing. This is achieved, first of all, by providing contrasts between sets of songs. Even an audience of one predominant age group does not want to hear one style of music continuously:

> To make them happy the key is to not let them get too bored with something they don't want to hear. You want to keep them moving from one kind of music to the other so you keep everybody as happy as possible.
> —*leader, early 40s, piano and vocals*

The phrase "keep everyone as happy as possible," which I heard frequently from bandleaders, points out a problem inherent in performing for audiences of mixed age groups: what pleases one segment of an audience may well displease another. Using as varied a repertoire as possible in order to satisfy the eclectic tastes of a mixed audience, the bandleader is bound to alienate some listeners who have very specific tastes in music. One leader used a somewhat exaggerated example to illustrate this point:

> We used to do one particular country club which had three segments. One segment didn't like music at all; they hated it. Another third wanted chamber music. The other third wanted to swing and have a good time. Now the bandleader walks into this lion's nest, into this cage. No matter what he does, he's got 66 percent of the people hating him. If he does nothing, he's got two-thirds of the people hating him . . . you really have to be a psychologist or psychiatrist, a priest, a rabbi. You have to be everything as a bandleader.
>
> —*leader, late 40s, trumpet and vocals*

Changing musical styles from one set of songs to another is the bandleader's first consideration. The length of these sets is also important. How long a set will be depends on the bandleader's interpretation of audience response to the music, but generally speaking, sets will be no longer than ten minutes and no shorter than four or five minutes. One- or two-minute sets would be impractical because not all guests get up to dance immediately when a set begins. By the time they have risen to dance a foxtrot, they might find the band switching to a rock number or a cha-cha. The sets are not very long for two reasons. First, people's enthusiasm for a single dance step or musical style will wane eventually, and the bandleader wants to end the set before this happens, leaving the dancers "up" in spirit. Second, people may wish to change partners between sets when the music stops. A set that lasts fifteen minutes or longer makes it difficult to change partners gracefully. The actual "stop" between sets may be only a few seconds long, but it at least indicates that one dance set is completed.

The format of the party provides the framework within which the bandleader makes the song and set choices. The goal of keeping the people interested and dancing is complicated by the fact that caterers do not allow dance music at all while dinner courses are being served or formal entrances or ritual ceremonies are taking place. At a four-hour party, dancing is rarely uninterrupted for more than forty-five minutes at a time. As an example, the following format would be typical for a four-hour bar mitzvah celebration:

1:00–1:40   guests arrive; cocktails and smorgasbord; minimum of dancing

1:40–1:55 band stops and moves equipment to the main dining room
1:55–2:15 guests find their dinner tables; dancing
2:15–2:35 bar mitzvah boy enters; candle-lighting ceremony
2:35–3:00 dancing
3:00–3:15 soup is served and eaten
3:15–3:35 dancing
3:35–3:50 main course is served and eaten
3:50–4:20 dancing
4:20–4:30 dessert is served and eaten
4:30–5:00 dancing; guests begin leaving

There will, of course, be considerable variation in the timing of this format from party to party, but the overall sequence of dancing versus nondancing segments is common to nearly all club date affairs. The format of a wedding reception, for instance, often includes even smaller time segments, because the many individual rituals such as cake cutting, throwing the bridal bouquet, and tossing the garter may require the dancing to stop.

The four-hour performance context is somewhat less restrictive for the bandleader if the clients choose to have the cocktail hour added to rather than part of the total four hours. The music for the cocktail hour may be provided by members of the band—often the guitarist and/or keyboard player—or it may be provided by a separate solo musician or ensemble playing light classical music. The bandleader seldom performs during this time. Club date offices will naturally try to sell this format both for the extra profit it means and because it allows more time for the bandleader to "develop" the party, to get and keep the audience dancing. (The cocktail hour in this format is referred to as a *preheat,* both in common parlance and on official union contracts—a wonderfully evocative term, implying that the hour is only preparation for the real "cooking" later on.) This format, of course, costs more for the party's sponsor and is consequently seen more often among wealthier clientele.

All the nonmusical "events"—rituals, entrances, dinner courses— naturally divert attention away from the music and work against the bandleader's primary goal of keeping the people dancing. The time between the events can be as little as fifteen minutes, and the bandleader must try to build as much audience interest and involvement as possible during those brief intervals. The task is to build and sustain the energy and momentum of the party in spite of the numerous anticlimaxes necessitated by these events. The total amount of time spent playing dance music may be only two or two and one-half hours, which explains in part why songs and medleys are often very short. Quite a lot of music must be represented during that short amount of time if the bandleader hopes to reach as much of the audience as possible.

Music *is* played during ceremonies and during the serving of dinner courses, but it is not intended for dancing, whether or not the songs used could be perceived as such in other circumstances. While dinner courses are served, the music is most often played by a keyboard or guitar player without the accompaniment of drums, at a relatively low volume, and often in slow rubato style—all characteristics intended to make it clear to the party guests that it is in fact nondance music.[4] Other means that I observed for making this interlude music clearly nondanceable included varying the time signature throughout the song and playing what would normally be a ballad at a very fast tempo. It is at the caterer's request that the bandleader calls for such music, since the dance floor must be clear for food to be served and eaten while it is hot (or cold). The intention is not always fulfilled, though, for a crowd of avid dancers is not easily coaxed to sit down.

The caterer's concern that this music be definitely nondanceable was made quite clear to me by one incident I observed at a wedding reception. The guitarist began performing an extremely slow, rubato version of "Over the Rainbow" as dinner was being served. The rhythm and tempo of the piece hardly seemed conducive to dancing, yet his performance was apparently very engaging, because many guests left their tables and began dancing. When the caterer saw what was happening, he rushed over to the guitarist and made his dissatisfaction clear in a few words. The song stopped immediately, and another began—this one even more deliberately arhythmical and also less familiar. The dancers were soon back at their tables.

The bandleader is obliged to comply with the caterer's stipulations as to when the nondance segments are to begin and end; after all, the caterer is also in the business of booking parties, and his recommendation can direct future clients to the bandleader. Clients frequently ask caterers to suggest bands, and a bandleader who disregards signals from the caterer is unlikely to be recommended. A good working relationship with the caterer is good for business:

First thing I'll do is go up to the caterer and tell him I'll work with him all the way—disarm him, psych him out. They can be very difficult, for instance, when you have trouble getting the people up, then he calls for you to stop for the next course. Many will not

wait the five minutes needed to keep the crowd dancing. But you
go with them.
    —*leader, early 50s, accordion*

I must work *with* the caterer. You have to coordinate your whole
party with the caterer. If the caterer does not work with you, you're
in a lot of trouble. . . . Once you find out who your caterer is, you
go over, fraternize with him, "Whatever you want, it's my plea-
sure." This way there aren't any surprises. I know when the cake-
cutting ceremony is, when the guy says the prayer over the bread,
when I bring the parents in, when I bring the bride and groom in.
    —*leader, early 50s, trumpet and vocals (1989)*

There will be an inevitable amount of conflict between bandleader
and caterer, however, because they are working toward different ends
in dealing with a single audience during a limited period of time. The
caterer is concerned with the proper presentation of the food and its
enjoyment by the guests. What goes on musically is not really the caterer's concern as long as it does not conflict with the food service.
From the caterer's standpoint, a party is a series of dinner courses
with interludes for dancing. From the bandleader's standpoint, a
party is a series of dance music segments with interludes for eating
food. The bandleader is concerned with the food only if it conflicts
with his presentation of the dance music. Bandleaders tend to feel,
understandably enough, that a successful party is one where people
are dancing rather than sitting and eating most of the time:

Caterers are worried too much about food and don't realize that if
the music isn't right the party won't be a success regardless of how
good the food is. They don't allow enough time to dance, to develop a party.
    —*leader, early 50s, piano*

The good affair is one where guests dance rather than eat. They
[the caterers] have plenty of time to show their food, and the people can decide what they want to do about it.
    —*leader, late 50s, trumpet and vocals*

If the time allotted by the caterer for dance and nondance periods
is either unclear, too long, or too short, the bandleader will have
difficulty in selecting and ordering songs in a way that will sustain au-

dience enthusiasm. If the bandleader, for instance, plans to end a dance segment with an up-tempo number, and the caterer signals for him to cut the music immediately while the band is playing a medium-tempo or slow song, the intended effect is lost. A caterer who gives unclear time indications causes similar problems, because the bandleader cannot be sure precisely when a dance segment should end. If the caterer times the dinner courses too closely together, the bandleader may not have enough time to get the people up and dancing between the courses. If the caterer decides to have the dance music resume only after all the guests have finished eating their main course—which can take up quite a bit of time with a crowd of 200 people—any momentum created by the bandleader before the dinner course will probably be lost. To avoid problems like these requires a good working relationship between caterer and bandleader, where each is sensitive to the needs of the other.

The specifications for the party are given to the bandleader by the caterer (through whom the party has been booked). These specifications, or *finals,* as some offices refer to them, list both the names of the guests to be announced and particular songs or musical styles that the clients want—or do not want—to hear. If a bandleader has seen these specifications before arriving at the event, he or she has at least a general idea of what kind of music the clients expect to hear. The bandleader may know, for example, that the event to be celebrated is a wedding and that both the bride and groom are from Irish families. This minimal amount of information lets the bandleader know that some of the standard wedding material—perhaps "Daddy's Little Girl" for the bride's dance with her father and "The Bride Cuts the Cake" (to the tune of "The Farmer in the Dell") for the cake cutting— as well as a few songs either from or about Ireland will be appropriate at some point in the course of the party. Specific requests may also be included—the bride's parents might want to hear some Dixieland music, for example, or the newlyweds may want Whitney Houston's "Greatest Love of All" for their first dance.

On the other hand, the bandleader may know little about the party beforehand other than its location and time. More than a few times I saw the caterer hand the specifications to the bandleader while the band was setting up equipment. This last-minute information can be quite a challenge, since it may include many specific song titles. It is common, for instance, at a bar or bas mitzvah celebration for the client to request particular songs to be played for each of the thirteen relatives or friends who will light candles on the birthday cake. Even though only eight measures or so of each song are played while the person comes forward to light a candle, *someone* in the band needs to know the song to come up with a recognizable version of those eight measures. The bandleader quickly checks through the list, making sure that at least one or two band members are familiar with each song. If no one knows a song, the bandleader must come up with a suitable substitute.

Once the party begins, the bandleader relies on past experience as a guide in selecting songs. The skill needed to determine what is right for a particular party and for a particular time within that party is known by bandleaders as "reading a party."[5]

I'm performing a service called "reading a party." You sense what is taking place at a party at a given time based on your past experience. What will make this group respond favorably to what you're going to present? Watching dancers, age groups. Sometimes one request will give you the key to the whole party.
—*subleader, late 50s, accordion*

What makes one guy more successful? The ability to read a crowd beforehand, have the wisdom to know what isn't working and get out of it. Caring enough to pay attention to what's going on and play accordingly.
—*subleader, late 30s, guitar and vocals*

During the first hour of the party, the bandleader will try out a variety of musical styles, all the time watching the guests for visual or aural cues as to what will or will not work at this occasion. The age mix of the audience provides some initial clues. A predominance of guests in their twenties or younger will make it clear that the rock and contemporary material should be fairly current. An older crowd will usually also want to hear rock, but the currency of the material is not as important:

You don't play up-to-date disco music when you play for sixty- to seventy-year-olds . . . for them, you might play "Proud Mary" [1968]—that's a new tune [in 1978]. You might play "Leroy Brown" [1972], they'd like that.
—*leader, early 60s*

Essentially, everybody wants to feel that they're very "in," that they're bright, that they know the latest thing that's in vogue . . . so you've got to give them the illusion of responding to that type of music. You can play three hours of straight rock—things the kids ask for—and they'll come over and say, "Don't you play any rock music?" This question prefaces "Proud Mary," which is the only number that they know. So if you don't play it, you didn't play any rock music.

—*leader, early 50s, piano*

Standards and Latin music are generally good choices with an audience of older adults, but even this is not a hard-and-fast rule. There are situations, particularly in the society area of the business, where the bandleader will find the college-age guests dancing to and requesting standard songs and styles:

What's coming along now is tunes from the big bands. The kids have taken it up. . . . They've heard their mothers and fathers play this, and they're a little fed up with rock, obviously. And they find this exciting. Strangely enough, the kids love a Viennese waltz. They may not know how to do it, but they will get out there and try. Because it's gay and a faster tempo, and they find it's exciting, too. They like a polka . . . the kids do a polka.

—*leader, early 70s, saxophone and vocals*

They're taking dancing lessons at Yale and Princeton, MIT, Harvard. Dancing lessons, mind you. Now the debutante parties that are coming up for me, they hardly want any rock. They want a variety of music. But I'll have rock. But it won't predominate anymore, which is a good thing.

—*leader, early 60s*

Even if people do not dance immediately, there are visual and aural cues that can be useful in judging the reception of different styles. Are people watching the bandstand during particular numbers? Is there applause after any of the songs? Do any of the guests approach the bandstand to "check out" the performers, ask questions, or request songs or styles? Once the dance floor is either partially or wholly full, the bandleader watches the dancers for further clues. Are the dancers moving smoothly and easily to the chosen tempo and rhythm, or are they, as one bandleader put it, "pushing one another around the floor, talking as much as dancing?" Again, just because the dance floor is full, the bandleader cannot be sure that the music is "right."

If the movements of the dancers seem less than smooth, the band-leader may try a similar dance style using a different tempo. Do the same dancers stay on the floor, and did the change in tempo make for easier dancing? Perhaps the style of music (foxtrot, cha-cha, rock) is not right for this audience; perhaps the real dancers in the audience have not yet made it to the dance floor; or maybe the guests are just not good dancers. Which of these is the case will become clearer as the bandleader chooses different dance styles and tempos, constantly keeping an eye on the floor to gauge the reaction to each selection.

All the bandleaders emphasized that the ability to read a party is largely intuitive and can be learned only through experience. Veteran performers of all kinds—musicians, actors, comedians, orators—may find it easy to judge the difference between an audience that is silent with rapt attention and an equally silent crowd that is bored or dis-tracted, but they might be hard-pressed to tell you how they know the difference. Club date bandleaders can talk of the skill of reading a party easily enough in general terms, but when pressed for specific examples of the process, most found the process very difficult to consider outside of the performance context. They would often begin responding to my questions by saying something like "Well, I've really never thought about it," or "I've never put it in words." Reading a party is evidently more a state of general awareness or attentiveness than a set of guidelines or rules for choosing the right songs. The awareness continues throughout the course of a party, but it is most important during the first hour or so, for bandleaders need to know early on what kind of music will allow them to "build" the party most easily.

Learning *what* music the audience will most enjoy does not tell the bandleader *when* that music should be played, that is, how to order the sets throughout the course of the four hours. Playing the right music *at the right time* requires a separate skill, known to bandleaders as "pacing":[6]

> It's the biggest key to doing a good job. You can have a potentially good party and blow it by hitting it too hard too early. You've got to make the thing last, and it's got to be interesting. A good danc-ing party, if you dance it very heavy at the beginning, will end up a turkey.
> —*leader, early 50s, piano*

Pacing takes place on three levels. There is the pacing of the four-hour affair considered as a single event with beginning and end, the pacing of sets for the dance segments within the four hours, and even the pacing of songs within a set. How a party as a whole is paced is more a reflection of a bandleader's approach to parties in general than a response to the requirements of a specific occasion. The pacing of the shorter time segments within the four-hour event—sets within dance segments or songs within sets—is more directly affected by the nature of a particular party. The caterer's timing of dance and non-dance segments and the audience's response to the music shape these smaller time segments, and these factors are different for each party.

On each of these levels, the goal of pacing is to build the interest and involvement of the audience gradually, so that a climax is reached at or immediately before a stopping point. Within a set of songs, the final song should provide the climax; within a dance segment, the final set before the guests are seated is the climax; during the course of the entire party, the dance segments following the dinner courses—usually the final one and a half hours—should include the most engaging dance music as a climax to the party as a whole. The object is to leave the audience both in high spirits and with a favorable impression of the band as they either leave the dance floor, take their seats for dinner, or leave the party.

There are certain general rules of pacing that apply to most club date performances. The only such rules I include here are ones that were either first noticed in observing performances and later confirmed by bandleaders or first mentioned by bandleaders in interviews and later confirmed through observation. Other rules may be at work as well, but I discuss here only those that appeared to hold true generally in both theory and practice. I have numbered the rules in the order in which they apply to the sequence of a party, not necessarily in the order of their relative importance:

1. *At least the first fifteen minutes of the music at a party should be "light" dance music.* Because the bandleaders want to build the intensity of the music gradually, they do not begin with the most rousing selections. Fast and loud rock numbers, horas, group participation songs, ragtime pieces, or disco music are all out of the question as opening songs. At the same time, they do not want to begin at the opposite extreme, with a long, slow ballad.

When the people are coming in, I don't expect that they'll dance right away, but the music *should* be gay. There's something wrong if you're playing slow ballads: there's no life; it's a letdown psychologically.
    —*leader, early 70s, saxophone and vocals*

At the beginning of the party, neither the music nor the dancing is the focus of attention. The guests are arriving, meeting friends and relatives they may not have seen for some time, and generally getting accustomed to the room as well as to the size and constituency of the party. They are also, in most cases, seeing the band for the first time. Bandleaders will generally keep both the music and their own personalities as unobtrusive as possible during this first hour. Very little is said over the microphone other than a short greeting to the guests, and the music remains largely in the background. According to a leader in his early fifties, the band should "begin with bubbly music, but not stuff that takes attention away from the party. Latin music, Bacharach does it."

How long each bandleader keeps to this light music varies considerably, but at least fifteen to twenty minutes at the beginning is the general rule. In some cases, it may be thirty minutes or more. For parties that include a preheat—the cocktail hour with music prior to the full band's performance in the main dining room—the dance music can begin immediately, since the audience is already "warmed-up" to an extent. A number of factors may compel the bandleader to begin calling for more engaging dance music. First of all, such a song may be requested. Second, if the bandleader sees a significant number of guests on the floor for even the "light" selections, it's likely that the crowd is eager to dance. Third, there is the noise level factor, which is familiar to anyone who has attended a cocktail party. As more people enter the room and begin talking and drinking, the ambient noise level increases considerably. The music must increase in volume, and usually tempo as well, if only to avoid being lost in the background. But this increase in noise level can also be taken as a sign that the guests are getting into the mood for active celebration and would enjoy the physical and emotional release of dancing.

Some bandleaders will begin very compelling dance music immediately following a short fifteen-minute set of light music without waiting for such cues, but they seem to be in the minority. Their reasoning is that the people will make it clear whether they want to dance once they hear the right music; if no dancers appear, the band can easily enough switch back to something lighter after a single chorus of the song.

2. *Rock music should constitute no more than one eight- to ten-minute set during the first hour of the party.* This is, again, in keeping with the bandleader's conception of pacing the party as a whole. Rock music, with its strongly accented beat and normally louder volume, is best saved for later in the party. Also, because rock is generally familiar to

all age groups (unlike older standards, which might be completely unfamiliar to younger guests) and requires no particular expertise from dancers, the bandleader can be fairly certain that a few strong rock numbers will draw people to the dance floor at almost any party. Most bands will play a few rock numbers—rarely more than two or three—during the first hour to let the audience know that the band *can* play rock, but the "heavy" rock numbers will not be chosen until the last two hours of the party.

3. *Avoid playing two consecutive sets of the same type.*[7]Contrast between sets allows the party to build gradually and also ensures that all segments of the audience are pleased at one time or another. Even with an audience that prefers one style of music in particular, a continuous serving of that one style will soon lose its effect. Too much of a good thing can make for a bad party.

4. *Never end a dance segment with a slow ballad.* This is perhaps the cardinal rule of pacing, and every bandleader I interviewed and observed followed it scrupulously. Slow tempos, which are naturally less conducive to a mood of excitement or merriment, are generally kept to a minimum throughout a party. Ballads are used primarily to provide contrast to the predominant faster dance tempos. A slow number played immediately before a period of silence—when the band is switching rooms, for instance—or the serving of a dinner course will tend to "drag out" the party (in one leader's words), to lower its energy level. Slow or rubato music will be played during the serving and eating of the dinner courses anyway, and a slow number before the serving would extend the period of "low-key" music.

Slow music's tendency to decrease the energy level at a party is sometimes used to do precisely that, if the circumstances warrant it. Such a situation arose once as I was talking with a bandleader near the end of an afternoon bar mitzvah party. The band had another job to do that evening, and this party was scheduled to end in half an hour, yet two tables of guests—about twenty people altogether—seemed to be getting more enthusiastic by the minute, dancing to every song, cheering and applauding, and generally becoming louder and louder. A couple of the band members mentioned this to the bandleader, since it seemed to be possible that these people would request the band to play an hour overtime. It was obvious that no one in the band wanted to do this, even though it would mean extra money. The bandleader simply said not to worry: knowing the host and hostess, he was quite sure they neither had the money to add the extra hour nor would want to extend the party. When I asked him how he could be so sure that the party would end on time, he said, "It happens all the time. Just one table can do it. If they're getting crazy, I do two slow songs back-to-back—that's sure to kill any party."

5. *The first dance number following a dinner course should be slow to medium slow in tempo.* If the guests have been sitting for ten minutes or more while eating a dinner course, they are not really prepared to begin dancing: their stomachs are full, and they are relaxed in their seats and engaged in conversation. They need to be coaxed gradually onto the dance floor.[8]

> If they've been sitting for a while and they're filled up with a big meal, I won't do anything fast, because they're feeling a bit sluggish. I'll do a slow ballad—a little "belly-rubbing" music so they'll get out there. And once they're out there, then I'll go into something else to get them uplifted a bit.
> —*subleader, late 30s, guitar and vocals*

6. *Game songs or group participation songs should not begin until the second hour of a party, usually not until the last two hours.* Because the party guests need to be "loosened" and in a party spirit for this material to be at all successful, it would not make sense to do it too early. The bandleader has to interact verbally with the audience for any game or group participation songs—inviting them up to the dance floor and giving them instructions—and both bandleader and guests must be, in a sense, "prepared" for the interaction. The bandleader needs time to learn about the nature of the audience and how it will react to such material; the party guests need time to get accustomed to the room, the band, and the party generally before they are ready to participate in the games or dances.

7. *The climax to the party should not be reached until the end of the third hour or later.* This rule is in keeping with the bandleader's pacing of the party as a whole. Bandleaders want the guests to leave in an uplifted, enthusiastic mood, and, since many guests begin leaving a party during the last hour, whatever music will bring the most dancers to the floor is best saved for the sets preceding this. The dance segments following dinner and before the party begins to break up are the most important ones for ensuring that guests leave the party with a positive impression of the band.

One of the finest examples I saw of skillful pacing on all three levels—within sets, within dance segments, and within the party as a whole—took place at an evening wedding reception (7 to 11 P.M.) in the fall of 1989. I include here a description of the hour-and-fifteen-minute portion of the party following the main dinner course, from

9:15 to 10:30, during which two climax points were reached, leaving the guests exhausted from dancing and hoarse from loud cheering and applause:

9:15: Medium-slow swing
1. *"Moonlight Serenade"*
2. *"At Last"*
3. *"Serenade in Blue"*
4. *"I Can't Get Started"* (tempo increase)
5. *"Little Brown Jug"*

9:22: Faster swing tempo
1. *"American Patrol"*
2. *"Tuxedo Junction"*
3. *"Take the A Train"*
4. *"In the Mood"*
5. *"Chattanooga Choo-choo"*

9:27: Slow 1950s (12/8 time)
1. *"In the Still of the Night"*
2. *"You Send Me"*
3. *"Silhouettes"*
4. *"The Wonder of You"*

9:33: Fast 1950s rock and roll
1. *"Rock around the Clock"*
2. *"Blue Suede Shoes"*
3. *"Hound Dog"*
4. *"Let's Twist Again"*
5. *"Johnny B. Goode"*
6. *"Shout"* (tempo increase)

9:42: Slow contemporary (best man's toast, cake cutting)
1. *"Love, Look What It's Done to Me"*

9:46: Medium-slow foxtrot (bride and father's dance)
1. *"I Wish You Love"*

9:50: Medium-slow rock
1. *"Feel Like Makin' Love"*

9:55: Medium tempo Motown
1. *"The Same Old Song"*
2. *"Can't Help Myself"*
3. *"Get Ready"* (tempo increase)
4. *"I Heard It through the Grapevine"*
5. *"Respect"* (tempo increase)
6. *"Devil with the Blue Dress On"*
7. *"Gimme Some Lovin'"*

10:22: Fast Rock (volume increase)
      1. "Cadillac Ranch"
10:28 Stop

The band for the affair had ten pieces: guitar, bass guitar, two drummers (one on trap set, the other on timbales and miscellaneous percussion), three horns (trumpet—the leader—trombone, and sax), keyboard synthesizer, and two female lead vocalists. The band members ranged in age from the guitarist in his late twenties to the keyboard player in his sixties. A week before the affair, the bandleader had spoken with the bride and groom and the bride's parents, who had requested both some big band and some Motown music. The bandleader called for neither type until after dinner, feeling he could count on both to work toward a climax near the end of the party.

The first big band number, "Moonlight Serenade," drew a few dancers out immediately, and the floor was nearly full by the end of this set. Some of the older adults began to leave the floor during the faster big band set, but they were replaced by the bride and groom and many of their friends, all jitterbugging like crazy. The bandleader still had about fifteen minutes before the toast and cake cutting, so he slowed things down a bit with the next set, hoping to keep the younger crowd with fifties material. Just as they seemed to be tiring of the slow tempo, he called for "Rock around the Clock," which picked them up and kept them on the dance floor. During this song, the caterer signaled to the bandleader that the guests would have to be seated in five minutes. By the time the band reached "Shout," the dance floor was completely filled with people doing both jitterbug and nontouch rock dancing. They applauded and cheered as the song ended and they were asked to be seated.

The toast, cake cutting, and the bride's dance with her father brought the energy level back down. The bandleader knew he could get the younger crowd dancing again, but he wanted to work into it gradually. The medium-slow rock number, "Feel Like Makin' Love," drew many couples back onto the floor, followed by many more, including the bride and groom, as the Motown set began. The floor filled again when Marvin Gaye's "Grapevine" began. The dancing got more and more enthusiastic as the set continued, with the bride and groom seeming to lead the crowd. Near the end of "Gimme Some Lovin' " the bandleader asked the bride and groom to come forward to the bandstand. As they did, the guitarist came out onto the dance floor to greet them and began the loud opening chords to Bruce Springsteen's "Cadillac Ranch." The drummer had gotten noticeably louder, using a heavy backbeat, with the other percussionist on cowbell.

The bass guitar player also jumped off the bandstand to join the guitarist, and he was soon joined by the three horn players—all of them in a semicircle in front of the bride and groom. By the time the first chorus of the song was over, the bride and groom found themselves dancing alone, surrounded by nearly half of the party guests— nearly 100 people—all clapping and cheering. The couple certainly didn't seem to mind: they smiled and laughed and danced enthusiastically. Four tall extension lights held by the photographers spotlighted the two dancers while cameras flashed and video recorders whirred. As the excitement reached a fever pitch, the bandleader signaled for the song's ending. The sax player, honking and screaming on his horn in true rhythm and blues style, leaped in the air; as he landed, the guitar player crashed into the final chord, accompanied by loud and wild closing riffs from the drummer. The audience exploded with applause, and the bride and groom beamed with laughter, looking a bit exhausted after such a frenzy.

The musicians returned to the bandstand and began a medium foxtrot set with the song "When I Fall In Love." Only half an hour remained of the party, and many guests were already beginning to leave. After a brief interlude for the throwing of the bridal bouquet, the band played a short set of two rock songs, a longer set of standard fox trots, and ended with Donna Summer's "Last Dance for Love."

When I spoke with the bandleader later that week, he remarked that he does not always play that much rock music, especially so many songs in succession. But, he said, "I had that crowd where I wanted them. I had them in the palm of my hand; they wanted those songs. When I said to the band, 'Alright, let's go into Springsteen,' I knew I had 'em where I wanted them. When they are on that dance floor— especially the friends of the bride and groom—for twenty or twenty-five minutes, then I will go into something like the Springsteen thing. . . . I always try to feature the bride and the groom, because they're the stars. . . . That's my experience, my judgment. Everybody cannot become a leader and expect to do these things overnight; it comes with experience."

The skills needed to become a successful bandleader can be learned partly through observation of experienced leaders in performance, but they must be applied in performance before they can be considered fully acquired. Simply knowing the rules of bandleading and being able to apply such rules in performance are two very different matters. One can know all the rules for being a successful orator, but such knowledge is of little value until it is applied before an audience.

Most of the bandleaders I spoke with had some experience as a sideperson in bands, which gave them the opportunity to learn what the position of bandleader required without being responsible for the end result. As one leader put it, "[You] watch the reaction to what the leader is then doing and decide if it's successful or not. You don't have to wait until tomorrow to find out—it's happening right that minute. And you learn that way." All the bandleaders emphasized, however, that whatever skills they displayed were, for the most part, learned while leading rather than beforehand through observation or advice. The learning process really begins only when a musician is placed in the role of bandleader. New skills are acquired and old ones refined through years of experience.

Notes

1. "For Lester Lanin, 50 Years of Music" C18.

2. In a different but related context, folk singer Sam Hinton speaks of the folk performer who will "pride himself on timing and other techniques designed *to keep the audience in his control*" ("The Singer of Folk Songs and His Conscience" 67 [my emphasis]; cited by Sanders, "Psyching out the Crowd" 267).

3. Nye, "The Social Organization of Time" 69. Nye notes that "Do not give the dancers time to sit down" is one of the "rules" that resort bandleaders seem to follow invariably (69).

4. Harold Branch and Irving Dweir refer to this simply as "dinner music" and admonish the aspiring bandleader: "NOTE: Play AD-LIB (not in tempo). This music is NOT for dancing!" (*Club Date Handbook* 14).

5. This process of "reading" or "psyching out" an audience is surely familiar to any seasoned performer, yet there is surprisingly little writing on the subject. Scholarly writings that do consider this element of musical performance, whereby the musician changes the nature of the performance through interpreting cues from the audience, include Lord on Yugoslavian epic singers; Keil on urban blues singers; Ferris on rural blues performers; Sanders on folk performers in Chicago; Leary on "old-time" musicians in Wisconsin; Schuyler on Berber musicians; and Nye on "resort bands" in the United States. Complete information on these sources is found in the bibliography.

6. The term *pacing*, like *reading* a crowd, is certainly not peculiar to the club date context, although I have come across only isolated and brief references to the concept as it is used in musical performance. One especially interesting reference to the technique is found in Leslie Gourse, *Every Day: The*

Story of Joe Williams, where Williams describes Count Basie's ability to "make puppets musically of an audience" (74) through pacing the momentum of a four-hour performance.

7. Nye ("The Social Organization of Time" 70) also makes note of the importance of contrast, although in reference to individual songs rather than sets of songs.

8. Ibid. 68. Another "rule" noted by Nye is to "coax the crowd gradually" following dinner.

5

Employers and Booking

Running a business is never a completely stable and predictable venture, whether the product is a tangible object or a service. Business volume is subject to many uncontrollable variables: the public's ability to pay for the product; the public's perception of its need for the product; and yearly, monthly, or even weekly cycles inherent to the nature of the business. The owner of any business seeks to create as much financial security as possible in spite of these restrictions.

The club date business is a luxury business, and as such its health depends on the health of the national and local economy. When money is tight, people are less likely to avail themselves of its services. Leaders who depend on organizations for much of their work may feel the pinch less immediately, but the entertainment budgets of both organizations and individuals are bound to be curtailed if the economy is experiencing recession or inflationary trends.

The business can also suffer from a change in public values. The marked decrease in the number of debutante parties during the 1960s is a prime example of this. As fewer and fewer daughters of the social elite felt "coming out" to be either necessary or desirable, both leaders and sidepersons working in the society field found themselves losing a considerable amount of lucrative work. The disc jockey phenomenon, which began in the 1970s, represented another such change in public values. A significant portion of people sponsoring private parties felt that recorded music was a suitable substitute for live music, and club date musicians again lost many work opportunities as a result.

The seasonal nature of much club date work is another limiting factor. In any given year there will be peak periods as well as very slow periods for the business: May, June, November, and December will normally be the busiest months, and the first months of the calendar year and late summer months will be the least busy. And within each week of the year, one night—Saturday—is when most clients will want a leader's services.

Most leaders work within these limitations as sole proprietors of their business—independent leaders. A much smaller number decide at some point to join in partnership with other leaders, either forming a new office or joining an existing one. The partnership offers, for one, the advantages of sharing overhead expenses for everything from renting office space and paying office personnel to advertising and purchasing business and musical equipment. There is the additional advantage of being able to share client referrals on a regular basis: working, in effect, as subleaders for one another in order to maintain a steadier flow of work. The disadvantages are those common to any business partnership: loss of direct control over all aspects of one's business and the realization that one's own reputation—and financial well-being—can be adversely affected by the actions of other partners.

There is no single career path that naturally leads a musician into the club date leader/employer role; rather, there are at least four different approaches. The first and simplest of these is for a musician to inherit the role: a father, for example, passes on the reins of an established business to his son or invites the son to become a partner in the business. This situation does not seem to be very common, and I encountered only one example of it. A second approach is available to any musician: the musician begins in club dates working as a free-lance sideperson, learns the ropes of the business and the art of bandleading while still a band member/employee, and books his or her first jobs through friends or relatives. The majority of leaders I spoke with began in this way. A third method of becoming a leader works almost entirely within the club date "office" structure. The musician begins working as a sideperson or subleader for an established partnership, eventually works exclusively as a subleader, and becomes a leader by buying into the partnership. There may even be an intermediate step in the process, whereby the musician buys into the office initially as a junior partner.

The fourth method of becoming a leader seems to be available only to piano players because of the nature of their instrument. Three of the leaders I interviewed, who all began doing club dates in the 1950s and early 1960s, had followed this route. They had been able to begin club date work in the leader's role, by-passing the sideperson's role completely. Before entering the club date business, they had worked frequently in piano bars and nightclubs as solo performers—a role not normally available to other instrumentalists. Their club and bar work not only provided them with a large repertoire of popular music but also gave them experience in dealing with audiences and in booking their own work. They developed club date clientele from contacts made at bars and clubs, beginning as solo performers for small parties only. This led to larger jobs requiring more musicians, and they eventually moved into club dates on a full-time basis. This same path may still be open to piano players today, especially in terms of repertoire, for the piano bar is one of the last performance venues outside of club dates where standards from all musical eras can still be heard on a regular basis.

Whichever path a musician takes to become a club date leader, the realization comes early on that the work is completely different from that of a sideperson. The sideperson is a free-lance performer who sells services to other musicians (leaders and contractors); the leader is a businessperson with a product to sell to the general public—musical entertainment in the form of a band. This product must be packaged, labeled, advertised, and sold like any other commodity. Overhead costs must be kept as low as is practical, and the price of the product as high as the market will reasonably bear. Individual leaders use a variety of methods to market their product. Some of these methods are common throughout the club date business; others are particular to the socioeconomic class of a leader's usual clientele.

A leader relies on party guests' recognition of his or her name to attract future clientele. Whoever happens to be the actual bandleader on a job, the name identifying the group will invariably include the name of the leader or office that booked the job, either as part of the band's name or added to it. The leader's own band, then, will be packaged and labeled as The George Smith Band, for instance. George Smith booked the job, and George Smith will also be the bandleader. (There is the implication as well that the group is a consistent unit, a "set" group, whether or not that is the case.) The important fact is that the unit remains identified as The George Smith Band as long as George Smith is the bandleader.

Of course, Mr. Smith may be booking work for some bands other than the one he himself directs. The traditional method of packaging and labeling one of these bands is simply to organize the unit according to the specifications of a particular engagement and identify the band by the name of the leader that booked the job—*a* George Smith Band, for example. Both bandleader and band members are relatively anonymous in this case. A single leader or office may have a number of such "pick-up" bands, as musicians refer to them, working at the same time, each one directed by a subleader and identified only as a group organized by George Smith.

This method of organizing the selling unit is used throughout the business, but it is especially characteristic of the society area, where the name of the leader/owner is the major selling point and evidently enough assurance of quality product for upper-class clients. As a musician in charge of booking at one of these major society offices explained it, "We depend on the credibility of the name, the influence. . . . The client never gets to meet our bandleader, never gets to speak to our bandleader. . . . Our clientele is much more upscale . . . and they will generally leave it up to us what the music will or will not be." Thus, although there is only one band known as The Peter Duchin Orchestra, there may be fifteen others playing on the same night, each one identified only as "*a* Peter Duchin Orchestra."

Interestingly, this method of using only the leader's name to identify a band led by someone else has never been very common outside of the society field. "*A* George Smith Band" is apparently not sufficient identification at the middle- or upper-middle-class levels of the business. If Mr. Smith hires Jim Jones to lead a band for him, it is most likely that the band will be called "the Jim Jones Band of George Smith Music." This generally holds true as well for bands led by subleaders and working for an office composed of two or more leaders as partners. Say the office or partnership is known as "Empire Orchestras." A band working for them will be known as "the Jim Jones Band of Empire Orchestras."

One other method used for packaging and labeling a band is to organize the musicians under a nonpersonal, descriptive name, such as "Elegant Touch" or "Good Times." This method is most commonly used for bands working for leaders or offices with a predominantly middle-class clientele. Society offices do not use this method at all; upper-middle-class offices and independent leaders use it, but more exceptionally than as a rule. The band members in this situation are all completely anonymous beyond the band name, and all bookings are managed by an office or independent leader. Many of these bands are composed entirely of younger musicians—in their twenties, for the most part—and to someone watching them perform it is not always clear who the bandleader is, if there is one at all. These nonpersonal, descriptive names seem to have most appeal for younger clientele, who recognize the same method used for naming rock groups. That may well be the reasoning behind such names, because the bulk of club date work at the middle-class level is for bar mitzvahs and wedding receptions.

Whether selling the leader's own band or that of a subleader working under the leader's name, performance itself is the simplest and most direct means for advertising the product. As a leader reaches a wider audience with each performance, it is hoped that both the number of jobs and the fee for each job will increase. People who hired the leader for their son's bar mitzvah may decide to do so again for another bar mitzvah or a wedding—a "repeat" job. More importantly, guests at the bar mitzvah or wedding may ask the leader to perform at their party—a "spin-off" job.

Spin-off jobs are especially important because they serve to spread the leader's reputation. Both leaders and subleaders frequently pointed out that, because of the possibility of spin-offs, their performance is often directed more toward pleasing the guests at a party than the host or hostess. The guests, after all, represent far more future job possibilities to the bandleader; the sponsors, on the other hand, are not likely to offer a repeat job in the near future. The host or hostess, regardless of his or her reaction to the performance, will usually be quite satisfied as long as the guests are pleased with the band. If the tastes of the party sponsors do not happen to coincide with those of the guests, it may be wisest for the bandleader to consider the guests first and sponsors second.

Repeat jobs for organizations can build a certain amount of predictability and security into a leader's business from year to year and are thus probably the most important single kind of work. Fraternal, labor, and civic organizations that contract a leader's services for their yearly festivities may well do so in future years, and they may often do so a year in advance. In the society field, charity groups and private clubs are a common source for repeat business. Many debutante balls, charity balls, and holiday parties are sponsored each year by the same group, and the music contracts are often signed a year or more in advance. Business clients can be an even more lucrative source of repeat jobs at all socioeconomic levels, since during a given year a single business firm may sponsor multiple events requiring music. Leaders will establish ongoing accounts with as many business clients as they can reasonably handle.

Work for organizations also tends to create continuity of clientele, because many people will attend various organizational affairs throughout the year. Party guests—all potential clients—have the opportunity to become familiar with one or more leaders and will naturally keep those leaders in mind when planning parties of their own. Working for organizations in the society field especially, musicians soon begin to notice familiar faces in the audience:

> Deb balls, charity balls, April in Paris balls all repeat every year. The same people attend the affairs, and they expect the same quality of music. Indeed, many attend a variety of the affairs, so the audience becomes more knowledgeable.
> —*sideperson, late 40s, trumpet*

This "sameness" from party to party was mentioned frequently by musicians in the society field: the same people, the same parties, the same music. It isn't really surprising that this should be the case; members of the upper class, after all, have a vested interest in keeping things the way they are. Uniformity from one social event to another reflects this conservative outlook.[1]

There is a similar continuity among individual clients outside the society field, though it is not as well defined. Leaders as well as party guests will, for instance, refer to "the bar mitzvah circuit." Jewish parents of a bar mitzvah boy or bas mitzvah girl will naturally know other parents with thirteen-year-olds and may themselves have other younger children—each child representing a possible future engagement for a club date leader. Both children and parents will attend a number of these celebrations and become familiar with various leaders and their product. This is true, but to a lesser extent, with parents of wedding couples: if their children are marrying, they are likely to know many other parents with children soon to marry. Both parents and children attend a number of weddings as the children reach college age and beyond, learning about club date bands and exchanging information about them, and a wedding "circuit" of sorts is created. With both bar mitzvahs and weddings, repeat and spin-off jobs are common, but they do not occur with the same regularity as organization-sponsored affairs.

For some leaders, reaching prospective clients through performance alone may be sufficient for establishing and building a business. But advertising through performance cannot establish contact with those who have never seen or heard the leader's product, so most leaders find it necessary to use other means to reach prospective clients. Such prospective clients are known as "blind leads"—individuals or organizations that are likely to need the services of a leader but with whom a leader has had no previous contact. In order to reach such people, some sort of active advertising and sales is necessary. Printed advertising matter can be sent to organizations—fraternal and civic groups or businesses, for example—and later followed up with phone calls or in-person meetings. Reaching individual clients—the parents of the bar mitzvah boy or the bride-to-be—requires different tactics, because the people celebrating such occasions in any given year represent such a small and diffuse segment of the population.

One traditional method of obtaining leads is simply to check engagement announcements in local newspapers, find the number of the young woman's parents, and call to offer your services. This method can be successful, but it is much less efficient and comprehensive than a method whereby one or more "sources" can provide continuous recommendations or referrals for *all* kinds of parties. In the society field the "social secretary" provided such a source—and still does, to a large extent. The social secretary is a person paid by an individual or organization to make all the necessary arrangements for a society affair, from sending invitations and decorating the hall to locating a caterer and hiring a band.[2] The sponsor of a party may never contact the leader directly, leaving it all up to the social secretary. One society leader recalled that, in the 1940s and 1950s, very little active selling was really necessary for the leader who had established connections with these secretaries.

The most useful source for recommendations and referrals outside the society field is the caterer or hotel banquet manager. Individuals planning private parties will usually contact a catering hall or hotel first to be assured of a definite location and date for the event, because the most popular locations can be booked two or three years in advance. The caterer or hotel banquet manager, then, has information that is very valuable to a leader—a list of persons planning parties, many of them as yet undecided about which leader, if any, to hire for their party. It is clearly to the leader's advantage to have access to such a list. The caterer may also be willing to recommend the services of one particular leader or office—all for a fee, of course.

No caterer or hotel banquet manager is going to offer lists of prospective clients or recommendation services to a leader at no cost. The money involved in such an agreement can run into the tens of thousands of dollars per year. Such agreements are called either *concessions, package deals,* or *kickbacks,* depending on who is describing them. The leader or office making such an agreement becomes, in effect and often in title as well, the musical director or consultant for the catering hall or hotel, and the leader's bands become the "house" bands. Such an arrangement does not mean that this one leader has exclusive rights to all parties at the particular location; rather, more of that leader's bands will perform there simply because the leader has first contact with so many of the clients using the facility. At one catering hall with such an agreement in effect about half the bands on any given night were connected with the club date office that had made the agreement.

The musicians union has always been strongly opposed to these package deals (the term frequently used in editorials in *Allegro*), but its power to stop the practice has been negligible. The union stance in the 1950s and 1960s was that such leader-caterer arrangements restrict the free competition of leaders for available jobs, favoring those who have enough money to pay for a caterer's recommendations and

referrals. As more club date offices were formed through leader partnerships and the capital available for such deals increased, numerous
articles, editorials, and official announcements in *Allegro* denounced
the practice. One notice, set on a full page in large type, appeared
repeatedly during 1960. It read: "A Message to Users of Live Music:
Local 802 is not in the catering business—caterers are not in the music business," followed by a brief admonition that the union would
take strong action against caterers involved in package deals with
leaders. In some early cases the union succeeded in reaching agreements designed to keep the halls open to all leaders on an equal basis.

These concessions—as leaders and offices refer to them—were not
actually illegal as long as they were not completely exclusionary, and
consequently the union was unable to stop them permanently. They
are very much a part of the club date scene today, and many catering
halls openly advertise their connection with a particular leader or
office. The larger halls have not only a banquet manager's office but
also a music office, a florist, and a photographer—"one-stop shopping" for party-givers. The union's main concern today is that the
high price of these caterer-leader agreements tends to depress the
club date pay scale, but there is little that it can do other than to stress
this point at the bargaining table.

Once a leader has made contact with prospective clients, the product still must be sold. This is done in a variety of ways, and again, the
particular methods correspond generally to the socioeconomic level
of the clientele. In the society field, active selling has traditionally
been a relatively minor consideration. These clients have less concern
with budget restrictions and tend to trust the society offices to provide
quality music. Offices and leaders without high-society connections
usually find it necessary to display their product in some way before a
client is willing to sign a contract. The method of display preferred by
leaders for its simplicity and convenience is to videotape their bands.
The band can be shown at its best—even though out of context—and
the client can check out the product at the leader's office. If this is not
assurance enough, the leader may arrange for the client to see a band
in performance. Leaders in general try to discourage such "auditions," both because of their intrusiveness and because a short portion of any band's performance gives the client a very limited view of
its capabilities. A number of these leaders, all of them well established
and working primarily for a wealthy clientele, spoke with disdain of
any client's need to "feel the goods," implying or saying outright that
it reflects lower-class values. Clients who could not accept them on
reputation alone simply did not interest them.

At the opposite end from the society field is the "showcase" phenomenon. Offices associated with large catering halls will present
four or more of their bands in an evening showcase set up in the hall's
largest ballroom. Complimentary soft drinks and snacks may be provided, and there is often a cash bar as well. Two hundred or more
people who are planning parties—many of them engaged couples
along with friends and parents—watch, listen, and take notes as each
band presents thirty minutes or so of its best party music. The bands
do their best to create enthusiasm in the audience, but because the
music is so completely out of context, they do not always succeed. The
showcase marketing concept seems to appeal mostly to the lower socioeconomic levels of club date clientele, where getting the most for
one's money is an overriding concern in planning a party. The relatively low fees charged by the bands and the halls are directed toward
clients working within limited budgets.

Once a client is prepared to sign a contract for a leader's services,
the leader will naturally try to maximize profit from the contract,
keeping in mind both the client's budget restrictions and the limitations of a party's size and location. In some cases, it may be clear early
on that there is no room for bargaining. A client having a very small
party—fifty or fewer guests, for instance—asks for a disc jockey or a
solo performer, and the contract is set as such, with no attempt by the
leader or office salesperson to increase the scope of the contract. A
larger band would simply not be appropriate in that case. For larger
parties, though, the leader may point out the advantages of a band
larger than what the client has initially considered or perhaps suggest
a cocktail hour as separate from the main four-hour party. The larger
the band and the longer the performance, the larger the leader's
profit. Again, though, the leader recognizes the limits involved. The
client will usually have some budgetary constraints, and there are
practical limits to the size of a band for most jobs. A sixteen-piece
band may be far too large considering the size of the party and the
size of the room where it will be held. At the same time, a ten-piece
group might be quite appropriate, even though the client at first envisioned an eight-piece band.

As in selling other large ticket items, the client may be presented
first with the "best" possible product (also probably the most expensive) and bargaining goes down from there. If a band is presented to
the client as a "set" group, where the personnel are supposedly always
the same, it is to the leader's advantage to present the unit as a large
one that can be reduced rather than the other way around. In negotiating the contract, it is more difficult to add to a stripped-down ver-

sion than to subtract from the "all-frills" model. Also, if the band was first presented as a six-piece unit, any added members might seem just that to the client—additions not integral to the usual group. For example, suppose a client initially asks for a six-piece band for a large wedding reception. The leader may normally work with a basic five-piece group but, considering the size of the reception in question, respond to the client that his or her band is a nine-piece unit. This gives the impression that any number less than nine would be an incomplete unit and perhaps a poorer product. The bargaining begins from there, rather than beginning lower and trying to work upward.

The final price for a band is seen in terms of dollars per musician, although it may not be presented to the client that way. Per musician cost to the club date client in 1989 was in the $300 to $600 range, each additional musician increasing the leader's profit by a set dollar figure or percentage. This figure covers pay to the musician, office expenses (including staff), catering concession fees, if any, and profit. The total cost for a five-piece band, then, runs from $1,500 to $3,000 or more; "more," in the case of very popular leaders, especially in the society field, can include well over an additional $1,000. A deposit is paid once a contract is agreed on and signed, and the balance is due immediately following the engagement.

Actually delivering the specific product that a client has contracted for is not always a simple task. Club date contracts may be arranged a year or more in advance, and no leader can absolutely guarantee that the personnel in the band will be identical to the personnel the client originally saw. Every leader will try to keep the personnel in bands as consistent as possible: it makes for better client relations, greater consistency of musical quality, and less difficulty conducting the group on stage. Even in the society area, where the particular musicians in a band may not be important to the client, consistency of personnel is still important for musical reasons.

A leader will try to keep the key members of any group—guitarist, keyboard player, section leaders, featured vocalists—working together as a unit by offering them guarantees, either written or verbal. In some guarantees the leader promises the sideperson a certain annual dollar amount as long as the musician agrees to work on an exclusive or at least semiexclusive basis for that one leader or office. Society offices may offer not a dollar figure but rather a first-call privilege to their most important musicians. The "first" guitarist working for a society office is guaranteed first call for the best jobs, usually those led by the leader/owner, in return for agreeing to accept such work precedent to any other offers.

These guarantees work to an extent, but they are hardly ever as exclusive as leaders would like them to be. Sidepersons need to keep their schedules as full as possible, and individual offices or leaders may not be able to do that for all of their key musicians. Most leaders and the contractors working for them recognize, though some very grudgingly, that they occasionally will have to use substitutes for musicians who are under guarantee. The leaders may overlook such occasional exceptions to their guarantee agreements as long as the jobs in question are not especially important ones, good substitutes can be found, and the offices are given sufficient advance notice. They realize that retaining exclusive use of musicians is not always a practical possibility, or as one leader put it, that "you can't own anyone in this business."

The contract between client and leader normally stipulates in regard to personnel only that the leader or subleader and a band of so many musicians agree to perform for the party. Even if substitute musicians are used at the engagement, the contract has been fulfilled, and the client may still be fully satisfied with the product received. Only if the leader does not appear at the performance when contracted to do so does a significant problem arise, and for a variety of reasons—most of them much less than legitimate—this *does* happen.

A single leader will sooner or later encounter the possibility of booking more than one engagement for a single time slot. This is most likely to occur during peak periods of the year or on Saturday nights throughout the year. The ethical leader who hopes to keep a second, third, or fourth booking for that single time slot will try to sell the client a band led by a subleader at a substantially lower price. The leader can still receive some profit from the job and, in satisfying the client, possibly derive later repeat and spin-off jobs from the engagement. Thus, a single leader may have three, four, or more bands performing on a single night. It is not uncommon for one office to have twenty bands performing on the same Saturday night during a busy season.

The unethical way of dealing with such situations is known as *double booking*. The practice is similar to the intentional overbooking of airline flights or hotel rooms. In the club date usage, though, the practice can be carried to an extreme. The term applies when a leader books more than one engagement for the same date and time but promises to be the bandleader for each affair. The leader, of course, will perform for only one complete party at the specified date and time; subleaders or substitute groups will have to perform at the extra parties. Musicians refer to these "extra" engagements as *trouble jobs* or *screamers,* the latter term referring to the client's reaction to the deception. In a more humorous vein, they will also call them *V.S. jobs,* the initials standing for "Vere's Sidney?" the scheduled bandleader.

Double booking probably does not happen in the society field, for both the names of the leader/owners and the events for which they perform are well publicized. If Lester Lanin didn't show up for one of his engagements, you can be sure that his absence would be noted in the society pages of the *New York Times.* Nor is double booking likely to happen with established leaders in other areas. Nonetheless, the practice clearly has been and continues to be a problem in the business, and every bit of publicity such incidents receive reflects poorly on club date leaders as a whole. At the showcases I attended, the office leaders who introduced the bands stressed repeatedly that "the band you hire is the one you get," and individual leaders often brought up the subject during interviews without my mentioning it:

> And I want you to know . . . that whoever is assigned to that job *goes* to that job. No horsing around. The King of England could call him, but if he's assigned to that job, he goes to that job. Integrity and honesty with the people—that's why our reputation grew.
> —*leader, late 60s, trumpet (1989)*

> We're a very ethical company; we never screw anyone. We never give screamers. If you're promised on a job, you're there. If a job comes in for ten or twenty thousand dollars and I'm already promised, I will never get off that job. When people hire us, they get who they hire.
> —*leader, late 50s, trumpet (1989)*

Sidepersons tended to talk of the practice with some hesitancy, perhaps because many of them had worked on trouble jobs in the past yet found it necessary to continue working for those leaders or offices later on. Both of the musicians whom I quote here spoke on the subject with the understanding that I would not identify them even by instrument or age.

> I'm going to be blacklisted if anybody hears this. But, what happens—a common practice in the club date business—you'll come to hear a band—Joe Schmoe and his boys. You like them and sign them up. Now, that's in July of 1978; your daughter's wedding is in July of 1979. You get there—no Joe Schmoe. "What happened to Joe Schmoe?" you say. Either he doesn't work for us anymore, he

died, his mother died, he's sick, he got into a car accident. In the meantime, Joe Schmoe is at another affair making more money.

I had a job a while ago. I got to the job—guys I had never seen before. I introduced myself. The leader introduces himself, "My name is Mark. Jerry [the scheduled bandleader] is supposed to have laryngitis today." I figured they had called the people that day, but then Jerry showed up at the job. He whispered to the woman [the hostess]. He actually came in a tuxedo and was obviously going to work someplace. The woman really believed it and was ready to give the guy something for his cold . . . that's the lengths they will go to.

The repertoire of excuses used by leaders who double book work and need an explanation for their inability to fulfill their contracts is familiar to any experienced club date musician. One musician related the story of a leader who had devised a standard excuse for such situations:

There's a great story about a leader who used to sign personal appearance contracts—four, five, six a night. So he had a fake cast made. He'd go to each hall and say, "Sorry, but I did something to my arm." And he'd put in a subleader. Then he'd go to the job that paid the most money and off could come the cast.

Whether this story is true or fictional was not clear to me, but the fact that it exists at all and that the musicians to whom I later mentioned the incident found it humorous underlines the reality of the situation it depicts.

If the clients at one of these trouble jobs can prove that leader X, whose mother supposedly died two days prior to the event, was in fact working elsewhere, they *can* bring the leader to small claims court for breach of contract. That usually will not happen, however, for a number of reasons. First, it would be difficult to prove unless the client had reason to expect the situation beforehand; second, going to court can be time consuming and expensive, and the final settlement may not justify the effort; and third, the clients probably believe the story as long as the leader's reputation for double booking is not widespread. The leader also banks on the general confusion and myriad last-minute details racing through the mind of the party's host or hostess to deflect attention from the deception taking place. In the end, the client may actually be satisfied with the substitute provided by the leader and even recommend the leader's services to friends.

Though it may occasionally succeed, however, double booking to any great extent is bound to harm a leader's reputation sooner or later. Not every client is going to be so understanding about the matter, and the angry client is certain to spread the word to more than a few friends. For those leaders with established reputations in the club date business, the risks involved in double booking far outweigh the financial temptation. Also, with the increase in the number and size of offices in the business, single leaders acting as partners risk harming the reputation of the entire office—and probable expulsion from the partnership—by engaging in double booking. Another factor limiting the practice is that many offices, as well as independent leaders, have expanded their operations to include such services as booking other, nonmusical entertainment, acting as agents for location work at hotels and lounges, or "total party planning"—providing whatever is needed from decorations and invitations to flowers and entertainment. With a broader base of income, there is less temptation to risk one's reputation through double booking. Yet the practice does continue, and it tends to tarnish the public's image of the business as a whole.

Once a party is underway, the business cycle begins again. As the leader is delivering the contracted product, the product is on display for possible future clients in the audience. As the leader's client base broadens over time, the number of jobs a leader does per year begins to reach a practical maximum, and income begins to stabilize. For independent leaders who book their own services only, the number of jobs per year will probably range from 100 to 200—an average of four per week, though that probably means six or more jobs during busy months and only a couple per week for the rest of the year. A leader who can realize $400 profit from each job after covering office expenses—a bit more than twice the 1989 union scale for sidepersons—would earn between $40,000 and $80,000. Of course, this may represent four or five full days of office work in addition to weekends on stage, which makes the real value of the total income a bit less than outstanding. Booking work for other bands, making more profit per job, and getting involved in work outside the club date field can increase this income considerably. I was given only very general income figures by some leaders and no such information at all from others, but I estimate the net income of most full-time leaders to fall within the $50,000 to $100,000 range. This represents roughly twice the income of a full-time sideperson. Considering the nature of the work, it is difficult to imagine a leader remaining in the business for long if income fell below this range. Partners working for large offices or

well-established society leaders certainly make far more than
$100,000 a year, though how much more is anyone's guess. Total in-
come for leaders who book the services of many bands other than the
one they themselves direct is limited only by the number of subleaders
or set groups they are able to control.

Notes

1. This concept of "sameness," keeping things stable and unruffled on the
home front, is the primary duty of the upper-class woman, who is also the
one responsible for party arrangements. It is a recurrent theme throughout
Susan Ostrander's *Women of the Upper Class.*

2. An interesting and informative account of the role of social secretaries
in planning debutante parties is found in Steven Birmingham, *The Right People* 81–91.

6

Employees and the Hiring Structure

How you get into club dates is—when you're off, between engagements, even with Tommy Dorsey. You get a break or vacation. He can take off for a month or six weeks because he's making the big bucks, but you can't. When you're in town you've got nothing. So you go down to the union floor. "Hey, what's happening?" "Oh, you want to work Saturday night?" And that's how you get into it. It's economics, that's all it is. Basic economics.

—former sideperson, presently a leader, late 40s, trumpet

Entering the club date business as a sideperson is not always an especially significant or difficult process. Particularly for those musicians who began playing club dates in the 1940s, club date work was just a way of "filling out their calendars" when other musical work was slow. Between Broadway theater jobs or during breaks in hotel or big band work, musicians could go to the union exchange floor and, using contacts already established from other work areas, find temporary work in club dates. There was enough similarity in repertoire between club dates and location work that the musical transition was not a big problem. The work was not difficult to get for the musician who was not particular about who offered the work or at what pay scale it was offered. In any case, it was not at all a matter of entering the club date field with the intention of beginning a career:

> People fall into the club date business. You start making a fairly steady income from it, and you keep doing it.
>
> —*sideperson, late 50s, trumpet*

One thing led to another, and before you know it, you're in the business . . . just fell in. I enjoyed it, and there was opportunity to do it.

—*sideperson, early 60s, saxophone*

I was so young—sixteen when I got into it—that I didn't have any
goals. My parents wanted me to be a school teacher. It's the parents
who have the goals, and they try to mold you in their image. If I
could augment my income by playing on weekends, they'd be satisfied.

  —*sideperson, late 40s, piano*

Many musicians who began working in the club date field in the
1950s and later also did so in such a casual fashion, although the repertoire requirements were becoming more of a problem. They learned
the basic requirements of the business from teachers, relatives, or
friends and began working on an irregular basis through these same
connections. The fact that club date work was or could be a business
or career hardly occurred to them; playing club dates was a way of
making extra money while going to school or pursuing other ends.

I didn't get into it because I wanted to. I got into it because my
older brother played in the band I was in, and the band was the
thing when I was growing up. Lots of kids had bands; and you
made some money, and it was a social thing. I never looked at it as
a business thing because I was good enough to just do it.

  —*sideperson, late 20s, guitar*

A minority of younger musicians began working on a regular basis
in the club date field soon after their first jobs. The ones who did so
were usually first hired as specialists: rock guitarists from the late
1950s onward or female vocalists beginning in the 1980s. For most
players who began in the field after the 1960s, it was only after playing club dates on a casual basis for a number of years, by which time
they had established many contacts in the business, that club date performance as a major source of income presented itself as a possibility.

Club date work is attractive to young musicians for a number of
reasons. Once a musician has a handle on the basic repertoire requirements, the work seems to pay very well for a relatively small investment of time. The work is not nearly as competitive or high-pressure
as recording or theater work, and the pay per job is much better than
nightclub work. In addition, because most club date jobs are concentrated on weekends, the work need not conflict with other employment, musical or nonmusical. All in all, it seems an ideal part-time job
for a young musician.

Union pay scale for club date work varies according to the day and
time of a performance. The scale is highest for Saturday night, a four-

hour Saturday night job paying $149 in 1989. Any time beyond the four hours pays $38.25 per hour. Jobs on other nights pay $129 for four hours, $33.25 per hour for overtime. In comparison with Local 802 scales in other popular music areas, the club date scale is fairly high, at least on a per-job basis. Union scale for nightclub work, for example, is $550 for a five-night week or $110 per night. Broadway theater work pays $847 per week for eight performances, or about $106 per job. Recording work is by far the highest-paying musical work in New York, but it is also highly competitive and offers steady work to very few musicians. Radio and television jingles, which are the most frequent recording work in New York, pay $78 to $84.30 per hour, depending on the number of musicians involved. Scale for a three-hour recording date is $227.57, additional time being prorated in fifteen-minute intervals.

The union pay scale for club dates is fine as long as a musician doesn't have to depend on club dates alone. Even so, the value of the scale is deceptive considering what the work actually entails. Musicians may be on stage for only four fours, but they normally must arrive at the performance location a full hour before a job begins to set up equipment and receive any last-minute instructions from the bandleader. Depending on where the job is in relation to the musician's home and the amount of traffic encountered on the way to the job, just getting to the location may take as much as two hours, and returning home the same amount. A musician who is to play a four-hour Saturday job from 9 P.M. to 1 A.M. will actually spend seven to nine hours: dressing, packing the car, getting to the job, and returning home mean starting as early as 6 P.M. and finishing as late as 3 A.M. The Saturday night pay of $149 seen as an hourly rate thus would be more like $16.50 to $21 per hour, not $37. This is, of course, the only job of the week that will pay this well. For an afternoon or non-Saturday evening job, the real hourly rate would be more like $14 to $18.

These figures may still seem attractive, but remember that the musician is self-employed. The amount of time spent driving to and from individual jobs is far more than an average commuter spends getting to and from work, and gas, tolls, other car expenses, and meals are paid out of pocket. There are also expenses for musical instruments and formal clothing plus a certain amount of money and time for buying recordings and learning current material. There are no paid vacations, and there is little in the way of workmen's compensation or retirement benefits. All these costs, which would normally be covered by an employer, come out of the $14 to $21 per hour. That the actual value of the union scale is much less than it seems at first glance becomes very obvious the longer a musician stays in the club date business.

Union pay scale and benefits increases in the club date field remain relatively low because full-time club date musicians are such a small minority of the business as a whole. The vast majority of musicians in the field are "moonlighting," and they already have benefits provided by their full-time weekday jobs. Between 1978 and 1989 the scale increased from $85 to $149 for a Saturday night engagement—a 75 percent increase, but this was well below the 93.7 percent rate of inflation for the same period.[1] The full-timers would naturally like to see more substantial increases, but they realize that such increases may well result in a work decrease. Any increase in union pay scale and benefits widens the gap between the price of union versus non-union bands:

> Raising wages for club date musicians is not the same as raising wages for the symphony orchestra or theater musicians. There you have a set number of musicians hired for a set period of time. Here, raising wages is like pricing a product in a competitive market. Will it sell? Will the markup justify the net profit in the end?
>
> I as a sideman must decide. If I get a raise, will I get the same number of jobs, or will these jobs be siphoned off into other areas? Will orchestra leaders who pay under scale get the jobs I've had with legitimate leaders?
> —*sideperson, early 50s, piano*

The means for establishing club date pay scale changed significantly in the 1960s, and this change has also contributed to keeping scale increases to a minimum. Scale changes had traditionally been agreed on by club date union membership as a whole, which included leaders as well as sidepersons. In 1968, however, following nearly a decade of litigation initiated against the union by leaders, a federal court ruled that leaders and sidepersons were required to engage in collective bargaining to establish scale and benefit changes. This increased the power of leaders, since they could act as one voice in opposition to sidepersons rather than as a minority of individual voices within the total club date union membership. Since collective bargaining has been in effect, club date pay scale has consistently decreased in actual buying power, and both union membership and the amount of union work in the club date field have decreased. The collective bargaining arrangement may not be entirely responsible for these changes, but many sidepersons feel that it has been a major contributing factor.

To make a living through club date work alone a musician *must* be able to average at least three or four jobs each week. A fairly busy sideperson, working exclusively in the club date business, will average between 200 and 300 jobs per year, or four to six jobs per week. At union scale, gross income would be $26,800 to $39,700—before any expenses are considered. The actual amount of time involved, disregarding time for practice, negotiating with leaders or contractors, and bookkeeping, would be twenty-eight to thirty-six hours per week for 200 jobs per year and forty-two to fifty-four hours per week for 300 jobs per year. For a sideperson without a family, the lower gross income ($26,800) might be suitable as a sole source of income, considering the cost of living in metropolitan New York City. On the other hand, trying to support a family at this level is difficult, if not impossible. The minimum level *can* be achieved by working steadily with a set group or for a single leader exclusively, though that seems to be the exception rather than the rule. To get beyond this minimum income level, musicians must work the free-lance hiring structure to their best advantage, seeking to maximize both number of jobs per year and pay per job. To do so successfully requires a certain amount of social and business finesse.

The free-lance hiring structure of the New York club date business is similar in many ways to the hiring structure in the studio recording industry as described by Robert Faulkner in his book *Hollywood Studio Musicians*. The club date musician, like the studio musician—or any other free-lance worker or independent businessperson—"competes for jobs in a market where his ability, reputation, tact and social contacts determine the nature and volume of his work."[2] The stakes for which the musician is competing, in terms of both money and status, may be considerably lower in the club date business than in the studio recording industry, but the two hiring structures are equally intricate.

The beginning club date player soon learns of the informal hierarchy of offices and leaders, corresponding generally to the socioeconomic class of the clientele they serve. From the sideperson's standpoint, this hierarchy represents different levels in regard to pay scale, musical quality, and working conditions. At the lowest end are leaders or offices that pay below union scale, are the least demanding musically, and perform frequently at large catering facilities, the function factories. An inexperienced musician with a minimum of repertoire and technical facility *can* get work from such an office or leader. At the opposite extreme of the hierarchy are leaders and offices that pay at or even above union scale, tend to hire more experienced musicians, and work in fairly exclusive locations. To begin working for these offices or leaders normally requires previous experience in the business and the reputation that comes with it. Between the two extremes of the hierarchy there are leaders and offices that display various degrees of selectivity and willingness to pay union scale to all sidepersons.

The hierarchy can, but does not necessarily, represent a "job ladder" for the individual sideperson. A musician may find, for example, that contacts at one level offer considerable job security, both in number of jobs and in money received for each job, since there may be the opportunity to sublead or even to move into the leader's role at a later time. Working with a set group at any level can have many advantages also: substantial and regular income, more musical satisfaction, and less need to rely on constant free-lance bargaining to fill out the musician's schedule.

The upper levels of the hierarchy generally involve better pay, better musicians, and a better working environment, and as a general rule, musicians who continue to work on a free-lance basis exclusively will aspire to work at these upper levels. This upper-level work is always at or above union scale, and the musician may be able to bargain for either a guarantee of sorts or higher pay per job. There is no assurance that musical quality will be high, but the musicians working at these levels are experienced professionals, making it at least more likely that the musical product will be more sophisticated and interesting. The performance locations are generally more exclusive—hotels, country clubs, or private homes—there is more likelihood of overtime on individual jobs, and there is often the possibility of out-of-town "flying" dates, which add some variety to the work.

The point in the hierarchy at which a musician enters the business depends on size and scope of repertoire, personal connections, and often the instrument the musician plays. For someone whose repertoire is very limited and who has no connections in the business, it is almost impossible to begin anywhere except at the lowest level:

> In this business, if you're starting out, you're a total beggar. Unless you're really hot stuff, forget it. You can't get into this business. You can't. If you went to any office and you didn't have any club date experience, why would they hire you when there's a handful of people that do know the business and also want the work? Why would they hire you? Only if they can make money on you.
> —*sideperson, late 20s, trumpet*

A successful audition or meeting with a leader or contractor may lead to the musician being hired, but this initial hiring may be only on a "trial" basis—a sort of training period. The sideperson will often receive something less than full union scale, and the leader or contractor will keep things that way as long as the musician will put up with it. Inexperienced players at this stage are often not even fully contributing members of a band: they only pretend to play on songs they do not know while the rest of the band carries the tune. The player is known as a *phantom*.

Performing as a phantom can provide valuable on-the-job experience, but unfortunately, the practice is somewhat less than legal or ethical. The client is being deceived into thinking that the entire band is playing and is probably paying the full price for each band member. The difference between union scale and what the phantom receives goes to the leader as pure profit. It is impossible to determine exactly how prevalent this practice is, but all musicians affirmed that phantoms are a widespread phenomenon, a few having been phantoms themselves during their first months in the business.

Whether working as a phantom or as a regular band member, the musician is able to build repertoire and learn the ropes of the business at the lowest level of the hierarchy. Whereas the studio players studied by Faulkner found they had to "pay dues" in other areas of musical work while waiting to be called back, the club date player can get on-the-job training in the business itself. The "ceremonial period of putting in his time" described by Faulkner takes place within the club date business.[3] The training period may last a few months or more than a year, depending more on how long the musician will accept the below-scale wages than on when the leader decides that the novice player has been fully trained. The novice club date musician may "mark time" for quite a while before a significant volume of work and movement upward in the hierarchy become possible.

Some musicians do find it possible to enter the business at higher levels of the hierarchy and as regular band members. A certain amount of basic repertoire can be learned as an outsider, either by home practice using advice from experienced players or by performance in other contexts, jazz and rock bands, for example. It is still safest, though, to begin at a lower level, because as Bruce Bergman stresses in his book on club date guitar playing, "the danger is in getting in the best group *before* your ability merits it. If this happens, you'll be a long time convincing the top echelon offices that the playing they heard was your earlier efforts."[4]

At whatever level of the hierarchy musicians begin, they are sub-jected to a semiformal screening process that determines the amount and type of future work available to them. The bandleader in charge of these initial jobs files a report, either written or verbal, on a new-comer's performance.Whether positive or negative, the report's con-tents will travel quickly among club date musicians either over the phone or at the union exchange floor, which one leader described as "a little henhouse." If the first report is unfavorable, the novice player may be out of work for a few weeks or months, after which time the same process will begin again. The musician who has failed the initi-ation is at this point in a state of limbo.

Because of the importance placed on this first report, it is safest for the musician to begin at a low level of the hierarchy. If the report is unfavorable, leaders and contractors at the upper end of the hierar-chy will probably hear nothing of it. They are, as a general rule, un-interested in inexperienced players and have access to enough experienced players that they do not need to be told whom *not* to hire. As a contractor for a society office explained,

> We don't train them in our orchestra. They have to get their train-ing in the field. The people who train are the ones who have twenty, thirty jobs a night and have no choice since not that many musicians may be available for that night.
>
> The ones I do choose from "surface" after a while, if they stay around long enough and the talk is good. It's passed by word of mouth from one musician to another, you know. I'll hear that this guy or that guy plays good, and I'll write his name down. When you reach our organization, you've risen like cream to the top.
>
> —*sideperson and contractor, late 40s, drums*

Once this initial screening process is passed successfully, the musi-cian begins to build a reputation in the business. The favorable first report at least establishes the fact that he or she can do an adequate job, even though subsequent reports might point out some weak-nesses. Unlike the situation in the Hollywood studio scene, where any more than a few mistakes from even an experienced player cannot be tolerated, a certain amount of ineptitude is expected and tolerated from new club date musicians. There is certainly some pressure felt by the novice to play as faultlessly as possible, for not all bandleaders are equally tolerant of mistakes, but the pressure is not nearly as in-tense as it can be in the studio recording situation. Also, very few club date players at this point are considering a career in the field, and they are consequently not as likely to attach overwhelming significance to this informal screening, if they are aware of it at all. Even unfavorable reports after an initial favorable report will not necessarily exclude a musician from the business (as might be the case in studio work) but rather serve to point out the musician's strengths and weaknesses: reliability, size and range of repertoire, knowledge of any ethnic repertoire, ability to improvise solos, on and offstage demeanor.

As the musician's reputation grows, movement in the hierarchy may at first be mainly horizontal rather than vertical. This is to be expected, for leaders and offices working at one level in the business have most of their contacts at that level. It is also just as well for novices, because it gives them a chance to get a feel for how the business works without taking work that might be too demanding. Besides learning repertoire and getting accustomed to the various routines used by different leaders, the novice is establishing personal connections with numerous leaders and, most importantly, contractors.

Contractors hold a position of considerable power in the club date business, and this power can be used justly or not. The contractor's criteria for hiring one musician rather than another can be quite straightforward and fair; on the other hand, they can also be very arbitrary and partial. Unfortunately, the process of hiring individual musicians for single engagements does not lend itself to easy regulation, whether by the musicians union or by an outside agency. So many individual musicians are hired for so many different jobs, with each contract governed by different criteria, that no set of regulations could ever be comprehensive and just to all. The musician hoping to establish a solid reputation in the business is wise to keep open all possible avenues of work by maintaining good relations with all contractors. A single contractor who does the hiring for a large office represents a number of leaders and the subleaders working under them. Poor relations with that one contractor can exclude the possibility of working for any of those leaders or subleaders.

Musicians who were playing club dates in the 1940s and 1950s recalled that, before the advent of large club date offices, currying favor with single contractors or leaders was not such an important consideration as it has become today. If relations with a single leader or contractor were unfavorable, ten or twenty others could be approached instead. As more leaders entered into partnerships, a smaller and smaller number of contractors began to control a majority of the available club date work.

Because hiring practices are largely unregulated and concentrated in the hands of a small number of contractors, individual musicians— and particularly those who have not yet established a reputation in the business—have little power to protest against unfair treatment. Paychecks may be consistently a bit shy of the figure agreed on; mileage, cartage, or doubling fees may be "forgotten"; the job location may be much farther away than the sideperson was led to believe when accepting a job; or the job may be noncontinuous although the sideperson was told otherwise. Or the leader or contractor may expect "favors" from the sideperson—playing underscale or playing an undesirable job in return for a promise of future work. The musician who protests any of these practices may jeopardize relations with the leader or contractor. Two musicians I spoke with recalled instances where they did protest being paid less than agreed on and subsequently were not hired by the leaders in question for over two years.

Although nearly every sideperson I spoke with mentioned these unethical business practices, they also singled out certain leaders and contractors as being thoroughly straightforward and ethical in their dealings with employees. Not surprisingly, those singled out were among those most successful in the business. Sidepersons are the first to admit that contracting can be a thankless job—whatever the contractor decides to do, someone is bound to be dissatisfied. The contractor follows a kind of pecking order in selecting musicians for jobs, from the first players on down, but even this cannot be followed strictly if the office or leader needs to rely on musicians further down the line to work for them during busy periods. If there are ten jobs on a Saturday and two jobs on Tuesday, obviously not everyone can work an equal amount. The contractor tries to spread the work around, from the busier weekend nights to the slower weeknights, but there isn't always a simple way to do it.

As musicians move into the upper levels of the hierarchy, they may still find it necessary to deal with unethical or illegal contracting situations, although the situations will tend to occur less and less. Periods of slow business may mean that the musician must be less selective about accepting jobs, and there may be situations where, as one sideperson put it, "you can't always be as honest as you'd like to be."

As the sideperson's reputation spreads through word of mouth, he or she can begin to be more selective in accepting work. The selectivity has two goals: (1) to increase the number of jobs per week and per year and (2) to move up the hierarchy to play with better musicians and for better pay. This selectivity involves some financial risks, but the musician who is unprepared to take them will never gain any control over the amount and type of work. It is at this point, when bargaining is seen as a possibility, that the idea of club date work as a career often enters the picture.

Maximizing jobs per week requires some finesse, because the sideperson is dealing with a number of leaders and contractors, all of whom are offering work that falls mainly on weekends. Suppose, for example, that leader A offers you, a sideperson, a single Saturday night job at a country club for a weekend that you still have open. You accept the job. Later in the week, leader B calls and offers you both a Saturday night and a Sunday afternoon job. The Saturday night job—a wedding reception given by a wealthy Jewish client for his only daughter—promises to go into overtime, whereas the country club job offered by leader A is unlikely to go past the contracted four hours, since the club has a fixed music budget for the year.

The offer from leader B is obviously the better of the two for the musician's pocketbook, ensuring at least $278 and possibly more. Leader A's offer, on the other hand, promises only $149 for one evening, and the sideperson will have to look elsewhere to fill out the weekend. Nevertheless, leader B's offer will probably have to be refused, because reneging on leader A's offer would call into question the sideperson's reliability.

If the sideperson can be fairly well assured that more than a single call will come in for each weekend, it may make sense to reject most offers for single nights and bank on the possibility of multiple-job offers. To the leader offering just one job, the sideperson might respond, "Sure, if you can give me one other night as well." It may also begin to make sense to refuse poorly paying jobs—ones either below scale or with little chance for overtime—in hopes that better offers will come up for the same dates. In either case, the musician is risking not working at all on the given date by refusing the initial offer. Coming up with three, four, or more jobs per week requires both a lucky combination of offers and skillful bargaining.

Certain financial risks may also be necessary in beginning vertical movement in the hierarchy. A musician may decide to accept even single-job offers from the better offices or independent leaders to get a foot in the door, even if accepting the jobs means working a bit less overall. If a society office, for example, offers a single job for one week and the sideperson can normally expect to do three jobs for an office lower in the hierarchy in the same week, a choice must be made between present financial security and the opportunity for upward mobility.

I was lucky to be motivated enough in the club date field to keep moving on—not to get satisfied with working five club dates a week

with an office that was inferior—below my level musically, intellectually, emotionally.
—*sideperson, early 30s, drums*

If this initial bargaining is effective, both the number and quality of the musician's jobs increase. As more and more of the individual's income is derived from club date work, depending on it as a primary source of income becomes more of a real possibility. At the same time, such sidepersons begin to recognize that they are valuable to certain leaders and contractors and consequently may be able to use bargaining further both to build some security into the work and to increase their pay per job.

Security can be increased either through a guarantee of sorts or a first-player agreement. Such agreements have advantages for both the sideperson and the leader or contractor. If the contractor or leader can count on a musician's services on a continuous basis, that means three or four fewer positions per week that must be filled. The contracted sideperson has a fairly steady source of employment and is at least partially freed from juggling the offers of so many different contractors to fill a schedule. Sidepersons are divided, though, on whether such contract agreements are better than working entirely free-lance, or *floating*, as some call it. If a contract is exclusive, the musician may find it necessary to refuse more lucrative work from other offices and to play many undesirable jobs. The guarantee or first-player agreement with a single office or leader also may not be enough to fill the musician's schedule. Free-lancing entirely, on the other hand, allows the sideperson to be selective in accepting work and also to accept work outside of the club date business for either short- or long-term engagements—theater jobs, touring shows, night-club acts, or recording. Most of the sidepersons I spoke with who were doing club date work as a primary source of income remained at least partially in the free-lance market, even though they might also have semi-exclusive arrangements with a single office or leader.

After working as a first player for one leader for some time, it may be possible to reach an agreement with the leader that the pay per job will be union scale plus some set figure. This tactic can be used as well by floaters, since the contractor would not call in the first place unless a need was there; there is thus bargaining power in this situation. Again, there is a risk involved, because the leader can refuse, either calling the musician's bluff or simply finding someone else. A sideperson will not normally broach the subject at all unless it seems that the time is right—that the association has been both lengthy enough and valuable to the leader. The actual figure beyond union scale may be from a few dollars to as much as $100.

Another way of increasing income per job is to begin working as a subleader. Not every sideperson is interested in subleading, but if the extra money is attractive enough and the sideperson is willing and able to do it, bargaining for subleading jobs only may be advantageous. Again, this might mean an initial decrease in number of jobs per week, but in this case, the pay per job is considerably higher as well. Musicians who are successful as subleaders and who can convince leaders of their value as regular subleaders may soon be doing as many jobs per week as before, and each job will bring 50 percent more than a regular sideperson's pay. Beyond this, the subleading experience may persuade such sidepersons to begin booking their own jobs and eventually to become leaders on a full-time basis. Such a step requires, of course, that the musicians accept the additional business responsibilities of the leader's role.

However skillful sidepersons may be in working the hiring structure to their advantage, they soon realize that there is a practical limit to the number of jobs a single musician can do in a year. There are also two other factors that limit the sideperson's job opportunities yet are, for the most part, beyond the musician's control: first, the instrument one plays; and second, age.

A dozen or more different instruments are commonly used by club date bands: electric guitar, synthesizer, drums, electric bass, acoustic piano, saxophone (with clarinet and flute double), trumpet, trombone, timbales, conga drums, violin, and accordion. And it is possible to specialize in any one of them and still be able to rely solely on club dates as a source of income. I met accordion and trombone players, for example, who were full-time club date musicians. Nonetheless, the business as a whole can provide full-time employment to far fewer players of those two instruments than to drummers, guitar, or keyboard players. Of course, it is probably also true that there are far fewer trombone players than guitar players competing for club date work, but the guitar player still has a wider range of options. The more demand there is for one's chosen instrument, the more selective one can be in accepting work.

It is not at all surprising that there should be a hierarchy of instruments in the club date business, whereby players of certain instruments are more in demand and consequently have more bargaining power. There are conventions of instrumentation in every style of music, and some instruments come to be considered by both musicians and listeners as more essential than others to the style. The big difference in the club date context, however, is that the conventions as they stand today are almost completely different from what they were thirty or forty years ago. Club date musicians who have been in the business from the 1950s until today have seen one group of instruments—those associated with pre-rock American popular music—gradually replaced by another group—those associated with rock music. The present hierarchy of instruments is approximately as I have listed them in the preceding paragraph, from the instrument most in demand, electric guitar, to that least in demand, accordion.

Trumpet, saxophone, trombone, violin, and accordion players, whose instruments were solidly in the club date mainstream when they entered the business, saw the demand for their skills eroding as rock music entered the picture. Small bands, emphasizing electric guitar, electric bass, and electric keyboards, began to replace the larger groups with trumpet, sax, and trombone at their core. The musicians could adapt to the situation in a variety of ways: switching to the electrified relative of their instruments (electric piano or electric bass); learning a new instrument (although I heard of no one actually doing so); competing for the decreasing number of jobs that still called for their instrument; or simply relying less and less on performance as a source of income. There are, unfortunately, no figures that I know of that show the exact nature and extent of this change—when the change began and how long it took to accomplish, or just how many musicians left the business as a result. What is very clear from speaking with older club date musicians is that the change did indeed drive many musicians out of club dates and often out of the music business entirely. Many of them were understandably bitter about the situation, having invested years of their lives establishing themselves in the business, only to find that someone seemed to be pulling the rug out from under them.

The recognition that age, too, can limit a musician's volume of work may be equally distressing. And again, the limitation usually becomes evident only after the musician has seemingly established a relatively stable career.

> The most dispiriting thing is that, as you get older, you realize that you cannot age gracefully in the club date business. I grew a mustache when I was younger to look older; now I've cut it off to look younger. There *is* a youth element. I don't know if it is a public demand, but the leaders perceive it as a public demand. Age is a definite factor.
>
> —*sideperson, early 50s, piano*

Guitarists begin to notice this emphasis on youth early in their careers, because their instrument is so closely associated with rock music. A guitarist in his mid-thirties said that he consciously avoided telling his age to leaders. If he was compelled to admit his age, a common reaction from the leader was something like "If you're that old, why are you still playing rock guitar? Can you still play the current tunes?" The fact that he might "look" too old to be playing rock guitar is never said directly, but the implication is clear. A fifty-year-old guitarist (1989) said that, yes, he was beginning to feel the restrictions of the leaders' youth emphasis but added that "I have my hair, hardly any gray, and I seriously think that makes a difference."

Many musicians pointed out this youth element during interviews even before the issue had been raised through questioning. A drummer, just over forty in 1978, who later expressed how fortunate he was to look much younger than his actual age, related the following incident involving a less fortunate musician not much older than himself:

Another thing I must tell you . . . I'm not sure if you're aware of this. Recently in club dates there's come a thing of image. They want a certain image on the bandstand—a youth thing. It can be really scary.

An excellent player who's not too old I recently introduced to a man [who needed a keyboard player]. I asked him a couple of weeks later if he ever called him, and he said, "No, he's not the image. He's too old-looking."

I've seen guys who are good players who aren't working as much because of that certain image. That's the way of the world. Let's face it: the youth thing is in.

Our society's fixation on looking, acting, and feeling young is certainly news to no one, and it is hardly surprising to find practical manifestations of this youth emphasis in the club date business. The increasing dominance of rock music in the club date repertoire is one main reason for this: the music has from its inception been associated with youth. In addition, club dates are a form of show business, and people will be "shown" things that they value. As a guitarist in his early 30s put it, "Audiences like to *look* at a band . . . and they want to take from it what they see . . . they want it to reflect. People want to look at something and get a feeling of youth and vigor. That's what entertainment is all about."

Many musicians forestall the inevitable decrease in employment by dyeing their hair. Others employ their musical skills elsewhere—in

Broadway shows or recording or teaching. Other seek work in fields unrelated to music. Those who choose to remain in club dates come to accept the importance of the youth element and recognize the restrictions it imposes on the future of their careers:

> Naturally, younger people have a slight edge. A young man who can do the same job I do will probably have an edge. This has to be expected. I expect a gradual turn-down of income and work. But I'm not going to fight it because it's inevitable. We *are* a form of show business. We *are* visual, and this is a cross we have to bear.
> —*sideperson, late 40s, trumpet*

The actual amount of money a sideperson can make in a year is hardly outstanding, even if scale-plus arrangements and subleading are added in. Working as a sideperson only and pushing the limit as far as jobs per week and dollars per job are concerned, maximum *gross* income in 1989 would probably be not much more than $50,000 per year. If the musician can work as a subleader exclusively, this figure might reach $70,000. It's a lot of work for the money, but as one guitarist pointed out:

> Nobody ever became a musician to make money at it. We all did it because we loved it. You start to play, and all of a sudden you've got some gigs, you're getting paid, and you're a musician . . . you're in the music business. And you just wanted to play.
> —*sideperson, early 50s, guitar and vocals*

Notes

1. *The Consumer Price Index,* January 1990 Report.
2. Faulkner, *Hollywood Studio Musicians* 44.
3. Faulkner, *Hollywood Studio Musicians* 98.
4. Bergman, *Rock Guitar* 73.

7

On Being a
Club Date Musician

Musicians' personal responses to playing club dates as their primary occupation range from very negative to very positive. The main factor that seems to determine which of these extremes an individual's overall evaluation of the work tends toward is whether the musician works as a leader or as a sideperson. A second significant determinant is the extent to which club date work conflicts with an individual musician's career goals.

The Leaders' Perspective

When I come on the job, I want to relax, enjoy myself. I wouldn't care if we did eight hours, ten hours. If it ever becomes a job to me, I'm out of the business. Why do it if you don't enjoy it?
—leader, late 50s, trumpet and vocals (1989)

Including both leaders and sidepersons in the general category "club date musicians" is misleading, if not inaccurate. Performing music—being a club date musician—is only one part of the leader's role: a leader is just as importantly an entertainer and a booking agent/employer. Consequently, a leader's perspective on working in the club date business is very different from that of sidepersons. Sidepersons and leaders do have some common concerns within the club date world, but their views of success and job satisfaction differ radically.

Leaders naturally have a much more positive outlook on their work than do sidepersons. They are, after all, able to control the nature of their work to a large extent. Becoming a leader was, for all but two of the leaders with whom I spoke, a career goal in their early years in the music business. The responsibilities of a leader are greater than those of a sideperson, but the challenges and the rewards, both emotional and financial, are greater as well.

Leading is *much* more interesting. You deal with the people; you
deal with the employer; you hire the men; you call the tunes.
—*leader, early 50s, accordion*

Every job is a challenge. It's tremendously satisfying when you're
successful at a party.
—*leader, late 40s, saxophone and vocals*

The leaders are well aware that sidepersons will frequently criticize
them for their poor taste in music, but as long as such criticism does
not get in the way of a smooth performance, it is more of a minor
annoyance than a real problem. Again, the leader is in control, and
the musician who does question the authority of the leader on the
bandstand is unlikely to work for that leader much longer:

The band doesn't play what they want. They play *my* phrasing, *my*
selections. If they don't want to, they don't work for me.
—*leader, early 60s*

If a guy is good and he comes on the job with the attitude, "Oh,
what are we going to play that song for?" I don't want him. He ru-
ins your attitude for the party.
—*leader, late 40s, trumpet and vocals*

Interview a sideman, especially a busy guy. You'll find out that they
all think the leaders are shitheads. We're corny or idiots or what-
not. The sidemen make a consensus among themselves of a repertoire that has nothing to do with the public. I could probably name
two dozen songs that these guys all think are fantastic. On the
other hand, if you take a random group of people who are supposed to buy this stuff, they don't know any of these tunes [names
"Watch What Happens," "What Are You Doing the Rest of Your
Life," "Here Comes That Rainy Day"]. . . . A miscellaneous bunch
of garbage that all musicians want to play. They all have a certain
cocktail lounge kind of feeling, for an audience that doesn't exist.
—*leader, early 50s, piano and vocals*

Whether this leader is correct in ascribing such esoteric and un-
marketable taste to sidepersons is really a moot point, because the
leaders make all the song choices. As to the aptness of those choices,
the leaders can point to their successes as evidence that the public
usually agrees with them.

All in all, leaders find very little bad to say about their threefold role of musician, conductor, and entertainer in the performance context. Outside of the performance context, they have the additional satisfaction of being either sole proprietors or partners in an independent business, which allows them to exercise nearly complete autonomy over their work life. They became leaders because they found the position to be challenging and rewarding, and they continue to find their work satisfying.

There are, however, two aspects of the work that many leaders do consider to be problematical; to a lesser degree, these problems face sidepersons as well. First, there is the question of actual financial rewards received in relation to type of work performed and amount of time and effort expended. The complaint is that the same amount of time, effort, and abilities needed to succeed in the club date business, if applied in another specialized field such as law, medicine, or corporate business, would yield much higher income. Of course, club date musicians are not alone in feeling that their income is not commensurate with their abilities and their application, but the perceived injustice of the situation can affect both work performance and the satisfaction received from it. Seeing one's age-peers working in other fields that offer high income, job security, benefits packages, and regular hours is a constant reminder of the limitations of club dates as a form of employment. A musician establishes a reputation over a period of years yet must constantly live up to the expectations of audiences, leaders, or both to maintain that reputation. There is no career ladder. As one leader put it,

> Unless you give every fiber of your body into the music business, don't get into it. It's not like being a carpenter or an electrician or so many things in life that one can be and be very successful. You're putting yourself under the gun—your whole life.
>
> I've been in the business since I was thirteen, and I'm still auditioning. You're only as good as your last job, only as good as your last note. You can't be an accountant in this business because you're not going to make any money. The most successful guys in this business are not doing near the average doctor's salary. For the money I make and the position I'm in, it's nothing.
>
> —*leader, late 40s, trumpet and vocals*

Another significant problem, which leaders again share with sidepersons, is that they are forced to lead a constricted social life, working while everyone else is relaxing from work. Club dates effectively exclude them from the social life enjoyed by their friends and relatives outside the music business. The situation is more problematic for most leaders, because even their weekdays may be taken up with office work.

> What I don't prefer about our business is that my weekends are not my weekends. I'm constantly out making other people happy on the weekend. I would have liked to have had more weekends off in my lifetime, unquestionably.
> —*leader, late 50s, trumpet and vocals*

> You have to have quite an understanding wife, and luckily I do. Our social life is limited to weeknights, and most of our friends happen to be others who work weekend jobs.
> —*leader, early 40s, trumpet and vocals*

Some of the musicians felt certain that the constricted social life necessitated by the business was a prime factor in the many divorces among their colleagues. The initial glamour of being married to a musician wears thin once the realities of making a living in music become clear.

In his 1941 article "The Professional Dance Musician," Carlo Lastrucci points out this social segregation as an important factor in shaping the dance musician's way of life, as does Howard Becker in his later work with dance musicians.[1] In both cases, however, the enforced segregation is seen in positive terms, because the musicians generally preferred not to socialize with nonmusicians anyway. Lastrucci's musicians "feel a deep scorn for most laymen,"[2] and Becker suggests that "much self-segregation develops out of the hostility toward squares."[3] Club date musicians, on the other hand, express very little, if any, scorn or hostility toward nonmusicians. Consequently, the restrictions on their social life, which are common to workers in all the performing arts, are seen as a definite disadvantage to their work. Nearly every leader and sideperson cited this problem when asked about club date work as a lifestyle; indeed, many offered their thoughts on the subject before it came up as a direct question.

The Club Date Stigma

> *There were times when I wasn't as diversified and I didn't like it because of the stigma attached to being a club date musician. I don't want to play with the people who consider themselves club date musicians. I consider them hacks. It's not enough to make a decent salary*

and play in those catering halls. It doesn't have to do with art or creativity or what really sustains me and makes me better as a human being. And that part of you is fighting when you're doing club dates with those people.

—sideperson, early 30s, drums

I seldom admit to the fact that I'm a club date musician. I think it's a way of earning a living, and there's very few musicians who haven't done them at one time or another.

—sideperson, early 40s, drums and vocals

Working as a sideperson in the club date business has traditionally been considered low status employment by musicians. Indeed, an *Allegro* article mentioned the "worn-out and out-of-date cliche [that] club date players are lousy players and incapable of doing any other kind of job in the music profession."[4] In the years when steady musical employment was more readily available in New York—hotel bands, ballroom bands, radio and later television staff orchestras— the club date business constituted a catchall for those musicians who couldn't compete successfully for location jobs. A stigma came to be attached to club date musicians, marking them as players who were just not good enough to find any other kind of work. The stigma remains today in the minds of many musicians.

One sideperson recalled that he was careful not to mention his previous involvement in the club date field when he began working in a pit orchestra for a Broadway show. Regardless of how musically proficient he was, he felt it necessary to disavow his connection with club dates to maintain a reputation among his fellow musicians in the orchestra. A singer in her early thirties was careful not to mention club dates when she worked in recording studios: "I don't want to be known as a club date singer . . . it limits you if other musicians get that impression." Frederickson and Rodney frequently encountered this same coping strategy among free-lance theater musicians in Washington, D.C.: by treating their work in pit orchestras as merely a "peripheral part of the self," players felt they could more easily maintain esteem among their non-free-lance musical colleagues.[5] To identify too closely with a group perceived as having low status is to run the risk of being trapped at that level.

The musicians who react most strongly against this stigma, which they feel no longer reflects the reality of club date work, are generally older musicians who spent their earlier years as members of radio and television staff orchestras or nationally known big bands. At present, they work at the upper levels of the club date hierarchy, particularly in the society area, and there is general agreement among club date musicians, both young and old, that their presence has served to increase the quality of club date music, however minimally. They not only have large repertoires but also can fake harmony well, improvise excellent jazz solos, and read nearly any music put before them (when backing a featured performer at a society ball, for instance.)

These well-seasoned professionals, however, constitute only a small minority of club date musicians. For the majority of musicians in the business, club dates remain a casual form of employment to augment their income from full-time work during the week. This diverse group of moonlighters, rather than the "inner circle" of musicians who work at the upper levels of the business, is most responsible for whatever image other musicians and the general public have of the "average" club date musician.

Club date musicians also meet with the common stereotype applied to all musicians in popular or jazz performance, however untrue or outmoded the stereotype may be:

> The attitude toward musicians as long as I can remember has been one which encompassed a room, a girl, a bottle of booze, and an iron cot. And the public has been led to believe that things aren't any different today.
> —*sideperson, late 50s, saxophone*

Evidence that this stereotype is still current comes not so much from party guests as from the other nonmusicians with whom club date musicians come in contact in their work—in particular, caterers and hotel banquet personnel. Even if it is not expressed in word or deed, the musician is often regarded as a member of the servant class. One musician, who had played for television staff orchestras, recordings, Broadway shows, and all the major society leaders and was, in 1978, a union official, described the rather discouraging situation:

> Almost everybody else—naturally there must be exceptions—has more security or gets more consideration or has in general more respect from the public than the musician. I'm not talking about the artist-musician who is a concert performer whose name becomes a household word or even a jazz star. I'm talking about the average employee musician, the professional musician who spends half his life developing his skills, and then he has to use the freight elevator in the hotels. The waiters and the maitre d's and everybody else tells him what to do.

With rare exceptions, I would say that musicians do not have a status commensurate with what they provide to society. Music seems to be the most expendable commodity.

—*sideperson, late 50s, trumpet*

A vocalist said that her club date colleagues would often joke about going to heaven and being asked by God to go through the kitchen.

The instances where the stereotype *is* expressed are understandably very disturbing to club date musicians. One musician described a striking example of this:

I played a date just last year at this time and was standing in front of the bandstand. There was a glass of cigarette butts behind me. Well, the caterer—a lady—came over to me, held the glass and said, "See? You see? See? You musicians are all alike." And she started to scream at me, "Why did you do this to me?"

I said, "Lady, I don't even smoke. Talk to your husband like that; don't talk to me like that." I mean, the club date does not change. They treat musicians like dirt. In the catering hall, you're a musician, so you're a lowlife. It doesn't matter how good or how professional you are.

—*sideperson, early 30s, saxophone*

Responding verbally in such a situation can, of course, jeopardize the sideperson's reputation both with the caterer and with the office or leader in charge of the job. Musicians who do fight back against this lack of respect are few in number, but they are respected for their efforts to change the situation:

A friend of mine refused to play at a certain country club because they made musicians use only the back door. My hat goes off to him, and I wish there were more of us like him.

—*sideperson, late 20s, piano*

Of course, whatever stigma or stereotype the lay public or other musicians apply to club date musicians does not elicit the same response from every club date player. For some, such inaccurate generalizations are of no concern whatever; they are not even worthy of a response. At the opposite extreme are sidepersons to whom such prejudgments are a major source of bitterness and anger. Nonetheless, all club date sidepersons recognize that the stigmas and stereotypes continue to exist and that club date work remains at the bottom of the musical totem pole as far as status is concerned.

Context and Musical Quality

Even if club date musicians eventually were to gain more respect from other musicians and the general public, it is unlikely that the work would become any more desirable from a musical standpoint. The music is often nothing more than background, and only occasionally is it the main focus of attention. What music is played and how it is played is dictated by the bandleader, who is in turn interpreting the tastes of the guests at a party. The guests are interested in music that is both danceable and recognizable, and because they are not only listening but also talking, eating, drinking, and dancing, they cannot be expected to listen for subtleties in the music. Indeed, the high ambient noise level at most parties precludes almost any subtlety.

> You have a room full of noise, and it doesn't matter really what the quality of the music is. If the music is mediocre, nobody knows it. Nobody knows what you're playing half the time.
> If you devote yourself to club dates and try to do what people expect of you, you deteriorate. You play too loud. Especially on piano it's damaging—it cramps your technique. . . . One of the subleaders [I used to work for] used to look over inside the piano to make sure the hammers were going up since he couldn't hear it from where he was standing. To make sure he was getting his money's worth.
> —*sideperson, early 50s, piano*

> I go shopping for earplugs now—most drummers do. We go shopping to find the best earplugs, and that's ridiculous! I don't mind playing loud when you're doing disco, fine. But when you come off the disco and go into a cha-cha, I see no reason to stay at triple *forte*. We call them earplug jobs—there's no variation, no coloring.
> —*sideperson, early 40s, drums*

The necessity of playing music continuously for four hours or more is another factor that makes club date work less than desirable to many musicians. Even if the bandleader is very concerned with musical quality and the musicians in the band are all very proficient players, it is difficult to maintain a high quality of music for such a long time without stopping. It is both mentally and physically demanding for musicians.

> It's a lot of work, between the packing and the driving and the playing. It's a very physical gig, especially for drummers or chord players who have to carry organs that weigh like a ton. And carry speakers. You play the smorgasbord in the basement and have to go two flights up for the party. Then, it's "Bang, bang, bang—keep that party going." You become a machine.
> —*sideperson, early 40s, drums*

In this respect, many musicians referred to club date music as "music by the pound," that is, ground out like hamburger.

When asked whether they received any musical enjoyment from their work, many club date sidepersons said that it was hardly a consideration. The main consideration for them seemed to be that the music not be too bad. If the music actually sounded good, it was a pleasant but infrequent surprise. Two types of sidepersons, though, tended to have more positive feelings about the music. The first type was horn players who had frequent opportunity to perform with large faking bands. They noted the challenging aspect of having to switch musical styles on the spot within a large group and to play harmony parts for any song called by the bandleader. The second type was those sidepersons who were members of set groups. If the set group is able to play together often over a long period of time, there is more opportunity to refine the music and to develop a group sound. This is, of course, assuming that the members of the set group are genuinely interested in increasing the quality of the music. Playing in a set group can also be a very repetitious or boring experience if there is little initiative for change from within the group.

Yet even a set group that the members consider to be of high musical quality cannot guarantee positive audience response. The best band led by the most experienced bandleader can still flop at a party if the chemistry is not right.

> People come to a party to have a good time. If they don't have a good time, regardless of how good the music may have been, the party was a flop to them and the band was no good.
> —*subleader, late 30s, guitar and vocals*

One musician recalled his experience as a member of a set group and his consequent inability to understand public taste:

> We really sounded good, even recorded some demos. But we got a range of reactions from people from "Best music I've ever heard" to "How can you play that junky noise?" I don't know how you define the taste of the public. I've been with bands that I felt like crawling into a hole and dying from embarrassment, and people will come up and say that it's the best thing they ever heard.
> —*sideperson, early 30s, saxophone*

The phrase "Best band I've ever heard" has become a standard in-joke among club date musicians, who use it as an ironic response to questions about how the music was at a recent job. The reply makes it clear that it was pretty bad, although the audience liked it—as usual.

Musicians who have the opportunity to play with bands at the upper end of the club date hierarchy, where the clientele is wealthier, the bands bigger, and the musicians generally more proficient, do feel it to be at least more likely that their work will be enjoyable from a musical standpoint. Yet even there, any musical enjoyment is limited by the party context. The wealthier clientele may be somewhat more discriminating musically than those with less money, but they too are interested mainly in having a good time, not in just listening to good music. The most striking example of this, which a number of sidepersons pointed out, is seen at society balls where the proceeds go toward supporting symphony orchestras in New York or elsewhere:

> For instance, symphony balls, which go on all over the country. Some of the things that will go on in the band you're almost ashamed of. And yet these people who are supposedly supporting the symphony orchestra, you would think they knew music. They are enthralled with what's going on. "This is beautiful" and "that's so beautiful," when it really was not.
>
> The leader will walk in late, and in five minutes he'll destroy the band as far as the music goes. The people will come up and say things like, "It wasn't a party until you were here" or "Now the music is wonderful."
> —*sideperson, early 60s, saxophone*

Again, the party's atmosphere and the bandleader's personality are more important than the purely aesthetic quality of the music. The guests judge the music in a way very different from how they judge a concert performance or, further removed, a recording.

At the same time, few club date musicians have a totally pessimistic view of their work. They realize the limited musical enjoyment inherent in the work, yet they rarely express the extreme hostility toward audiences and the performance context that, for instance, Howard Becker found among the dance musicians whom he studied in the late 1940s.[6] They accept the musical limitations of the work as a compromise necessary to make a living as a musician. Also, very few of the musicians work exclusively in the club date business. Although club dates may account for 90 percent or more of their income, they still work occasionally in other musical areas—Broadway shows, record dates, jazz performances, concerts, arranging, composing, or touring shows—and that allows them to see their club date work in perspective. Club dates come to represent their "steady" work to which they can always return, almost like a "day gig," as one musician said.

There are also certain positive aspects to the performance context that many musicians noted. First of all, because most of the parties involve a celebration of some kind and because many of the guests know one another beforehand, the context tends to have a friendly, festive mood even before the band arrives. Musicians contrasted this especially to the scene at nightclubs, which many described as very negative, often depressing places to perform at night after night. Those who did recording work noted difference between the relaxed atmosphere of club dates and the high-pressure, no-mistakes-allowed situation in the studio. At a club date, party guests may well have a good time in spite of the band. (There is, of course, a downside to the party atmosphere, which many musicians also pointed out: what one musician considers "festive and friendly" may be raucous, loud, and unsettling to another.)

Second, even if the party and the music are not very pleasant, the musician has the consolation of knowing that the affair usually lasts only four hours. The next job will be another situation entirely—a different location, a different audience, often an entirely different group of musicians. The musicians Becker studied in the 1940s were working mainly in bars, where it was likely that both the group and the location would remain set for more than a single night, often for a period of weeks or months.

This is not to say that club date work is endlessly varied; it can be very repetitive and tedious. New songs may be added to the repertoire frequently, but even those are played again and again as long as the leaders feel the material is popular. And older songs that become part of the general repertoire are played thousands of times by active club date players. The musicians who react most strongly to the repetitive nature of the repertoire are those who work often in the society field, where standards far outnumber contemporary songs. As a piano player in his late 30s put it rather bluntly, "It's the same old shit. I mean, how many times can you play that stuff and really make it sound like you're enjoying it? So the guys just chop away and let the guy out front worry about smiling and all that."

Still, such statements do not necessarily mean that the speaker would rather be doing some other kind of work. Many of the musicians who expressed negative feelings about playing the same songs so many times were also quick to point out that the club date field is hardly peculiar in that respect. One trumpet player groaned as he recalled a seven-year period when he played the same Broadway show eight times weekly; he remembered hating to go to work at all, even though the pay was good, the work was steady, and the musicians were very proficient. A sax player in his thirties welcomed the variety of club date repertoire as a break from the incessant repetition of jazz standards from the 1930s and 1940s that he found himself obliged to perform in order to continue working in the jazz field. Many others recalled the boredom they experienced in playing five or six nights each week at nightclubs, with the audience constantly asking for the same songs. Even symphony musicians experience tedium in their performance, as Robert Faulkner discovered in talking with former orchestral players working in the Hollywood studio scene. Statements he heard from former symphony players are not so different from those I heard from many club date players: "It would be all right if you could play different music all the time in a symphony. But what can a guy think when he's going out to do the Brahms C Minor for the 31st time?"[7] Or again, "An orchestra's quite a grind. There's really not a chance to play . . . you're just a small cog in a big piece of machinery."[8] Club dates are hardly unique to the world of music in their reliance on a similar repertoire from one performance to the next. Specializing in any area of music requires almost by definition considerable repetition of material. As in any field, greater specialization means a more limited scope.

Experienced players in the field do not seem to mind that most of the music in the club date repertoire is of the American popular variety. Indeed, many enjoy the genres of music played on a typical club date. The introduction of rock and roll to the repertoire, for instance, was welcomed by many older musicians, even though there was some initial adverse reaction to it:

We would even scratch out some backgrounds, some pieces of music that we would use. We had some intricate backgrounds, arrangements, lines we would play for intros, endings, or riffs in the middle. There was quite a bit of musical leeway. And that music [rock] was much more satisfying, more exciting than the society tunes we were playing, more satisfying than playing a lot of [pre-rock] pop tunes . . . no question about it.

—*sideperson, late 50s, trumpet*

I liked rock because I saw some of the vitality in it. There is obviously a vitality in it. It isn't any worse than the old pop scene. People forget there was so much garbage in the old days too. There's always a resentment of new developments.

—*sideperson, early 50s, piano*

There are also younger musicians who enjoy much of the club date repertoire, and they are not at all apologetic about it:

I've always liked the American song form—Porter, Kern, Gershwin—and club dates are really the only place where you get much chance to work with that form.

—*sideperson, late 20s, trombone*

To tell you the truth, I really like pop music. I like classical music too, but I can honestly say that with few exceptions I really like most of the stuff that's being recorded today—disco stuff, non-disco, ballads, and up-tempo rock. I like the music, and I don't mind playing it at all. And I'm lucky, because if I didn't like the music, I probably wouldn't want to be playing it.

—*sideperson, late 20s, guitar and vocals*

Sure, you're going to have to play "Feelings" and "New York, New York," but, really, there's not that much bad music out there . . . it's your attitude about it.

—*former sideperson, presently a leader, early 30s, vocals (1989)*

The pay is good compared to clubs, plus it gives you an opportunity to sing a variety of styles you wouldn't normally come across in other music areas.

—*sideperson, early 30s, vocals (1989)*

I do get a kick out of playing a polka once in a while. I do get a kick out of playing Jewish music. There's something about ethnic music—a ritual quality—that old standard music doesn't have. It just sets people on fire. It has a ritual quality that was absent in popular music until rock and roll came about.

—*sideperson, early 40s, drums*

Although some sidepersons spoke of "tuning out" the audience, at least an equal number found that neither necessary nor desirable. In particular, younger musicians or those who only recently began doing club dates on a regular basis—perhaps representing those who have not yet become "hardened" to the business—expressed the importance of audience reaction for their own enjoyment of their work. As undiscriminating musically as the audience may be, these musicians are still interested in seeing them have a good time:

I enjoy seeing them grooving, you know. I don't care who it is. If you get them swinging, they're going to swing. They're going to have fun . . . I'm always interested in audience reaction.

—*sideperson, early 40s, drums*

The most important element is probably the people you're working for, how uptight or un-uptight they are. You can play in the best of surroundings at a millionaire's mansion, and it can be no fun at all.

—*sideperson, early 30s, drums*

I definitely try to make the music happen to the audience. I really love it when the people come up—especially the young people— when you're getting across to them. And they just won't feel "Oh, it's just another band at my cousin's wedding."

—*sideperson, late 20s, piano*

For most of the sidepersons with whom I spoke, the musical standards of the audience were not a critical issue, as perplexing as they might be. More than a few felt that the audience members were, in a sense, innocent victims of the poor musical judgment of leaders— both in their selection of songs and their hiring of musicians. The issue of song selection in particular came up frequently in talking with sidepersons who worked regularly for society bandleaders. Although recognizing that society parties do generally require bands to rely heavily on older standard material, especially Broadway show tunes, these sidepersons still feel that the leaders are overly conservative in selecting songs. The leaders tend to choose material that has worked for them in the past rather than trying newer, untested songs that might work just as well:

> It's the attitude: you've got to sing this; you can't do a club date without that. . . . I don't think anything *has* to be done. People are having a party, they're dressed up, they feel good, and they're drinking, and it's very hard to have a bad time. Duchin doesn't *have* to play "Anything Goes." We don't *have* to play every standard in the book. Everyone has their tried and true routines, and they're convinced that that's what one *must* do. I don't think there's any one way to win over anybody.
> —*leader (formerly a sideperson), early 30s, vocals (1989)*

> When I work with my own group, people think we're tremendous. I look at it musically. I can size up an audience, the kinds of tempos they'd like, the kinds of music they'll like, their age groups. But I've been through this. The average [society] leader has not. The average leader has not been a sideman. He's like a general who went to West Point and was never a soldier.
> —*sideperson and subleader, late 40s, trumpet*

> As a subleader, I can call my own musical shots, establish my own musical levels. I don't have to stick to the tried-true, hackneyed repertoire that most leaders call for. And I've been quite successful at it.
> —*sideperson and subleader, late 40s, piano*

How well the selections are played is partly the leader's responsibility and partly the responsibility of the band members themselves. If the leader hires musicians who are not very proficient technically, play out of tune, have limited repertoire, or cannot fake harmony well, the sideperson who *is* concerned with the quality of the music has a right to put the blame for the poor quality on the leader:

> I'm paid by the hour or the job, not according to the difficulty of what I'm doing. If I'm leading a sax section where it's only 50 percent functioning because of poor musicianship, I don't get paid any more for the extra headaches. So I make sure I know who the leader is hiring before I accept the job.
> —*sideperson, late 50s, saxophone*

Unfortunately, a lot of leaders feel that the number one requisite is repertoire. So, if a guy has a terrible sound or plays out of tune, it doesn't matter. Most of the time the leader doesn't know it because he isn't a musician himself and doesn't know that the sound is terrible.

—*sideperson, late 40s, trumpet*

It upsets me that the audience doesn't react more negatively when the band is bad. When I'm in a band or see a band that's bad, I really wish that the band would suffer—especially the leader.

—*sideperson, late 20s, piano*

Sidepersons also acknowledge that the poor musicianship in a band is not always the leader's fault. The musicians hired by the leader may be quite proficient on their instruments and possess a large and varied repertoire, but they can very easily spoil a job from a musical standpoint because of a negative attitude. They may simply be in a bad mood or dislike the leader and as a result be unconcerned with the quality of their playing. Neither the leader nor the party guests may notice the difference, but the other musicians in the band still have to suffer their compatriots' sloppy playing for the entire job.

Many sidemen have simply lost the desire to play. They don't care whether they play well or whether the band sounds good, as long as they get their paycheck. It's very difficult to get any musical enjoyment from your playing when you've got guys like that in the band.

—*sideperson, early 50s, trumpet*

If you're in a miserable situation where the guys are saying, "I hate this. It's awful"—if you work with people with attitudes like that, who play like that—then the music is going to stink.

—*leader (formerly a sideperson), early 30s, vocals (1989)*

I like to see the musicians in a band have commitment to their playing. Many get lax in their playing, since they don't get much negative reaction from the audience. Maybe they take it for granted that they can do that as professionals, but even professionals shouldn't do that.

—*sideperson, late 20s, piano*

On Being a Musician

One musician mentioned rather casually at the beginning of an interview that "you don't usually get to play good music on a club date." I later asked him what he considered to be "good" music in the club date context, and I'm sure that most club date musicians would agree with his response:

> When a band is swinging—the rhythm section is really cooking, and the guys are playing in tune. They're phrasing together . . . there are some solos that come off well—that's good.
>
> —*sideperson, late 40s, trumpet*

The music doesn't have to be jazz or any other specific genre; the important thing is that it is done well. I heard many variations on the statement that "a good club date is far more enjoyable than a poor jazz gig." One guitarist felt that his attitude toward the music had evolved over his years in the business:

> There are dates that I enjoy being on both musically and personally. If you had asked me this about fifteen years ago, I would have said, "Anything that is more jazz oriented, I would tend to gravitate toward." My answer now would be, "Anything or situation where the music is done well, at a high level of quality." It could be the dumbest little jingle or a very hokey Christmas song, but if it's done properly, everybody's doing their job and is pleasant about it as well, then it's an enjoyable date. I guess that comes from doing so many club dates over the years. There's a certain amount of acceptance or non-aesthetic that you develop.
>
> —*sideperson, late 30s, guitar (1989)*

Unfortunately, all club date players do a certain amount of work that is not at all musically satisfying. Whatever satisfaction they derive from their work in those situations becomes largely a personal matter. There is some satisfaction, for instance, in knowing that they have played a particular piece or job well—the "sense of pride in craft rather than art" that Frederickson and Rodney found among freelance theater musicians.[9] Recognition comes, if at all, from fellow band members, not from the audience.

> As long as I'm playing my best, whatever else goes on musically doesn't bother me. I'm satisfied.
>
> —*sideperson, early 40s, drums*

There is a certain satisfaction knowing that you've served your function and served it well.

 —sideperson, late 40s, piano

It's a great feeling to play something very well and to have the people around you—the musicians—appreciate it.

 —sideperson, early 40s, piano

I try to keep my instruments up, even though I don't really need all the skills I have for club dates. If I play as well as I can every time I go out, I'm more satisfied with myself, plus it means that I can still do jazz jobs, record dates, concerts, since I've got the chops.

 —sideperson, early 50s, saxophone

Most musicians who rely on club dates for their primary income eventually come to see their work primarily in practical and economic terms, and only secondarily in musical ones. Job satisfaction comes both from earning a living doing what one enjoys and from performing a service, fulfilling a function well. Artistic considerations may not be unimportant, but they are clearly secondary.

I like the jobs where I stand the chance of making the best paycheck. . . . In general, in the club date business—again, using the word *business*—you usually go on a job and say, "Okay, let's play it, and let's go home." Pick up your money. It's not that stimulating.

 —sideperson, late 50s, saxophone

To me, being a musician is like doing any other kind of a job. There are some differences—certain aesthetic satisfaction you get sometimes—but basically it's something in return for which you're paid *x* amount of dollars. A lot of musicians are fantasizing all the time . . . they're on ego-trips; they all think they're artists. They're not. It's a business. It's primarily a business.

 —sideperson, early 50s, saxophone

This businesslike attitude toward performance may perhaps disillusion those who have romantic visions of what it means to be a professional musician. Both musicians and their listening public learn early on the ideal picture of a life devoted to music. Our society instills in musicians, through formal training as well as through the media, the artistic ideals and expectations of the concert stage, even though the field of concert performance is available as a career to a very small minority of trained musicians. Any musical work outside of the concert context is a sign of relative failure in pursuing those artistic ideals. The notion that musical performance can be regarded as a craft or a skilled trade rather than an "art"—with all the cultural baggage that the word carries—is unfamiliar to the lay public, and it is also very difficult to accept for many musicians. It should not be surprising, then, that those musicians who express the most negative criticism of club date performance are those who are unwilling to view club dates as work only and tend to judge performances using standards from other musical contexts. Anyone whose ideal is to do recording or jazz work only and judges club dates according to jazz or recording standards will be very dissatisfied with the work. Such a musician may have had specific musical goals outside of club dates from early on, or maybe such goals became apparent only after a number of years in the field; in any case, the realization that these goals remain unfulfilled while the club date business has become a career leads inevitably to feelings of entrapment and bitterness.

Although there are many club date musicians who feel this entrapment, having initially "fallen into" the business without ever entertaining the notion that it could become a career, even they find some consolation in being able to make a living from music performance alone. They may not be concert performers, but they *are* musicians, and they realize that much of the general public views them with a certain amount of fascination and even envy for that simple fact. There is, for example, the question frequently heard from party guests and circulated in a humorous vein among club date sidepersons: "So, what do you do for a living?" The assumption is that surely one doesn't just "play" for a living, and certainly not "just" club dates. Indeed, why should anyone be paid for "playing" when I, a party guest, work for my living?

Max Kaplan, in an unpublished Ph.D. dissertation titled "The Musician in America: A Study of His Social Roles," treats in depth this concept of play and what it means for the career musician. He concludes that "the musician in American life is an enigma to his fellow men . . . he deals with experiences which are not ordinary, but must be equated with ordinary kinds of activities in order to pay for his services: what, for instance, is a recital 'worth'?"[10] And what is a club date worth? Probably considerably less than a recital, since it lacks the social sanction of dealing with "art" or "serious" music. Popular music can mean high status and high finance, but not in the club date field, where the music has already been popularized by other performers, the musicians are anonymous, and recording is rare.

Yet club date musicians *are* being paid, and many of them make a living from that pay. That in itself commands a certain amount of respect.

> People in the audience think it's wonderful that music is what you do for a living.
> —*sideperson, early 30s, piano*

> People—and young people especially—are very much aware of creativity, and, even if club dates aren't really a creative area of the music business, I think that they are impressed when they hear that I just make a living from music—and in only two days a week.
> —*sideperson, late 20s, trumpet*

> I think it [status] has gotten better in the last decade or so. A couple of things are involved: first, the hopelessly materialistic way we have of according status whereby a man with a doctor before his name can be a wife-beater and still be respected. With music such a big business and the possibility of becoming a star or at least fairly wealthy off of it, it's become accordingly higher in status to be a musician.
>
> Second, there's the post-Beatles' attitude among younger people of making your own choices, doing what you want to do rather than someone else. A person who chooses to be a musician has a certain amount of respect from his peers because it is a risky but glamorous venture in their eyes, a kind of statement of strong personal values.
> —*sideperson, early 40s, drums*

Professional music offers financial security to a precious few, and those few have, in a sense, beaten the odds. The question "What do you do for a living?" *may* be perceived as a put-down, a way of belittling club dates as an occupation. The musician, however, probably is polite enough not to respond as he or she might like to: "Well, unlike yourself, I'm not trapped in a nine to five desk job that I hate. I love music, and I'm self-employed as a musician. Whatever financial security I have today and for the future I have acquired on my own." Older club date players in particular, whatever criticisms they had of their work, nearly all expressed a certain amount of pride in the fact that music, rather than some other field, had always been their livelihood:

Naturally, it becomes less challenging after a while . . . less stimulating maybe. . . . But I never thought of doing anything else. That's always what I wanted to do. And I was able to make a living at it, get married, had my own home—all done with the music business. I always made money as a musician.

—*sideperson, early 60s, saxophone*

I'm fortunate enough that I've made a living out of it all my life. Whether I taught, whether I played with big bands, whether it was club dates—but it was always music. I didn't have to become an accountant or anything like that.

—*sideperson and subleader, early 40s, trumpet and vocals*

Notes

1. Carlo L. Lastrucci, "The Professional Dance Musician" 169; Becker, *Outsiders* 97.

2. Lastrucci, "The Professional Dance Musician" 170.

3. Becker, *Outsiders* 97.

4. *Allegro* (2 April 1977): 2.

5. Jon Frederickson and James F. Rodney, "The Free-Lance Musician as a Type of Non-Person" 234.

6. Howard Becker, *Outsiders* 79–120.

7. Faulkner, *Hollywood Studio Musicians* 71.

8. Ibid. 64.

9. Frederickson and Rodney, "The Free-Lance Musician" 235.

10. Max Kaplan, "The Musician in America" 262.

1989: The Changing Scene

Changes that take place in the club date business are nearly all direct reflections of changes in the popular music scene at the national level. The most frequent and obvious changes in the club date business occur first in the repertoire; these in turn affect other aspects of the performance context and eventually the structure of the business context as well.

The most significant change during this period has been the increasing emphasis on rock and contemporary music rather than standard songs from the theater and Tin Pan Alley traditions. When asked about differences in the business between 1978 and 1989, every musician I spoke with noted this change, and all the performances I observed were clear evidence of the difference.

When I decided to observe performances in 1989, my intentions were twofold: (1) to establish new contacts with musicians and (2) to make note of general differences in the makeup of bands and their style of presentation. I expected that the repertoire would have changed, for the emphasis on currency of songs was already evident in 1978: songs that were popular in 1978 would naturally have been replaced again and again by new material over the years. I did keep track of songs at each performance, but I didn't expect the lists to show much beyond a new collection of current songs. And, true enough, none of the hits from 1978 appeared in 1989; indeed, of the titles that were five years old or less in 1978, only one appeared in 1989.

But when, two months after the performances, I combined the individual lists, it was clear that there was more going on than just the substitution of one group of current songs for another. Some of the differences could, of course, have been a result of differences in the sample of parties used in 1978 versus 1989. My 1978 sample included nine parties: four bar or bas mitzvahs, two weddings, two Gentile dinner-dances, and one society dinner-dance; the 1989 sample included only five complete parties: three bar or bas mitzvahs, one wedding, and one mixed Gentile/Jewish dinner-dance. But the differences are large enough to indicate an overall change of emphasis, even though the particular occasions are not directly comparable. In 1978, out of 520 songs, standards constituted 40.4 percent of the sample and rock 20.6 percent; in 1989, of 302 songs, standards were 24.5 percent of the sample and rock 45 percent. The rock and contemporary pop categories combined—in a sense, the "current" material—constituted 35.1 percent in 1978 and 58.2 percent in 1989 (see appendix B for further details).

The more I thought about this difference, the less surprising it seemed. After all, the club date audience was aging, which meant that more and more party guests each year had grown up listening to (or at least having been exposed to) rock music. Parents of a thirteen-year-old bar or bas mitzvah child in 1989 could be thirty-five years old or even younger—born in 1954, as rock was just beginning. Even parents forty-five or fifty years of age—those of wedding couples, for instance—were likely to have spent their teens and early twenties listening to rock music. Club date bandleaders are aware of this, and they have tailored their performances accordingly.

Current rock songs are still a very important part of the repertoire—a bit over 10 percent of the total—but rock music in the club date context now has a historical component that was hardly evident in the 1970s. Every band I heard in 1989, both those in the sample and eight others, played at least one set of fifties rock songs and one set of sixties Motown songs. Other subcategories I heard were medleys of songs by formerly popular rock artists—the Beatles and Carole King, for instance. This historical aspect of rock music on the club date scene, of course, reflects a national trend that has spawned innumerable "oldies but goodies" and "classic rock" radio stations as well as nightclub bands specializing in earlier rock genres and eras.

I occasionally heard sets of 1950s songs played by club date bands in 1978, but the 1960s Motown material was virtually nonexistent. The revival of Motown music, whether on club dates, radio, or at nightclubs, seems to have begun with the appearance in 1983 of the movie *The Big Chill,* which featured Marvin Gaye's "Heard It Through the Grapevine." That piece has become almost a theme song used by many club date bands to introduce their Motown sets: its introductory instrumental measures usually succeed in drawing a wide range of party guests to the dance floor.

There are still club dates where standards constitute the vast majority of songs: charity balls in the society area, for instance, where the average age of guests is higher than on the wedding/bar mitzvah circuit. But the relative importance of standards has obviously decreased in all areas of the business. One genre of standard songs, however, does seem to have made a comeback in the last decade: big band songs from the 1930s and 1940s. Nearly every band I heard in 1989 included a medley of big band songs—"In The Mood," "Tuxedo Junction," "Moonlight Serenade," "Take the A Train," and so on. And in nearly every case, the set was followed immediately by a fifties rock set and often a sixties Motown set as well (as in the example at the end of chapter 4). This sequence seems to be very effective in drawing guests of all ages to the dance floor and building party momentum as the styles and tempos change and move forward chronologically. Neither this routine nor the big band medley alone were common in 1978.

The continued emphasis on current rock material and the new emphasis on older rock styles have effected changes in instrumentation and band personnel. For example, in 1978 almost all piano players had found it necessary to own an electric piano—often a Fender Rhodes—to achieve what was then a contemporary sound. As recording technology became more sophisticated, however, and synthesized sounds more prominent throughout popular music, the simple electric piano no longer sufficed. Keyboard synthesizers are the norm for piano players these days, and they are capable of reproducing the sound of studio recordings with uncanny accuracy. It is no longer "humanly impossible" to "reproduce the aesthetic . . . of particular commercial recording sessions," as was the case in the 1960s and 1970s for the Top 40 rock bands studied by Bennett.[1]

Indeed, the line between recorded and live sound can become very fuzzy. At one catering hall I observed a solo keyboard player/vocalist performing current Top 40 songs, and the only thing that seemed to be missing was the physical presence of a band of musicians. The sound itself was nearly indistinguishable from what I had heard on the radio earlier that day. Nevertheless, there are no signs that either these solo keyboard players or disc jockeys are taking over the club date business, which might seem to be the logical extension of the public's insistence on having the music sound "just like the record." The listeners' attitude is ambivalent: although they want to hear what they have heard on the radio or on records, they still want to *see* live musicians doing the reproduction.

The keyboard player has consequently become an indispensable member of club date bands. One leader remarked that he could easily find good substitutes for every member of his set group—even the lead vocalist—*except* the keyboard player, because so much of the sound texture of the current songs depended on him. The keyboard player who is also a strong vocalist has become perhaps *the* most important single band member. To retain these keyboard players on a regular basis, leaders will often make guarantee or scale-plus arrangements with them, realizing that the keyboard player/vocalist can very easily work solo if need be.

The concept of the guitarist as solely a rock specialist is almost gone from the business, hanging on only in the society field. In fact, many of the guitarists, now in their late thirties or forties, who entered the business as rockers are now leaders or regular subleaders. This is a very convenient arrangement, because beginnings and endings on many contemporary songs are often done by guitar and drums alone, which reduces the need for constant hand signals from the leader. Also, the guitarist/vocalist can perform requests with drum accompaniment only even if no one else in a band knows the particular song. Guitarists working in the society field, where the "rocker" concept has held on the longest, have noticed more often in recent years that they are at last getting substantial musical support from other band members on rock material. There are still some bands where sidepersons will sit out the rock numbers, but those situations are becoming a rarity.

The doubling combination of horn and violin, which I found so fascinating in 1978, is virtually extinct today. Two explanations were offered by leaders for this change: (1) that there is less demand for the combination, especially in light of the contemporary emphasis in the music, and (2) that many of the musicians who were capable of playing club date material on both horn and violin—*violin doublers,* as they are known in the business—have retired since 1978. The number of club date musicians playing violin only is also diminishing rapidly. The increasing use of synthesized string sounds by keyboard players has been one major reason for this decline. In addition, few young violin players know the club date repertoire, and leaders thus find it difficult to replace the violin players who retire from the business.

The most immediately noticeable change in the makeup of club date bands is the ubiquitous presence of female vocalists. *Every* band I saw in 1989 had at least one female vocalist; some had two, and one had three. I asked leaders, sidepersons, and a number of the vocalists themselves how this change had come about. Evidently, leaders had used female vocalists occasionally in the past, although I saw not a one in 1978, nor did anyone mention women as club date band members. Part of the reason for the absence of women in the business was simply the strength of tradition: club date bands had generally been all male, and no one thought to change that. Also, the vast majority of standards were performed instrumentally, and female sax, trumpet, or trombone players were then and still are a rarity. The one major exception to this rule was the Latin American female vocalist, who appeared with bands in the 1940s and 1950s playing maracas and singing on the few Latin tunes done in an evening.

Another reason given for the absence of women in club dates, particularly as lead vocalists, struck me as very unconvincing at first, but I heard the same explanation from enough musicians, both male and female, that it surely has some foundation in fact. It was apparently often the case that the mother of a bride—or even the bride herself—would request specifically that no female vocalist be included in the band. The reason: the vocalist threatened to steal the limelight from the bride—the "star" of the occasion. This attitude has changed gradually for a number of interrelated reasons: the increase in the number of female pop vocalists at the national level, making it only natural for a woman to sing their songs; the increasing presence of women throughout the society in traditionally male roles; and the increasingly later age at which women are marrying, making them more secure in their own self-image and consequently less threatened by the female vocalist as a competitor for the spotlight.

Another factor was also involved in the Jewish part of the business: the more orthodox the family sponsoring a party, the less likely they would even consider the presence of a female entertainer for traditional religious reasons. And even the more reformed Jews were not always comfortable with a female musician on stage while the rabbi was in the room. One female vocalist recalled occasions when she had to leave the room until the rabbi left—this was in the 1980s. This situation has become less common, for the religious aspect of bar and bas mitzvahs in particular is most often separate both in time and place from the catered reception.

Leaders began hiring female vocalists in the late 1970s and early 1980s both as a response to perceived public demand and as a selling point to make their product seem more current and versatile. Donna Summer, who had a string of disco hits in 1978 and 1979—"Last Dance for Love," "Hot Stuff," and "Bad Girls"—was the single national vocalist most responsible for this change. Her song "Last Dance for Love" became a standard evening closing song for many club date bands, and it still is today in many cases. The first female vocalists in the business held a position similar to that of the Latin singer in the 1940s and 1950s or the rocker in the 1960s and 1970s: she might sing only five or six songs the whole evening, doing occasional harmony or simply shaking a tambourine on other songs. A vocalist who began in club dates in the early 1980s described the scene: "All you needed to be able to do was 'Bad Girls,' 'Last Dance' and 'Hot Stuff.' If you could do those three songs, you were a girl singer" (the term *girl singer*, dated as it is, is still in common use in the business). The role of the female vocalist was similar to the rocker in one other respect: she effectively displaced another musician, usually a horn player. In a five-piece band including trumpet and saxophone, the female vocalist would normally replace the trumpet.

In a relatively short time the female vocalist has become a standard feature in nearly every club date band. There are also some female instrumentalists—most often keyboard players—but they are not nearly as prominent as the vocalists. A small minority of the women in club dates work as bandleaders; the percentage of them who do so is probably not so different from the number of musicians in general who turn to bandleading, which requires skills and responsibilities different from those of band members. There is also some resistance from established offices to the idea of a female bandleader. One vocalist who now books much of her own work recalled the reaction she received when she suggested to an office president in 1985 that she begin subleading:

> His response was, "No, really, I don't think musicians want to be taking orders from women. I don't think caterers want to give orders to women, and I don't think the clients want to speak to women." I couldn't believe it. After all, there are old leaders, and some people don't want them. And there are really young leaders, and some people won't want them. But, hey, what world do you live in? Half the time people come up to me at a job and think I'm the leader. . . . So I left, and I've never had a problem. People are thrilled to deal with a woman.

This same woman pointed out later on that 90 percent of the people in charge of planning parties are women.

The increasing demand for female vocalists in combination with the popularity of the Motown sound also brought many black musicians into the business. The mainstream of the club date business, which offers enough work paying at least union scale that leaders and sidepersons can rely on it as a primary source of income, serves a predominantly white, middle- to upper-class clientele, and white males had traditionally been the only musicians in the field. Leaders began offering their clients bands with black vocalists, both male and female, in the early 1980s partly as a marketing strategy—a new feature to make their product more versatile and attractive—and partly in response to perceived public demand. When they saw that client response to the addition was clearly positive, it wasn't long before bands throughout the business had one or more black vocalists, followed soon by both black and Hispanic instrumentalists. A few all-black bands also began working for offices and have been very successful. As with the addition of the rocker and the female vocalist, what began as a unique marketing feature soon became a standard part of the business.

Things have changed since 1978 in club date offices as well as on the club date stage, and the changes are all directly or indirectly related to the increasing predominance of rock music in the repertoire. Leaders, sidepersons, and union officals all agree, for one, that the volume of union club date work has decreased since 1978. Where a leader in the 1970s might commonly do 200 or more jobs in a year, the same leader may find 150 or less as a limit today. Many sidepersons find it impossible to work for one office exclusively and still make a livable income.

The increasing demand for rock music on club dates has made it much easier for rock bands that might normally work only the nightclub circuit to sell their services for private parties as well. Because the historical approach to presenting rock music is popular in nightclubs as well as on the club date scene, the transition from nightclub to club date becomes less difficult each year. The traditional club date difference—being able to play music on request from *any* era—seems to be less and less a public demand. The cost of hiring one of these bands can also be far less than the cost of a band working through a large club date office: operating independently with little overhead costs, they can charge far less while still making a substantial profit. And the pay for band members is often higher than union scale even though the overall cost of the band is less for the client.

Offices at the upper levels of the club date hierarchy continue to buy out smaller offices, cultivate concessions with caterers, and diversify their entertainment services to spread their economic risk, but this also tends to push the cost of their product higher. Union work in the club date business is concentrated more and more in the hands of those leaders and offices serving the upper-middle- and upper-class clientele. At these levels, a decrease in total number of jobs per year can more easily be offset by charging a higher price per individual job.

The disc jockey phenomenon *has* displaced many musicians in the club date field, but its effect overall has been far less than musicians expected a decade ago. Disc jockeys were especially prominent in the late 1970s and early 1980s while disco music and dancing were the current craze. Club date musicians in 1978 were seriously concerned that live music at private parties might soon become a thing of the past:

> I can see that there's not going to be much business for our type of musician. Kids don't even care for live music anymore. . . . I was talking to some kids, and this was their argument: Let's say we have the Bee Gees—great group. Actually, they only have four or five songs that we really like. So, if we hear them for four hours, we'll hear those four songs, which will take fifteen or twenty minutes. For the other three hours we have to listen to stuff that doesn't mean anything to us. When we go to a disco . . . we hear the best of everybody. . . . The fact that it's not live makes no difference. They've gotten used to records, and they don't know the difference.
> —*sideperson and subleader, late 50s, trumpet and vocals*

> We are on the borderline between staying in business and being put out of business by disc jockeys . . . because, quite frankly, some of the music you get out of a disco machine can be much more exciting than what you'll get out of a live band.
> —*leader, late 50s, trumpets and vocals*

Disc jockeys are still popular for private parties, but the interest in them has clearly waned since the 1970s. Many club date offices today offer disk jockey services as well as live bands, but the disk jockeys are hired mainly for either small parties (fifty or so people) or "resets" after a regular band has played the four-hour main party. The real effect of disc jockeys as well as synthesizers has been indirect, because they have displaced so many musicians in other areas such as nightclubs and recording studios. More and more high-caliber musicians who at one time could rely on work outside of club dates to support themselves are finding it necessary to supplement their income with club date work.

This has both advantages and disadvantages for mainstream club date offices. It is advantageous mainly because the quality of musicians willing and able to do club date work has increased; it is disadvantageous because these same musicians are less willing to ally themselves exclusively with any one office or leader and are often much more interested in booking their own work on a part-time basis than working for an established office. For individual sidepersons, this influx of newcomers to the field simply means more competition for jobs. The total supply of musicians seems to outweigh the demand for their services in the club date field, and even though the total number of parties per year probably remains fairly constant, the amount of work available to individual musicians has decreased.

Some club date leaders have responded to the continued importance of imitating records by shifting their emphasis to set groups instead of bands composed entirely of free-lance musicians. They feel that a band working together regularly is more capable of imitating recordings authentically, and the product is more easily marketed because it remains relatively consistent over time. The bands can produce good record copies even without formal rehearsal, because musicians who are familiar with a band's instrumentation and personnel will find it easier to predict how a part learned from a recording will work with the rest of the band.

Of course, these same leaders don't mention that their logic can work both ways: a set group can also use substitute members fairly easily, since everyone in the business is copying their parts from the same recordings. Recordings today play a role similar to that of the stock arrangements used by the big bands in the 1930s and 1940s: they provide a common source of both songs and arrangements that guarantees a certain amount of continuity from one club date band to another. As long as the instrumentation and particular songs are not significantly different from band to band, parts learned for use with one band can probably be used with any other club date band. In any case, the set group concept has certainly not taken over the business. Most sidepersons still do much of their work on a free-lance basis, even though they may also work with a set group or have informal ties to a single leader.

The society offices have not followed the set band route as yet, but they may eventually, for they are beginning to see the limitations of the traditional all–free-lance club date band. Although there is still a lively market for bands specializing in show tunes and other standards with a smattering of rock, more and more upper-class clients—especially younger ones—want to see and hear a band before hiring them. If the band is organized only *after* a contract is signed—the traditional society band method—that is impossible. Clients who are looking for groups that emphasize authentic-sounding rock will find them outside the society field. A guitarist who tried to sell the idea of hiring set, Top 40–type groups to some society offices explained his lack of success:

The offices were reluctant to go in that direction, and the one reason I think is that it would change the selling strategy, since customers would get used to buying a group as a whole and not need to rely so much on the office. That gets them shopping in another market, and naturally the offices are trying to avoid that. I'd say they're trying to avoid the inevitable, since it's definitely going in that direction. There's more and more of the Top 40–type jobs and less and less of the society.

—*sideperson, late 30s, guitar and vocals (1989)*

The society bands remain the most "traditional" part of the club date business. Show tunes and other standard repertoire are their specialty, and their horn and string sections are capable of harmonizing nearly any popular song called by a bandleader—without written music, of course. But the days of such bands appear to be numbered, both because the demand for them is decreasing and because the number of musicians who know the standard repertoire and can fake harmony is rapidly dwindling. This was already a problem in 1978 and is more acute today. Fewer and fewer younger musicians coming into the business are familiar with the older repertoire, even though there is still a market for the music, and faking harmony is, of course, out of the question for the player who does not know the tunes in the first place.

The concept of large bands performing without written arrangements seems to be a time-bound phenomenon, a product of particular historical circumstances. The conditions that gave rise to "faking" bands—a fairly homogeneous repertoire that was commonly performed by big bands with horn and string sections, along with the availability of many musicians who were experienced in section playing and willing to do club date work—have disappeared. Some leaders have already begun to use written arrangements with their larger bands, if only for a portion of each performance, and it seems inevitable that large faking bands will disappear altogether in the near future. Another decade or two may find entire club date audiences—and bands—with virtually no knowledge of standards and the associated dance styles, simply because they have not had occasion to be exposed to the music.

Note

1. Bennett, *On Becoming a Rock Musician* 155.

Conclusion

The late Meyer Davis, who began his career as a society bandleader in 1913, reputedly had eighty-nine orchestras and 1,100 musicians across the country playing under his name in 1941.[1] In the previous year Mr. Davis had conducted a seventy-five-piece orchestra at a party given by the Widener family. The Atwater-Kents, not to be outdone, required an orchestra of ninety pieces. Meyer Davis Orchestras were grossing over four million dollars a year—a minor musical empire at the time. The society orchestras in New York City, led by Mr. Davis, Lester Lanin, and a handful of others, were in full swing, and they were virtually synonymous with the club date business as a definable structure of any sort. Bandleaders whose clientele happened to be less than upper class were a very loosely organized group—a "push-cart peddler operation," as one leader put it.

The scene began to change soon after World War II. The demise of the big bands brought many high-caliber musicians into the field, and their experience as section players using stock arrangements allowed club date leaders to phase out the use of written arrangements. Also, the nonsociety part of the business was growing rapidly, responding to major social changes experienced throughout the country—increasing general affluence, mass migration to the suburbs, and the beginning of the baby boom. By the late 1950s it was clear that providing music for parties outside of the society area could be and was a full-time venture for many leaders—even a big business for those who began to form club date offices through partnerships. Sidepersons as well were finding that the strength of the suburban club date circuit allowed many of them to rely on club dates as a primary or even sole source of income. Club date work in all areas was active enough that it seemed to offer at least as much stability and security as any other work in the field of popular music.

The 1960s were the heyday of the business as a whole, but the decade also seems to have held the seeds of decline. Rock music began making its way into club dates during the 1960s, and although it may not have seemed to be a major event at the time, the new music eventually changed nearly every aspect of the business.

The young guitarists—the rockers—who were added to club date bands had at first only minor effects overall: each rocker displaced one other musician, but beyond that, adding a few rock tunes on each job simply meant that older musicians sat out a few songs. As the demand for rock music increased, however, other changes soon followed. Accordion players, horn players, and older musicians generally began to see their work load decreasing, and everyone had to learn the new music—not a simple task, for rock represented a musical conception very different from that of the standard repertoire.

Club date bands also began to decrease in size, both because of rock's reliance on small units and because the national economy was experiencing a downtrend in the 1970s. Large faking bands with full horn and string sections were becoming a less significant part of the business with each passing year. Finding young musicians who knew the repertoire and could improvise harmony became more and more difficult.

The disc jockey phenomenon and rock music's increasing dependence on synthesized sounds displaced musicians in the club date business as well as in the New York nightclub and recording fields. More musicians were entering the club date field, and each job these newcomers took meant one less job that went to leaders and sidepersons already in the field. Beginning in the early 1980s, many of these newcomers competing for the work were women and blacks—a bit late in coming, perhaps, but still a major change for veterans of a business that had always been populated almost exclusively by white males. Many leaders throughout the business expanded the scope of their work beyond club dates alone as they saw the business declining, and fewer sidepersons found it possible to rely solely on club dates to make a living.

The club date business is not disappearing by any means. People still value live music for celebrating important life events, and club date leaders adapt their product as well as they can to continue providing that service. The society bands are still swinging, but even they are "rocking" more and more as time moves on. It isn't likely that "I Can't Get Started" and "Chattanooga Choo-Choo" will simply disappear from the club date scene, nor will "The Girl from Ipanema" or "The Alley Cat." Those songs will just become an increasingly smaller fraction of the total repertoire. Club date musicians will still need to "know the tunes" in order to work; the tunes they must know, though, are more likely to include Billy Joel than Cole Porter. Just how many musicians will be on stage to play the songs and what instruments they will be playing will continue to change in response to fads, fashions, and economics.

But a club date is still a club date. Consider the musician mentioned in chapter 7 who, after recounting a heated exchange he had had with a caterer, remarked somewhat despairingly that "the club date just does not change." He was not exaggerating for effect; he was stating a simple truth. The club date as a social form and the dynamics inherent in that form do not really change significantly over time. As important as it is to recognize the changes in repertoire, instruments used, bandleaders' routines, and ways of organizing and conducting the business of club dates, the club date of 1990 fulfills the same social function as the club date of 1940, and the role of music and musicians in that context remains much the same. It is this relatively static nature of the club date performing context that, more than any other single factor, shapes club date musicians' views on their occupation—what it is and what it means to them.

The dynamics of a social gathering tend to clarify and test the mental images we have of ourselves and our places in society. These images are constantly being formulated and revised as the mind establishes priorities for us in relation to whatever situations it encounters, whether the circumstances are immediate and physical or hypothetical and future-oriented. Perhaps this is the work of our survival instinct, whereby we are—or are at least trying to be—constantly aware of what is most and least important to us. Most of the time, the nature of these personal priorities is evident to the individual only; in a social gathering, however, our physical and verbal behavior can reveal quite a bit of this "inside" information to those we encounter. Erving Goffman suggests that these physical and verbal cues allow us to evaluate more precisely the nature and extent of each individual's "involvement" in a social gathering and, in turn, the dynamics of the occasion as a whole.[2] He speaks of *dominant* and *subordinate* involvements in various aspects of an occasion, all participants allocating their attention according to the values they carry into the situation. The occasion succeeds as a social gathering when most of the participants find that their dominant involvements are both pleasant and unrestricted.

We can view the club date as a social gathering wherein one particular focus—the celebration of the marriage, the bar mitzvah, the anniversary, the holiday—is expected to be the dominant involvement for all participants at various times during the affair. Of course, very little time may actually be devoted specifically to this central focus at the occasion itself: speeches, ceremonies, and rituals account for only a small portion of the four-hour party. During the remaining time, various other elements vie for party guests' attention: food, drink, music, dancing, conversation, or just surveying the sights and sounds as the party proceeds. The scene is, after all, intended to be a pleasant diversion from daily life. It succeeds in this purpose especially because there is little or no compulsion for participants to focus on any one element—the precise opposite of the usual work environment. One's dominant involvement throughout the course of the affair is allowed to shift again and again, and even the background elements—subordinate involvements—are pleasing to the senses, again, in contrast to the workplace. The dominant involvement for most party guests most of the time is undoubtedly conversation. Music may be essential to the overall ambience of the affair, but it is primarily a constant background presence.

The subordinate role of music in the club date context is very much at the root of the negative image that the public has of club date musicians. We might note, first of all, that because music is not often the focus of attention, it is likely that few party guests give much thought to the musicians and their role as performers. After all, the club date context does not really accord well with common notions of what constitutes a music performance. "Music performance" commonly evokes an image of a seated audience facing one or more musicians on a raised concert stage. Most people would initially envision such a work environment on learning that a person performs music for a living. Whatever type of music is being performed, the simple fact that the musicians are at least intended to be the center of attention—the dominant involvement—for the audience tends to legitimize their status as musicians.

The recording studio is the one alternative work environment in which one's status as a musician is "legitimized" even though no audience is present. The occupational title "studio musician" carries a certain amount of status with it, both because of its association with the recording, television, and movie industries and because of the high pay associated with the work. The music played may be simple commercial jingles, Muzak, or background for soap operas, but the work still commands respect from the general public.

When there *is* an audience, but one whose attention is lacking (as it is much of the time in the club date context), a couple of interconnected assumptions follow naturally. For one, we might expect that most musicians, assuming that they are "serious" about their work, would not like playing club dates very much. We assume that a person who takes the time to learn an instrument and earn a living from music aspires to be heard in a typical concert situation, or at least in a nightclub, where music is still a central focus for audience attention. No one aspires to play background music. A corollary to this is that the musicians in a club date band probably are not really serious professionals. They are either losers who have not succeeded in a more amenable performance venue, or they are not full-time professionals at all, just moonlighters making a few extra dollars on the weekend.

The kind of music being played by club date performers is closely related to its subordinate role, and this adds yet another strike against the musicians' status in the public mind. The music is familiar, commercial, popular music, both old and new—much the same repertoire you would hear in the office or on an elevator. As the purveyors of Muzak have known for years, familiarity along with formal simplicity are key components of successful background music, which must demand little or no conscious engagement of the listener. The fact that club date musicians are playing such a "something for everyone" potpourri of pop music rather than "classical" music, jazz, or original pop songs tends to keep them low on the status ladder.

The subordinate role of music in the club date context and the consequent low status accorded to its performers is an issue of far less importance for club date bandleaders than for sidepersons. This is explained by the very different nature of the bandleader's involvement in the performance. The bandleader's dominant involvement at a party is not simply "the music"; it is, more specifically, the adaptation of the music to the social context. The skills of reading a crowd, pacing, and building a party are what separate the bandleader from the sideperson. And the bandleader receives fairly clear indications as to how effectively these skills are being employed. The number of dancers on the floor, the amount of applause, spoken compliments at the party or written ones later on, and the spin-off business in the future provided by satisfied clients and their friends—all of these inform the bandleader that his or her skills are appreciated. That the bandleader's technical proficiency as an instrumentalist or ability to conduct an ensemble are less noticed or appreciated by the audience assumes relatively less significance. The bandleader is at least acknowledged and appreciated by the audience—directly or indirectly, verbally or nonverbally—and this is a major factor contributing to a musician's satisfaction with any work situation.

In a sense, bandleaders use the subordinate role of the music to their advantage. They realize that, for the most part, the music must not intrude too much upon an affair, yet they must also sense those times during a party when the music should come to the fore. At such times, the party guests are invited to change their involvement in the music from subordinate to dominant, to share temporarily the bandleader's dominant involvement in the context. Yet even then, care is taken not to overwhelm the celebration or to monopolize attention for too long. The bandleader continues to "play" the audience and the energy of the party to his or her best advantage and is rewarded when the party goes well.

In contrast, sidepersons' involvement in the social context is far more circumscribed by their role and also far less obviously appreciated by most party guests. Performing whatever music the bandleader calls for is really the only involvement expected of them. Whether that is actually the dominant involvement for all sidepersons is another matter. Just as a party guest who would rather be somewhere else can easily enough carry on a casual conversation while mentally planning more enjoyable activities later on, the sideperson who has little interest in the music and can perform quite acceptably with a minimum of conscious attention may be mentally involved in matters far removed from the music at hand. This is one common response to the fact that music, although it may be the musician's livelihood and dominant involvement throughout life, is relegated to subordinate status in the club date context. Of course, the idea flowing from this, that club date musicians are not "good" or "serious" musicians, often can become something of a self-fulfilling prophecy. Musicians entering the business with the "low-status, poor musician" image in mind all too frequently decide that there is no reason to give their all, to uphold any kind of musical standards, to play any better than the bandleader requires them to play. This tends to perpetuate the negative image, and for good reason.

But this is not at all the only attitude reflected by musicians who play club dates as their primary source of income—for some it is, but for most it is not. Many of these musicians eventually come to accept the fact that music can be appreciated and successful and yet not be at the same time "concert perfect." It is a hard lesson to learn, especially for musicians who have been socialized much of their lives to accept concert standards alone. From my own experience as a private party musician and from talking with experienced players in New York, it is clear that there *can* be satisfaction—though perhaps of a different order—in playing a party that is itself a success, almost regardless of the strictly "musical" quality of the sounds coming from the stage.

There is, at what seems to be a different level of acceptance, yet another way of appreciating the context as a full-time club date performer. A musician comes to acknowledge the fact that no audience—not even an audience for the New York Philharmonic—is completely attentive to the music or understands in any precise way what the musicians are doing. The club date context is no different in this respect. As encouraging as it may be to receive compliments or praise from the audience or even one's peers, such praise is small consolation if the individual musician is not really satisfied with his or her work. On the other hand, there is satisfaction in feeling that one has performed well, even though other elements of the context may have been somewhat less than ideal.

Club date sidepersons change their views of their work over time, as the work moves from a subordinate to a dominant involvement within one's personal career path. Musicians today enter the business, as did musicians in the 1940s and 1950s, on a casual and part-time basis. What begins as just another way to make money by playing music becomes, almost willy-nilly, the way to make a living. Hundreds of transactions for individual jobs, no single one seeming especially significant, together translate into a significant whole—the musician's occupation. Along the way, as more is learned about the business, the musician makes choices: in which area of the business and at what level of the club date hierarchy to concentrate; which roles to play— sideperson, subleader, leader, contractor; and within each of these roles, which strategies to employ to maximize income and still exercise selectivity in accepting work. In the end, club dates have become the musician's livelihood, even career, without ever having been a goal.

The pathway is familiar to us from the social circuits we travel from day to day. We find ourselves taking part in different social groups, led to each by a mixture of motivations, preferences, expectations, and chance. We learn the rules of the game as we go—interacting with others, playing the appropriate roles as best we can, and experiencing degrees of both success and failure in the process. And we find that, with the passage of time, an identity has taken shape, a niche has been carved out for us, which may or may not be what we intended. The realization that this process has taken place can be very disturbing and perplexing at first, forcing us to question just who it is we are (or would like to be) and why it is we do what we do. It is encouraging, of course, to realize as well that we are not alone in experiencing the process. The more closely we look at the work and life path of others, the more clearly our own lives come into focus.

Notes

1. "Businessman, Bandleader," *Time* 37 (January 20, 1941): 54–55.
2. Erving Goffman, *Behaviour in Public Places* 44 ff.

Appendix A: Interview Method

I arranged the first two interviews through my connection with the caterer whose son had been in my band in 1977. The next eight interviews I arranged with musicians after meeting them at performances. These musicians often suggested names of other club date musicians who were experienced in the business and could provide me with useful information. They would say, for instance, "You know who you should talk to who *really* knows the business?" or "You should really talk to guys at the union," or "You should talk to some society leaders." In each case I was then given names and phone numbers for future contacts. I made it a point to ask for suggestions even if the musician didn't offer names during the interview. At first I asked only for names of those who were experienced in the business. Later, I would specify particular kinds of musicians I wanted to speak with—sidepersons or leaders, younger or older, specialists on particular instruments—to achieve a wide range of viewpoints.

My first two interviews were with leaders who each worked in a different area of the business—one mainly in the society area, the other in the middle- and upper-middle-class suburban area. The contacts they provided me with seemed at first to spread in two separate directions, but very soon they began to overlap, because so many sidepersons worked in more than a single area. When I asked for names at the end of an interview, I was usually asked whom I had already contacted. After I had completed about fifteen interviews, everyone seemed to recognize most of the names I mentioned as previous contacts, but there were always a few they did not know because they were working with different offices or independent leaders. I made initial contacts for interviews in 1989 through musicians I already knew from the 1978 interviews.

It was not always a simple task to arrange interviews with these musicians, all of whom had very busy and erratic schedules. Ten of the musicians whom I first contacted by telephone refused to be interviewed for various reasons, and eight could not be reached at all, either because they would not respond to messages left with their answering service or because they were out of town for an extended period of time. The interviews that I was able to arrange often required a number of telephone calls to confirm or reschedule them.

Table 4. Distribution of Ages of Interviewed Club Date Musicians

Age	1978	1989
25–29 years	5	1
30–34	5	4
35–39	2	1
40–44	6	2
45–49	5	1
50–54	7	4
55–59	8	2
60+	4	4
Total	42	19

Although I interviewed most of the musicians at their homes, I also interviewed eight at their offices, one at the union hiring hall—with a vacuum cleaner running and other musicians talking and laughing nearby—two at restaurants, one during an hour-long break at a performance while a calypso singer was being featured, and eight by telephone.

The sixty-one musicians ranged in age from twenty-five to seventy-two. Table 4 shows the distribution of the musicians' ages at the time I interviewed them (the ages are grouped in five-year intervals).

According to primary instrument played, the sixty-one musicians divide as follows: accordion, 2; piano,11; drums, 6; guitar, 10; trumpet, 12; trombone, 1; saxophone, 11; clarinet, 1; violin, 1; voice, 3; conductor only, 3.

The three vocalists were women, as were two of the piano players; all the other musicians were men. Twenty-two of the instrumentalists also performed as vocalists.

Twenty-five of the musicians worked primarily as bandleaders; thirty-six as sidepersons. Eight of the leaders were subleaders, and the others were leader/owners. There were thus seventeen employers and forty-four employees altogether.

I used two general formats for the interviews, one for sidepersons and the other for leaders and subleaders. Other questions were added depending on the musician's particular experience in the business—for example, as a union official, as a specialist on one instrument, as a specialist in ethnic work, or as an independent versus an office leader. All the interviews began with an open-ended question about how the individual first became involved in music, which allowed me to become better informed for later questioning.

Following are the two basic sequences of questions that I used. Not all the questions were asked in every interview, because specific questions were often answered by a response to more general questions. Also, some of the most basic questions were omitted in later interviews. Questions that were directed only to older musicians, contractors, or ethnic specialists are listed after the basic format.

Interview Questions—Leaders and Subleaders

1. How did you first become involved in music? Did you have any specific goals in mind?
2. When and how did you get involved in club dates? Have you done musical work outside of club dates?
3. Did you begin as a band member? How did you learn to lead?
4. Did you have any problems establishing a reputation in the business?
5. Do you work with a set group? Do you rehearse?
6. Do you call all of the tunes? Do you use lists?
7. Do you use hand signals to indicate upcoming songs?
8. How do you arrange the music when leading a faking band?
9. How would you describe the leader's role? What should the leader do and not do at a party?
10. Do you speak to clients before an affair? Do you prepare beforehand?
11. Do you follow any general patterns in pacing a performance?
12. When would you use shtick and when not?
13. Are there combinations of set types or song types you would not normally put together in sequence?
14. What is the distinction between dinner music and dance music?
15. What kinds of indications do you receive from the audience as to the best music to play? How often do you receive direct requests?
16. What do you do if the band is not entirely familiar with a requested song?
17. Do you find certain events more or less challenging as a leader?
18. Do you notice a difference in musical tastes from party to party?
19. To what extent does the caterer affect your presentation?
20. Do you get musical enjoyment from your club date work?
21. What kind of advice would you give to an aspiring club date leader?
22. What do you think of the business as a life-style?
23. Do you feel that the amount of money you receive for your services is commensurate with the amount and kind of work you do?
24. How do you see the state of the business today? In the future?

Additional questions for older leaders or subleaders:

1. Has the size of club date bands changed over the years?
2. When were the most active years of the business?
3. When did rock first enter the club date scene?
4. Was there much resistance to rock from musicians?
5. When did faking begin? Do you have any idea how or why it began?

Additional questions for office leaders:

1. How many bands does your office have? What is the number of bookings per year?

2. What were the reasons for forming a partnership? What are the advantages and disadvantages?

3. Could you explain concessions with caterers to me?

4. How does a single musician begin working for your office?

Interview Questions—Sidepersons

1. How did you get involved in music in the first place? Did you have any particular goals in mind?

2. How did you become involved in club dates? Did you work in other musical areas as well?

3. How much of your income is from club date work? Do you have any idea how many musicians in New York rely on club dates as their primary source of income?

4. Did you have any initial problems in learning the necessary repertoire? How did you go about it?

5. Did you have any problem in establishing a reputation in the business?

6. What kinds of club date work have you done? Do you notice differences in the music used in the different areas of the business?

7. How do you go about keeping up on the current tunes?

8. Do you ever work with a set group? Do the bands you work with ever rehearse?

9. Do you get musical enjoyment from your work in the club date field? Do you feel any conflict between your own musical standards and the kind of music you play on a typical club date?

10. Do you keep the audience in mind when you're playing?

11. Have you done any subleading? Do you like it?

12. What would you say makes a sideperson valuable to a leader other than repertoire alone?

13. Do you feel that the financial rewards you receive for club date work are commensurate with your skills?

14. What do you think of the business as a life-style?

15. What do you think about the business as a means of making a living?

16. How do you see the state of the business today? In the future?

17. Can you suggest other musicians who would be useful to contact?

Additional questions for older sidepersons:

1. When did club date bands begin playing without written music?

2. Has the kind or amount of work you do changed since you began in the field?

3. Was rock a major change for you?

4. Do you have any idea how the term *club date* originated?

Additional questions for horn and string players:

1. When did bands begin faking?

2. How did you learn to do it?

3. Could you explain in musical terms how faking is done?

Additional questions for sidepersons working as contractors:

1. How do you decide which musicians are best suited to the jobs for which you are contracting?

2. How large is the pool of musicians from which you draw?

3. How do you contact the musicians—by phone, at the union floor, etc.?

Additional questions for sidepersons who worked frequently in the society field:

1. Do you find there is a musical difference in working for society leaders?

2. Is the performance environment different for musicians?

3. What kind of work is done today in the society field—debutante parties, work for individuals or organizations?

Additional questions for sidepersons with ethnic area experience:

1. What kinds of ethnic work have you done?

2. Which leaders contract the work and how?

3. Do you get musical satisfaction from playing ethnic repertoire?

4. How did you go about learning the repertoire?

Additional question for sidepersons who were also union officials:

1. How are pay scales established? What are they today?

2. What are minimums? How are they established?

3. Are there union records that would tell me how much work is done by independent versus office leaders?

4. How does the club date business differ from similar businesses in other cities?

5. What have been the major changes in the business over the years as far as the union is concerned?

6. What kinds of problems does the union have that are peculiar to the club date business?

7. Are there union records that would tell me how much work is done in the society area versus the Jewish, Gentile, or ethnic areas?

Appendix B: Repertoire Samples

This appendix lists the song titles from two repertoire samples. The first, from 1978, contains songs from nine club date performances, representing thirty-six hours of music; the second, from 1989, contains songs from five performances, or twenty hours of music. The lists from the samples provide a precise picture of just what kinds of popular music a club date musician's repertoire includes. The lists also indicate the size and scope of the repertoire.

I have included here all song titles from the three main categories of club date repertoire—standards, rock, and contemporary pop. These three categories constitute the bulk of the repertoire, and each of them experiences significant change over time. For the other three categories—Latin, ethnic, and group participation—I include only the number of songs in each category. These three together represent less than one-quarter of the repertoire, and none of them showed significant change from 1978 to 1989.

I remind readers that the songs are categorized according to their *function* in the club date context, that is, which dance styles accompanied the songs and which age groups the songs seemed to appeal to. Consequently, some titles are bound to seem misplaced. "Day by Day," for example, from the rock musical *Godspell,* may seem out of place as a standard in the 1989 sample, but at the party where I heard it, all the dancers were doing either a foxtrot or a modified Latin step; it thus fulfilled the function of a standard song. Likewise, Barry Manilow's "Can't Smile without You," although it did appear on the *Billboard* Hot 100 charts in 1978, is hardly what most people would consider a rock song. Yet the teenage guests at the party where I heard it—the only people on the dance floor—were all dancing in nontouch rock style.

The realities of my role as participant-observer made it impossible to identify every song at every performance. Not being allowed to record any of the music, I relied on written notes alone. I was also frequently engaged in conversations while trying to keep track of songs. Musicians sometimes supplied me with titles when I was unfamiliar with particular songs, but there were not many opportunities to ask them for the information.

With these qualifications in mind, I provide here a statistical comparison of the 1978 and 1989 samples (see table 5), as well as the lists of song titles from which the comparison is drawn (tables 6 and 7).

Table 5. Distribution of Repertoire Categories

Category	1978		1989	
	Frequency	Percentage	Frequency	Percentage
Standards	210	40.4	74	24.5
Rock	107	20.6	136	45.0
Contemporary pop	76	14.5	40	13.2
Latin	52	10.0	28	9.3
Ethnic	57	11.0	18	6.0
Group participation	18	3.5	6	2.0
Total	520		302	

Table 6. 1978 Repertoire List

Standards			
Title	Composer	Year	Frequency
Heart of My Heart	A. Mack	1899	1
Bill Bailey Won't You Please Come Home?	H. Cannon	1902	1
The Entertainer	S. Joplin	1902	2
Alexander's Ragtime Band	I. Berlin	1911	3
Darktown Strutter's Ball	S. Brooks	1917	1
Smiles	L. Roberts	1917	1
For Me and My Gal	G. Meyer	1917	1
Carolina in the Morning	W. Donaldson	1922	1
Charleston	C. Mack/J. Johnson	1923	1
The One I Love Belongs to Someone Else	I. Jones	1924	1
If You Knew Susie	J. Meyer	1925	2
Yes, Sir, That's My Baby	W. Donaldson	1925	1
Sweet Georgia Brown	B. Bernie/K. Casey	1925	1
Someone to Watch Over Me	G. Gershwin	1926	1
Bye, Bye Blackbird	R. Henderson	1926	3
It All Depends on You	R. Henderson	1926	1
Mountain Greenery	R. Rodgers	1926	1
'S Wonderful	G. Gershwin	1927	1
My Blue Heaven	W. Donaldson	1927	1
The Best Things in Life Are Free	R. Henderson	1927	1
Mack the Knife	K. Weill	1928	1
I Can't Give You Anything but Love	J. McHugh	1928	2

Table 6. (continued)

	Standards		
Title	*Composer*	*Year*	*Frequency*
Star Dust	H. Carmichael	1928	2
Body and Soul	J. Green	1930	1
Embraceable You	G. Gershwin	1930	1
I Don't Know Why	F. Ahlert	1931	1
I'm Sorry Dear	J. Scott	1931	1
Dream a Little Dream of Me	W. Schwandt/F. Andre	1931	1
Just Friends	J. Klenner	1931	1
All of Me	S. Simons/G. Marks	1931	1
In a Shanty in Old Shanty Town	J. Young/J. Siras/ J. Little	1932	1
Fascination	F. Marchetti	1932	1
I'm Getting Sentimental over You	G. Bassman	1932	1
I Get a Kick out of You	C. Porter	1934	1
Solitude	D. Ellington	1934	1
Summertime	G. Gershwin	1935	1
I'm in the Mood for Love	J. McHugh	1935	2
Cheek to Cheek	I. Berlin	1935	1
I Can't Get Started	V. Duke	1935	2
Begin the Beguine	C. Porter	1935	2
Stompin' at the Savoy	B. Goodman/C. Webb	1936	1
I've Got You under My Skin	C. Porter	1936	1
Moon of Manakoora	A. Newman	1937	1
Where or When?	R. Rodgers	1937	4
Have You Met Miss Jones?	R. Rodgers	1937	1
The Lady is a Tramp	R. Rodgers	1937	3
Once in a While	M. Edwards	1937	1
It's Raining Sunbeams	F. Hollander	1937	1
Cherokee	R. Noble	1938	1
September Song	K. Weill	1938	1
Moonlight Serenade	G. Miller	1939	3
Little Brown Jug	G. Miller(Winner)	1939(1869)	1
All the Things You Are	J. Kern	1939	1
Over the Rainbow	H. Arlen	1939	2
Our Love	B. Emmerich	1939	1
Tuxedo Junction	B. Feyne/E. Hawkins/ J. Dash/W. Johnson	1940	4
In the Mood	A. Razaf/J. Garland	1940	1
Chattanooga Choo-Choo	M. Gordon/ H. Warren	1941	1

Table 6. (continued)

	Standards		
Title	*Composer*	*Year*	*Frequency*
This Love of Mine	S. Parker/H. Sanicola	1941	1
You're Nobody till Somebody Loves You	R. Morgan/L. Stock/J. Cavanaugh	1944	2
Sentimental Journey	B. Green/L. Brown/ B. Homer	1944	2
Laura	D. Raskin	1944	1
We'll Be Together Again	F. Laine/C. Fischer	1945	1
It Might As Well Be Spring	R. Rodgers	1945	1
You Make Me Feel So Young	J. Myrow	1946	1
Stella by Starlight	V. Young	1946	2
Everybody Loves Somebody Sometime	K. Lane	1948	1
Daddy's Little Girl	B. Burke/H. Gerlach	1949	1
I Will Wait	M. Colclough	1950	1
When I Fall in Love	V. Young	1952	2
Here's That Rainy Day	J. VanHeusen	1953	1
The Happy Wanderer	F. Moller	1954	1
Misty	E. Garner	1954	2
I Left My Heart in S.F.	G. Cory	1954	2
Love Is a Many-Splendored Thing	S. Fain	1955	1
I Wish You Love	C. Trenet	1955	1
Around the World	V. Young	1956	1
Mr. Wonderful	J. Bock/G. Weiss/ L. Holofcener	1956	1
The Party's Over	J. Styne	1956	2
I Could Have Danced All Night	F. Lowe	1956	1
On the Street Where You Live	F. Lowe	1956	1
Just in Time	J. Styne	1956	2
Witchcraft	C. Coleman	1957	2
Satin Doll	B. Strayhorn	1958	6
My Favorite Things	R. Rodgers	1959	1
I've Got a Lot of Livin' to Do	C. Strouse	1960	2
Where Is Love?	L. Bart	1960	1
Consider Yourself	L. Bart	1960	1
Put On a Happy Face	C. Strouse	1960	2
Hey, Look Me Over	C. Coleman	1960	2
A Taste of Honey	B. Scott	1960	1

Table 6. (continued)

Standards			
Title	*Composer*	*Year*	*Frequency*
Try to Remember	H. Schmidt	1960	1
More	R. Ortolani/	1963	7
	N. Oliviero		
Hello Dolly	J. Herman	1963	3
It Only Takes a Moment	J. Herman	1963	2
Who Can I Turn To?	L. Bricusse/A. Newley	1964	4
Watch What Happens	N. Gimbel/	1964	2
	M. Legrand		
On a Clear Day	B. Lane	1965	2
What the World Needs Now	B. Bacharach	1965	1
Strangers in the Night	B. Kaempfert	1966	2
Cabaret	J. Kander	1966	6
Willkommen	J. Kander	1966	2
Mame	J. Herman	1966	5
Somewhere My Love	M. Jarre	1966	2
My Way	P. Anka/J. Revaux/	1967	3
	C. Francois		
Love Me Tonight	L. Pilat/M. Panzeri	1969	1
Unknown Titles			37
			—
Total			210

Rock			
Title	*Performer*	*Year*	*Frequency*
Native New Yorker	Odyssey	1978	2
Copacabana	B. Manilow	1978	3
Stayin' Alive	Bee Gees	1978	3
Feels So Good	C. Mangione	1978	1
Can't Smile without You	B. Manilow	1978	1
Night Fever	Bee Gees	1978	1
Short People	R. Newman	1978	1
Don't It Make My Brown Eyes Blue?	C. Gayle	1978	1
Theme: Close Encounters	J. Williams/Meco	1978	2
Keep On Dancin'	Bohannon	1978	2
Theme: Star Wars	J. Williams/Meco	1978	2
On and On	S. Bishop	1978	1

Table 6. (continued)

Title	Performer	Year	Frequency
Rock			
Keep It Comin'	K.C. & the Sunshine Band	1978	1
My Way(disco)		1978	2
Our Day Will Come(disco)		1978	2
Baby Face(disco)		1978	4
Play That Funky Music	Wild Cherry	1977	3
You Make Me Feel Like Dancin'	L. Sayer	1977	4
Whatcha Gonna Do?	P. Cruise	1977	1
Car Wash	R. Royce	1977	2
Sir Duke	S. Wonder	1977	1
Walkin' in Rhythm	Earth, Wind & Fire	1977	1
Keep Rockin' Me Baby	S. Miller	1976	1
Cherchez La Femme	La Belle	1976	1
Shake Your Booty	K.C. & the Sunshine Band	1976	3
I Wish	S. Wonder	1976	2
Lowdown	B. Scaggs	1976	2
Isn't She Lovely	S. Wonder	1976	1
The Hustle	Van McCoy/Soul City Symphony	1975	9
Get Down Tonight	K.C. & the Sunshine Band	1975	2
That's the Way I Like It	K.C. & the Sunshine Band	1975	2
Ease on Down the Road	Consumer Rapport	1975	3
Love Will Keep Us Together	Captain & Tenille	1975	1
Feelin' Stronger Every Day	Chicago	1973	1
Smoke on the Water	Deep Purple	1973	2
Bad, Bad Leroy Brown	J. Croce	1972	1
I Believe in Music	Gallery	1972	1
Evil Ways	Santana	1971	1
Beginnings	Chicago	1971	1
Joy to the World	Three Dog Night	1971	1
Birthday	Beatles	1968	1
Revolution	Beatles	1968	1
Proud Mary	Creedence Clearwater Revival	1968	3
Jumpin' Jack Flash	Rolling Stones	1968	1
Sweet Caroline	N. Diamond	1968	1

Table 6. (continued)

| Rock | | | |
Title	Performer	Year	Frequency
Eight Days a Week	Beatles	1965	1
The Twist	C. Checker	1959	1
Rockin' Robin	B. Day	1958	1
Johnny B. Goode	C. Berry	1958	1
Chantilly Lace	Big Bopper	1958	1
At the Hop	Danny & Juniors	1957	1
Jailhouse Rock	E. Presley	1957	1
Hound Dog	E. Presley	1956	1
Blue Suede Shoes	E. Presley	1956	3
Rock around the Clock	B. Haley	1955	3
Shake, Rattle & Roll	B. Haley	1954	1
Kansas City	Little Richard	1954	2
Unknown Titles			7
Total			107

| Contemporary Pop | | | |
Title	Performer	Year	Frequency
Slip Slidin' Away	P. Simon	1978	1
How Deep Is Your Love?	Bee Gees	1978	1
You Light Up My Life	D. Boone	1978	3
Just the Way You Are	B. Joel	1978	4
Evergreen	B. Streisand	1977	3
At Seventeen	J. Ian	1977	1
After the Lovin'	E. Humperdinck	1977	1
I Write the Songs	B. Manilow	1977	1
Feelings	M. Albert	1976	4
What I Did For Love	Inner City Jam Band	1976	4
The Way We Were	B. Streisand	1973	3
My Sweet Gypsy Rose	T. Orlando	1973	2
Feel Like Makin' Love	R. Flack	1973	1
You Are the Sunshine of My Life	S. Wonder	1972	5
Tie a Yellow Ribbon	Dawn/T. Orlando	1972	2
Alone Again(Naturally)	G. O'Sullivan	1972	1
Speak Softly Love	A. Williams	1972	1
Killing Me Softly	R. Flack	1972	1

Table 6. (concluded)

	Contemporary Pop		
Title	*Performer*	*Year*	*Frequency*
Color My World	Chicago	1971	1
Sing	Carpenters	1971	3
You've Got a Friend	C. King	1971	1
Everything Is Beautiful	R. Stevens	1970	1
Make It with You	Bread	1970	1
Close to You	Carpenters	1970	1
Raindrops Keep Fallin' on My Head	D. Warwick	1969	2
This Guy's in Love	H. Alpert	1968	2
I'll Never Fall in Love	D. Warwick	1968	1
Do You Know the Way to San Jose?	D. Warwick	1967	2
I Say a Little Prayer	D. Warwick	1967	1
Up, Up and Away	Fifth Dimension	1967	1
Can't Take My Eyes off You	F. Valli	1967	1
Fool on the Hill	Beatles	1967	2
A Day in the Life	Beatles	1967	1
Light My Fire	Doors (J. Feliciano)	1967	1
Here, There and Everywhere	Beatles	1966	1
Everybody's Talkin'	Nillson	1967	2
Georgy Girl	Seekers	1966	1
Goin' Out of My Head	Lettermen	1964	1
And I Love Her	Beatles	1964	1
Downtown	P. Clark	1964	1
Unknown Titles			6
			—
Total			76

Latin: 52 songs; ethnic: 57; group participation: 18.

Table 7. 1989 Repertoire List

	Standards		
Title	*Composer*	*Year*	*Frequency*
Ain't Misbehavin'	F. Waller/H. Brooks/ A. Razaf	1929	1
As Time Goes By	H. Hupfeld	1931	2

Table 7. (continued)

	Standards		
Title	*Composer*	*Year*	*Frequency*
Through the Years	E. Heyman/ V. Youmans	1931	2
Autumn in New York	V. Duke	1934	1
I Can't Get Started	V. Duke	1935	2
At Last	S. Lewis/C. Tobias	1935	1
Our Love Is Here to Stay	G. Gershwin	1938	1
Moonlight Serenade	G. Miller	1939	2
Little Brown Jug	G. Miller(Winner)	1939(1869)	2
In the Mood	A. Razaf/J. Garland	1940	3
Tuxedo Junction	B. Feyne/W. Johnson/ E. Hawkins/J. Dash	1940	3
The Nearness of You	N. Washington/ H. Carmichael	1940	1
Take the "A" Train	B. Strayhorn	1941	4
Chattanooga Choo-Choo	M. Gordon/ H. Warren	1941	2
Serenade in Blue	H. Warren	1942	3
Sentimental Journey	B. Green/L. Brown/ B. Homer	1944	2
New York, New York	B. Comden/A. Green	1945	2
When I Fall in Love	E. Heyman/V. Young	1952	2
Here's That Rainy Day	J. VanHeusen	1953	1
I Left My Heart in S.F.	G. Cory/D. Cross	1954	2
When Sunny Gets Blue	M. Fisher/J. Segal	1956	1
I Wish You Love	C. Trenet	1963	2
Watch What Happens	N. Gimbel/ M. Legrand	1964	2
Cabaret	F. Ebb/J. Kander	1966	1
Willkommen	F. Ebb/J. Kander	1966	1
Call Me	T. Hatch	1967	1
I've Gotta Be Me	W. Marks	1968	1
What Are You Doing the Rest of Your Life?	A. & M. Bergman/ M Legrand	1970	1
Day by Day	S. Schwartz	1971	1
What I Did for Love	E. Kleban/ M. Hamlisch	1975	3
One	E. Kleban/ M. Hamlisch	1975	1
Unknown Titles			20
Total			74

Table 7. (continued)

	Rock		
Title	*Performer*	*Year*	*Frequency*
The Way That You Love Me	P. Abdul	1989	4
Get On Your Feet	G. Estafan	1989	3
This Time I Know It's For Real	D. Summer	1989	2
I Get So Emotional	W. Houston	1989	2
My Prerogative	B. Brown	1989	2
Baby Don't Forget My Number	Milli Vanilli	1989	2
Givin' You the Best That I've Got	A. Baker	1989	2
Rock Witcha	B. Brown	1989	1
Wild, Wild West	Escape Club	1989	1
With Every Beat of My Heart	T. Dane	1989	1
Listen To Your Heart	Roxette	1989	1
We Didn't Start the Fire	B. Joel	1989	1
Room to Move	Animotion	1989	1
Batdance	Prince	1989	1
Don't Rush Me	T. Dane	1989	1
Walk the Dinosaur	Was (Not Was)	1989	1
Iko, Iko	Belle Stars	1989	1
Every Little Step I Take	B. Brown	1989	1
I Feel The Earth Move	Martika	1989	1
She Drives Me Crazy	Fine Young Cannibals	1989	1
Mixed Emotions	Rolling Stones	1989	1
Pink Cadillac	N. Cole	1988	4
Out of My Dreams, into My Car	B. Ocean	1988	1
Roll with It Baby	S. Winwood	1988	1
Dancin' on the Ceiling	L. Ritchie	1986	1
Papa Don't Preach	Madonna	1986	1
Born in the U.S A.	B. Springsteen	1985	1
Just a Gigolo	D. Roth	1985	1
Dancin' in the Dark	B. Springsteen	1984	1
Let's Dance	M. Jackson	1983	1
Mony, Mony	B. Idol	1981	4
Keep on Lovin' You	REO Speedwagon	1981	1
Celebration	Kool & the Gang	1981	1
Cadillac Ranch	B. Springsteen	1980	1
We Are Family	Sister Sledge	1979	1
You're Sixteen	R. Starr	1974	1
Smoke on the Water	Deep Purple	1973	1

Table 7. (continued)

	Rock		
Title	*Performer*	*Year*	*Frequency*
Feelin' Alright	J. Cocker	1972	1
Bobby McGhee	J. Joplin	1971	1
It's Too Late	C. King	1971	1
Heard It through the Grapevine	M. Gaye	1968	4
Respect	A. Franklin	1967	2
I'm a Man	Spencer Davis Group	1967	1
Get Ready	Temptations	1966	1
Devil with the Blue Dress On	M. Ryder	1966	1
I Can't Help Myself	Four Tops	1965	4
How Sweet It Is	M. Gaye	1965	2
My Girl	Temptations	1965	1
(I Feel Good) I Got You	J. Brown	1965	1
Day Tripper	Beatles	1965	1
It's the Same Old Song	Four Tops	1965	1
Dancin' In the Street	M. Raye	1964	3
I Saw Her Standing There	Beatles	1964	2
Baby Love	Supremes	1964	1
Baby I Need Your Lovin'	Four Tops	1964	1
The Way You Do the Things You Do	Temptations	1964	1
Heat Wave	M. Raye	1963	1
Wipe Out	Surfaris	1963	1
Shout	Joey Dee	1962	2
Do You Love Me?	Contours	1962	1
Locomotion	Little Eva	1962	1
Let's Twist Again	C. Checker	1961	1
La Bamba	R. Valens	1959	2
So Fine	Fiestas	1959	1
Johnny B. Goode	C. Berry	1958	3
I Only Have Eyes for You*	Flamingos	1958	2
Rockin' Robin	B. Day	1958	1
Silhouettes*	Rays	1957	2
You Send Me*	S. Cooke	1957	2
Great Balls of Fire	J. L. Lewis	1957	1
Blue Suede Shoes	E. Presley	1956	3
Hound Dog	E. Presley	1956	2
In the Still of the Night*	Five Satins	1956	1
Rock around the Clock	B. Haley	1955	3

Table 7. (continued)

Rock			
Title	*Performer*	*Year*	*Frequency*
Shake, Rattle & Roll	B. Haley	1954	1
Kansas City	Little Richard	1954	1
Unknown Titles			17
Total			136

*These fifties ballads do not fall neatly into either the rock or contemporary pop categories. I include them in rock because they are used on club dates for their immediate association with the early years of rock and roll, always accompanying a "fast" fifties song or set of songs.

Contemporary Pop			
Title	*Performer*	*Year*	*Frequency*
Wind beneath My Wings	B. Midler	1989	3
Shower Me with Your Love	Surface	1989	1
Angel Song	Great White	1989	1
I Will Always Love You	T. Dayne	1988	2
Greatest Love of All	W. Houston	1986	3
That's What Friends Are For	D. Warwick	1986	2
Arthur's Theme	C. Cross	1981	1
Sailin'	C. Cross	1980	1
Look What You've Done to Me	B. Scaggs	1980	1
Honesty	B. Joel	1979	1
Just the Way You Are	B. Joel	1978	1
You Light Up My Life	D. Boone	1978	2
Evergreen	B. Streisand	1977	2
This Masquerade	G. Benson	1976	1
You Are So Beautiful	J. Cocker	1975	2
Feel Like Makin' Love	R. Flack	1974	1
You Are the Sunshine of My Life	S. Wonder	1972	2
Color My World	Chicago	1971	1
You've Got a Friend	C. King	1971	1
Close to You	Carpenters	1970	1

Table 7. (concluded)

	Contemporary Pop		
Title	*Performer*	*Year*	*Frequency*
Something	Beatles	1969	1
Eleanor Rigby	Beatles	1966	1
Unknown Titles			8
			—
Total			40

Latin: 28; ethnic: 18; group participation: 6.

Song Lists

Under the first category, standards, songs are identified by title, composer, year of copyright, and number of times the song appeared in the performances in each sample—again, nine performances in 1978 and five performances in 1989. The list progresses from oldest to most recent to give an idea of the wide age range of the standard songs. The mean year for the standards in 1978 was 1942.4; for 1989, 1944.5.

Songs in the rock and contemporary pop categories are identified by title, performer, latest appearance on the *Billboard* Hot 100 chart, and the number of times the song was played at the performances. They are identified by performer rather than composer because rock and other contemporary songs are so closely associated with particular recorded performances rather than sheet music versions of the songs. The rock and contemporary pop lists progress backward in time, from most recent to oldest songs, because of the importance placed on the currency of this portion of the repertoire in the club date context.

Composer, performer, and copyright information on the songs derives from four sources: *The Great Song Thesaurus,* by Roger Lax and Frederick Smith; *An Annotated Index of American Popular Songs,* edited by Nat Shapiro; *The Billboard Book of Top 40 Hits: 1955 to Present,* by Joel Whitburn; and *Billboard's* weekly "Hot 100," 1984–89.

Glossary

Book band: A dance band that reads from a "book" of arrangements in performance. Opposite of a *faking band.*

Cartage: Money added to union scale for musicians who have to transport large instruments or amplification equipment.

Continuous job: An engagement where a band is paid to play fifty-five minutes of every hour.

Contractor: The person who hires musicians for engagements booked by a leader. The leader may also act as contractor.

Double booking: Booking one's own services as a leader for two or more jobs scheduled for the same date and time.

Doubling: Playing more than a single instrument at a performance. Union regulations require that musicians receive a specified dollar amount beyond scale for each extra instrument.

Fake book: Sheet music collections of popular songs presented in simplified form, often with only melody and chords for a single chorus of each song.

Faker: A horn or string player capable of faking harmony.

Faking: Playing harmony or improvised backgrounds without using written music. A band that does this is a *faking band,* in distinction to a *book band.*

Finals: The specifications for a club date engagement, or the process of finalizing those specifications before the engagement.

516 job: A club date taking place outside of Manhattan, usually on Long Island, where the telephone area code is 516.

First player: A musician who has a written or verbal agreement with a leader to receive first call for all engagements that the leader's own band plays This band is known as the leader's *first band.*

Floater: A sideperson who works entirely on a free-lance basis, having no written or verbal ties to a particular leader or office.

Fly date: An engagement outside the New York area requiring air travel. Such engagements are common only in the society area of the business.

Guarantee: A written or verbal arrangement with a leader or office whereby a musician receives a specified minimum salary for the year and is expected to work exclusively for that leader or office.

Independent leader: A leader who is not involved in a business partnership with any other leader.

Interlude music: Music played while guests at a party are seated for dinner courses, sometimes referred to simply as dinner music.

Job set: The main four-hour segment of a party, following a *preheat* and preceding a *reset* or any overtime hours.

Leader: The employer ultimately responsible for booking engagements and hiring musicians, whether or not he or she performs at the engagement.

Location work: Steady musical employment at one location, such as a hotel, nightclub, or theater. Contrasts with single engagement work, where musicians are hired for one performance only at a given location.

Noncontinuous job: An engagement where the band is paid to play twenty minutes of every half hour. Uncommon in the club date field today.

Office: An agency formed by two or more leaders in partnership. Such leaders are referred to as *office leaders,* in distinction to *independent leaders.*

Pacing: Selecting music that allows the momentum and excitement of a party to build gradually.

Phantom: An inexperienced musician who is hired at less than union scale and who is expected to act as if he or she is playing on all songs, whether or not that is actually the case.

Preheat: A cocktail hour preceding the full four-hour party, or *job set.*

Reading a party: The process of selecting music appropriate for a party relying on visual cues and intuition.

Repeat job: An engagement sponsored by the same individual or organization that sponsored a previous party where the same band was performing.

Reset: Any hours beyond the four-hour *job set* where a specialty band or disc jockey is featured.

Rocker: The electric guitarist in a club date band who is responsible for playing rock music, usually exclusively so. Synonymous with *rock 'n roller.*

Screamer: An engagement that has been double booked.

Set: A medley of songs, usually using the same rhythm and tempo.

Set group: A band that is hired as a unit and uses the same personnel for most engagements.

Shtick: Any show-type entertainment at a club date, usually involving much verbal interaction between bandleader and audience. Dance step demonstrations and game songs are common types of shtick.

Sideperson: A bandmember hired by a leader or contractor who is not expected to lead the band.

Spin-off job: An engagement sponsored by a person who was a guest at a previous party where the same band was performing.

Subleader: The bandleader for those engagements at which the leader who booked the job will not perform.

Trouble job: Synonymous with *screamer.*

Bibliography

Allegro. Newspaper. New York: Associated Musicians of Greater New York, Local 802, American Federation of Musicians.

Becker, Howard. "The Professional Dance Musician and His Audience." *American Journal of Sociology* 57, no. 2 (September 1952): 136–44.

——. *Outsiders*. Glencoe, N.Y.: Free Press, 1963.

——. "Art as Collective Action." *American Sociological Review* 39, no. 6 (December 1974): 767–76.

Behague, Gerard, ed. *Performance Practice: Ethnomusicological Perspectives*. Westport, Conn.: Greenwood Press, 1984.

Bennett, H. Stith. *On Becoming a Rock Musician*. Amherst: University of Massachusetts Press, 1980.

Bergman, Bruce, and Fox, Dan (ed.). *How to Make Money Playing Rock Guitar: The Professional Club Date Rock Guide*. New York: Schirmer, 1976.

The Best of Cole Porter. New York: Chappell, 1972.

Bethany, Marilyn. "The Duchin Touch." *New York* 22 (29 May 1989): 24.

Billboard. Magazine. New York: Billboard Publications.

Birmingham, Stephen. *The Right People*. Boston: Little, Brown, 1968.

Branch, Harold, and Dweir, Irving. *The Club Date Handbook*. Plainview, N.Y.: Harold Branch, 1968.

Breznick, Alan. "Bookings for Orchestras Swing into the Big Time." *Newsday*, 22 December 1986.

Bunce, Alan. "When His Orchestra Plays, Society Sways." *Christian Science Monitor*, 11 December 1987.

Chambers, Iain. "Some Critical Tracks." In *Popular Music 2: Theory and Method*, ed. Richard Middleton and David Horn, 19–36. Cambridge: Cambridge University Press, 1982

Chappell Collection of Great Theater Composers. New York: Chappell, n.d.

DeVita, A. Ray. *Standard Dance Band Music Guide*. Bayside, N.Y.: 1975.

Directory. New York: Associated Musicians of Greater New York, Local 802, American Federation of Musicians, 1977 and 1989.

Faulkner, Robert R. *Hollywood Studio Musicians: Their Work and Careers in the Recording Industry*. Chicago: Aldine-Atherton, 1971.

Ferris, William, Jr. *Blues from the Delta*. London: Studio Vista, 1971.

"For Lester Lanin, 50 Years of Music." *New York Times*, 3 August 1987.

Frederickson, Jon, and Rodney, James F. "The Free-lance Musician as a Type of Non-Person: An Extension of the Concept of Non-Personhood." *Sociological Quarterly* 29, no. 2 (1988): 221–39.

Goffman, Erving. *Behaviour in Public Places: Notes on the Social Organization of Gatherings.* New York: Free Press, 1963.

Gourse, Leslie. *Every Day: The Story of Joe Williams.* New York: Da Capo, 1985.

Groce, Stephen B., and Dowell, John A. "A Comparison of Group Structures and Processes in Two Local Level Rock 'n' Roll Bands." *Popular Music and Society* 12, no. 2 (1988): 21–35.

Hughes, Phillip S. "Jazz, Jazzmen and Jazz Audiences." *Institute of Race Relations Newsletter,* October 1962, 29–32.

Kanner, Bernice. "Strike up the Bands." *New York* 19 (29 September 1986): 24.

Kaplan, Max. "The Musician in America: A Study of His Social Roles." Ph.D. diss., University of Illinois, 1951.

Keil, Charles. *Urban Blues.* Chicago: University of Chicago Press, 1966.

Lastrucci, Carlo L. "The Professional Dance Musician." *Journal of Musicology* 3, no. 3 (winter 1941): 168–72.

Lax, Roger, and Smith, Frederick. *The Great Song Thesaurus.* New York: Oxford University Press, 1989.

Leary, James P. "Old Time Music in Northern Wisconsin." *American Music* 2, no. 1 (spring 1984): 71–82.

Lewis, George H. "Take out My Guitar and Play: Recruitment of Popular Music Performers." *Popular Music and Society* 7, no. 1 (1979): 32–36.

Lord, Albert. *The Singer of Tales.* New York: Atheneum, 1960.

Merriam. Alan P. *The Anthropology of Music.* Chicago: Northwestern University Press, 1964

Merriam, Alan P., and Mack, Raymond W. "The Jazz Community." *Social Forces* 38, no. 3 (1960): 211–22.

Mullen, Kenneth. "The Impure Performance Frame of the Public House Performer." *Urban Life* 14, no. 2 (July 1985): 181–203.

———."Audience Orientation and the Occupational Rhetoric of Public House Performers." *Popular Music and Society* 11 (1987): 15–29.

Nye, William P. "The Social Organization of Time in a Resort Band: Or, 'Moments to Remember.' " *Popular Music and Society* 10, no. 4 (1986): 63–71.

Ostrander, Susan. *Women of the Upper Class.* Philadelphia: Temple University Press, 1984.

Porter, Sylvia. "Wedding Costs." *The Middletown Press* (Conn.), 11 March 1991.

Roberts, John Storm. *The Latin Tinge: The Impact of Latin American Music on the United States.* New York: Oxford University Press, 1979.

Sanders, Clinton R. "Psyching out the Crowd: Folk Performers and Their Audiences." *Urban Life and Culture* 3, no. 3 (October 1974): 264–83.

Schuyler, Philip D. "Berber Professional Musicians in Performance." In *Performance Practice: Ethnomusicological Perspectives,* ed. Gerard Behague, 91–148. Westport, Conn.: Greenwood, 1984.

Shapiro, Nat, ed. *Popular Music: An Annotated Index of American Popular Songs.* 6 vols. New York: Adrian, 1964–73.

Single Engagement Club Dates: Wage Scales and Minimums. Handbook. New York: Associated Musicians of Greater New York, Local 802, American Federation of Musicians, 1977.

Stebbins, Robert A. "The Conflict between Musical and Commercial Values in the Minneapolis Jazz Community." *The Minnesota Academy of Science Proceedings* 30, no. 1 (1962): 75–79.

————. "Class, Status and Power among Jazz and Commercial Musicians." *The Sociological Quarterly* 7, no. 22 (spring 1966): 197–213.

U.S. Department of Labor, Bureau of Labor Statistics. *Consumer Price Index.* Report. Washington, D.C.: GPO, 1990.

Warren, Virginia. "They Call the Tune for Society's Dancing Feet." *New York Times,* 18 September 1966.

Whitburn, Joel. *The Billboard Book of Top 40 Hits: 1955 to Present.* New York: Billboard, 1983.

Wicke, Peter. "Rock Music: A Musical-Aesthetic Study." In *Popular Music 2: Theory and Method,* ed. Richard Middleton and David Horn, 219–43. Cambridge: Cambridge University Press, 1982.

Index

Bruce MacLeod received his doctorate in ethnomusicology from Wesleyan University in 1979. He has published articles on American popular and African-American folk musics and has taught at Wesleyan, Hamilton College, and the University of Pittsburgh. In addition to his scholarly pursuits, Mr. MacLeod has also played jazz and club date engagements throughout New England.

Books in the Series Music in American Life

Only a Miner: Studies in Recorded Coal-Mining Songs
Archie Green

Great Day Coming: Folk Music and the American Left
R. Serge Denisoff

John Philip Sousa: A Descriptive Catalog of His Works
Paul E. Bierley

The Hell-Bound Train: A Cowboy Songbook
Glenn Ohrlin

Oh, Didn't He Ramble: The Life Story of Lee Collins,
as Told to Mary Collins
Edited by Frank J. Gillis and John W. Miner

American Labor Songs of the Nineteenth Century
Philip S. Foner

Stars of Country Music: Uncle Dave Macon to Johnny Rodriguez
Edited by Bill C. Malone and Judith McCulloh

Git Along, Little Dogies: Songs and Songmakers of the American West
John I. White

A Texas-Mexican *Cancionero:* Folksongs of the Lower Border
Americo Paredes

San Antonio Rose: The Life and Music of Bob Wills
Charles R. Townsend

Early Downhome Blues: A Musical and Cultural Analysis
Jeff Todd Titon

An Ives Celebration: Papers and Panels of the Charles Ives
Centennial Festival-Conference
Edited by H. Wiley Hitchcock and Vivian Perlis

Sinful Tunes and Spirituals: Black Folk Music to the Civil War
Dena J. Epstein

Joe Scott, the Woodsman-Songmaker
Edward D. Ives

Jimmie Rodgers: The Life and Times of America's Blue Yodeler
Nolan Porterfield

Early American Music Engraving and Printing: A History of Music
Publishing in America from 1787 to 1825, with Commentary
on Earlier and Later Practices
Richard J. Wolfe

That Half-Barbaric Twang: The Banjo in American Popular Culture
Karen Linn

Hot Man: The Life of Art Hodes
Art Hodes and Chadwick Hansen

The Erotic Muse: American Bawdy Songs
Second Edition
Ed Cray

Barrio Rhythm: Mexican American Music in Los Angeles
Steven Loza

The Creation of Jazz: Music, Race, and Culture in Urban America
Burton W. Peretti

Charles Martin Loeffler: A Life Apart in Music
Ellen Knight

Club Date Musicians: Playing the New York Party Circuit
Bruce A. MacLeod